Create and Edit DVDs with Ease

DVD BURNING
SOLUTIONS

Project Simulation

Our Trip to Vegas

Before the T...

SigmaTel Audio

| File | Edit | View | Favorites | Tools | Help |

Back · → · 🔍 Search 📂 Folders ✕ ↺

Address 🖳 My Computer

My Computer

Select an item to view its description.

Displays the files and folders on your computer

3½ Floppy (A:) System (C:) Data (D:) Multimedia (E:)

Control Panel Compact Disc (F:) Compact Disc (G:)

Brian Lich

DVD Burning Solutions

Senior Vice President, Retail Strategic Market Group: Andy Shafran

Publisher: Stacy L. Hiquet

Credits: Senior Marketing Manager, Sarah O'Donnell; Marketing Manager, Heather Hurley; Manager of Editorial Services, Heather Talbot; Acquisitions Editor, Todd Jensen; Senior Editor, Mark Garvey; Associate Marketing Manager, Kristin Eisenzopf; Retail Market Coordinator, Sarah Dubois; Development Editor, Brian Proffitt; Production Editor/Copy Editor, Jenny Davidson; Technical Editor, Ryan Williams; Proofreader, Sara Gullion; Cover Designer, Chad Planner, *Pop Design Works*; Interior Design and Layout, Susan Honeywell-LJ Graphics; Indexer, Katherine Stimson.

Library of Congress Catalog Number: 2003108387
ISBN: 1-59200-087-8
5 4 3 2 1

Educational facilities, companies, and organizations interested in multiple copies or licensing of this book should contact the publisher for quantity discount information. Training manuals, CD-ROMs, and portions of this book are also available individually or can be tailored for specific needs.

Muska & Lipman Publishing,
a Division of Course Technology
25 Thomson Place
Boston, MA 02210
www.muskalipman.com
publisher@muskalipman.com

About the Author

Brian Lich has worked in the Information Technology industry for almost ten years. He is currently the Network Administrator and Systems Coordinator for the Indiana University School of Dentistry in Indianapolis. Brian has a degree in Electrical Engineering Technology from Purdue University and is a Microsoft Certified Systems Engineer. He currently resides in Indianapolis, Indiana.

Dedication

To my loving wife, Lesley, and new baby boy, Miles.

Acknowledgments

At Course Technology, I would like to thank Todd Jensen and Mark Garvey. Their combined efforts helped me mold this into the book that it is today.

I would like to also thank Brian Proffitt (my development editor for the majority of the book), Jenny Davidson (my production editor), and Ryan Williams (my technical editor). Each of these editors kept a watchful eye on the book and made sure I stuck to the task at hand.

Next, I would like to thank John Gosney who served as my mentor on this book.

Finally, I would like to thank my wife, Lesley, who was patient enough to pick up my slack in caring for our newborn baby while I was writing this book.

Contents at a Glance

Contents

Introduction

You decide to take the plunge and get married to your longtime sweetheart. To be spontaneous, you decide to elope to Las Vegas, the marriage capitol of the world. Because of this extreme spontaneity, the taxi cab driver that drove you to the chapel was your best man. Along with the wedding video from the chapel, the chapel photographer took many pictures of the ceremony. You also took a lot of pictures of your long weekend in Las Vegas.

Because of the short notice, family and friends did not have enough time to attend the trip. Some family members may have felt left out since they could not come. To make up for this, you decide to create a DVD to document your weekend of bliss.

Enter *DVD Burning Solutions*—this book serves as a guide to the multimedia experience of creating a DVD. Rather than a boring, dry, technical guide, this book will give you the experience that you need to create a DVD in a light-hearted atmosphere. This book will do the following:

> ▶ Explain what a DVD is and the different formats available
>
> ▶ Show you how to install a DVD burner into your computer
>
> ▶ Clarify the terms that are used when creating a DVD (menus, chapters, and so on)
>
> ▶ Compare and contrast four DVD authoring applications to help you choose the application that suits you best
>
> ▶ Present two case studies—each with different multimedia requirements—and see how they use a DVD to enhance their lives

Who Is This Book For?

DVD Burning Solutions is for anyone who is interested in burning their own DVDs. Among other things, if you are interested in installing a DVD burner, choosing a DVD authoring application that best suits your needs, digitizing home movies, and creating slideshows—this is the book for you.

How This Book Is Organized

This book is split into four parts.

> ▶ **Part One**—DVD Hardware Fundamentals—This part is designed to introduce you to a DVD by explaining the history of how the DVD was developed, the many copyright issues surrounding DVD authoring, the different formats that are associated with DVDs, and step-by-step instructions of how to install a DVD burner into your computer.

▶ **Part Two**—DVD Software Fundamentals—This section will compare and contrast four separate DVD authoring applications—Easy CD and DVD Creator, DVD MovieFactory, MyDVD, and iDVD—by quickly creating a DVD with each so you will have the knowledge to choose the software application that is right for you.

▶ **Part Three**—Creating a DVD with Easy CD and DVD Creator 6—Using one of the applications from Part Two, namely Easy CD and DVD Creator, we will dig deep into the DVD authoring process and look at each step that is required to burn a DVD, from digitizing your home movies to creating an efficient menu structure that is easy for anyone to navigate.

▶ **Part Four**—Putting It All Together—In this part, you will be introduced to two case studies, Bart and Lili. Bart, a retired police officer who is very active in his retirement village, has been asked to create a documentary of the village's annual Las Vegas trip, while Lili, a soon to be retired actress, is starting her own talent agency and would like to hand out electronic advertising tools to potential clients. While each case study weighs their distribution options, they both decide to use a DVD.

Conventions Used in This Book

The following are a list of conventions that are used throughout this book to draw your attention to important text.

Tips give shortcuts or hints so you learn more about the ins and outs of a certain process.

Notes offer more detailed information about a feature, food for thought, or guidance to help you avoid problems or pitfalls in your work.

Cautions alert you to pitfalls and problems you should avoid.

Part One
DVD Hardware Fundamentals

Chapter 1
DVD Burning Overview

By now, almost every person has heard of DVDs—they're taking the world by storm. In its short six-year history, the DVD player has found its way into 50 percent of American homes, mostly due to its rapid price decrease. Today, a DVD player can be purchased at any major department store for fewer than one hundred dollars. This explosion of DVD player sales has outpaced the personal computer, the CD player, and the television. By the end of 2002, according to the DVD Entertainment Group, DVD manufacturers had sold 54 million players in the United States. According to the group's research, it took thirteen years for VCRs to sell 13 million units. And while it only took eight years for CD players to sell 13 million units, DVD players sold that many units in five years.

Since the DVD format was introduced in 1997, the rate at which DVDs are making their way into people's homes has been phenomenal. According to Centris, a consumer research company that focuses on household technology, 70 percent of DVD households rent between one and ten DVDs per month. Centris also said that 40 percent of movie rentals are for DVDs! On average, DVD households buy sixteen DVDs per year, and in 2001, Americans spent more money purchasing DVDs than they did buying VHS tapes. Whereas it took the VCR 25 years to become a standard addition to home entertainment systems, it is forecasted that the DVD format will take no more than twelve years. With over 15,000 DVD titles available for purchase and more than 100 new titles being released weekly, it's clear that DVD players are here to stay.

In this chapter, we're going to learn DVD basics. We'll take a look at all the fun and useful ways you can use DVDs, and we'll cover some of the legal issues surrounding the burning of DVDs. Finally, we'll talk about copy protection technologies.

What Is a DVD?

While CDs were invented with audio in mind, DVDs were created for use with video. A DVD disc is identical in size to a compact disc and is comprised of two 0.6mm substrates—metal foils bonded together—enclosed in a hard plastic, or polycarbonate, material. Before the metal is put between the plastic, indentions representing digital data in the form of bytes and bits are stamped into the metal in a distinct pattern; that's how mass quantities of pre-recorded DVDs are made. A DVD disc is read by passing a red laser over the DVD. The laser follows the tightly packed indentations (or exposed substrate) across the DVD and sends the results to a decoder chip in the form of 1s or 0s that convert it from digital data into visual and auditory information that you can see and hear.

Video is compressed when it's burned to a DVD. Without compression, it would be impossible for a full-length movie to fit on a DVD disc, or on two DVDs for that matter. The compression technique used with DVD is called MPEG encoding. MPEG stands for Moving Pictures Experts Group. The MPEG name is given to a set of standards that apply to a digitally compressed format used for audio and video encoding. MPEG compression is a sophisticated technology, and a detailed study of it would be well beyond the scope of this book. Simply put, MPEG technology is the means by which the program material on a DVD is compressed. There are two common MPEG formats:

▶ MPEG-1 encoding
▶ MPEG-2 encoding

MPEG-1 encoding was released in 1993 and was the first compression of this type. MPEG-1 can be compared to VHS in its video quality. You may see some low-budget DVDs that are encoded with this compression, but for the most part, DVDs will be encoded in MPEG-2.

MPEG AUDIO
MPEG encoding is not just for video, but audio as well. An MP3 audio file is actually a MPEG-1 encoded audio file.

Most DVDs that you buy or burn should use MPEG-2 encoding. With MPEG-2, you can achieve near studio-video quality, which is not possible with MPEG-1. MPEG-2 encodes by using what is called a *lossy* compression, which means it stores only those portions of the image that change from one frame to the next, not the whole frame itself. For instance, let's say you recorded someone standing perfectly still for five seconds. After five seconds, the person you were filming waved at you. The MPEG compression would store the first frame of the person standing there and would not store another frame until the person started to wave. MPEG compression removes the duplicate frames. Table 1.1 compares the MPEG-1 and MPEG-2 formats.

Table 1.1 Comparison of MPEG-1 and MPEG-2

Type	Optimal Resolution (pixels)	Year Introduced	Industry Use
MPEG-1	352 × 288	1993	CD-ROM or Video CD
MPEG-2	720 × 576	1995	DVD or Broadcast

Another MPEG video compression format that has been making a name for itself is MPEG-4 encoding. The compression rate of this format far surpasses that even of MPEG-2. The most popular MPEG-4 encoder/decoder, or CODEC, is called DIVX. It is possible to encode one two-hour MPEG-4 video onto a single CD-ROM.

DECODING DVDS ON A PERSONAL COMPUTER

Keep in mind that once the data has been encoded, or compressed, it must be decoded in order for the video to play back. All stand-alone DVD players have an MPEG decoder chip built in, but you may run into decoding problems if you are trying to play a DVD on a computer. A good rule is to always use an industry standard CODEC. A way to stick to this rule is to only use CODECs that are built into the major media players, such as Microsoft's Windows Media Player or Apple's QuickTime Player.

What Are Bits, Bytes, and Kilobytes?

In the digital world, everything is composed of the 1s and 0s of the binary numbering system. The binary system is the language of computers. Each of these 1s and 0s is called a bit. Simply put, a bit is an electronic signal that is either on (1) or off (0). Another way to think about this is that a bit is the smallest unit of information the computer uses. As you can imagine, a bit is extremely small, and trying to express a large number of bits in a reasonable fashion would be impossible. This is where a byte comes in. Put simply, a byte equals eight bits.

So, how are bytes expressed in larger increments?

> 1000 bytes = 1 kilobyte
>
> 1000 kilobytes = 1 megabyte
>
> 1000 megabytes = 1 gigabyte

A single layer, single-sided DVD can hold up to 4.7 gigabytes. This is equivalent to 74 minutes of high-quality surround audio or 133 minutes of compressed MPEG-2 video.

What Does DVD Stand For?

Upon its birth, DVD stood for Digital Video Disc. After the technology matured a bit, it was discovered that it could be used for more than just video. At this time, the meaning changed from Digital Video Disc to Digital Versatile Disc. The DVD Forum, an evolved version of the consortium that invented the technology, decided that even the Digital Versatile Disc label did not do justice to its potential. Eventually the DVD Forum agreed to disagree and settled on the letters DVD. Here are some "alternative" meanings that were proposed, but didn't seem to catch on:

- ▶ Delayed, very delayed (referring to delayed releases of different formats)
- ▶ Dead, very dead (thought up by VHS die-hards)
- ▶ Diversified, very diversified (referring to the plethora of formats that are available)

History of the DVD

DVDs were invented to replace both CDs and VHS tapes. In 1994, DVD technology started as two competing formats. The first, introduced by a partnership between Philips and Sony, was called Multimedia CD. This format had exceptional video quality that surpassed the quality of both laser discs and VHS tapes. The other format was called Super Disc. This format was introduced by a partnership between Time Warner and Toshiba. Each partnership raced to get its format declared the new standard. There were two major technical differences between the formats. First, the Super Disc was double-sided, allowing for ten gigabytes of space, whereas the Multimedia CD was capable of holding only five gigabytes. Second, the densities of the two discs were different. The Super Disc was much thinner, which allowed for a faster data transfer rate and quicker manufacturing times. In early 1995, Toshiba announced that they were releasing an improved format that was dual-layered. It appeared as though the Super Disc was winning the race to the new standard.

Fortunately, in this same year, the two competing brain trusts joined forces and settled on one standard. It is said that the reason for this alliance was strictly political. Many of the hardware and software giants such as Apple, IBM, HP, and Compaq refused to support two standards, thus forcing a settlement. The alliance decided to take Sony and Philips' data coding methods (called EFM Plus) and use the physical characteristics of the Super Disc from the Toshiba/Time Warner side. If it had not been for this settling on one standard, DVD technology likely would have ended up like VHS and Betamax, with each one fighting to become the standard in video-tape technology, thus slowing down the integration of videotape technology into the home.

How Are DVDs Burned?

When you first hear the term "burning a DVD," many things may come to mind—frustrated computer users who have had enough and are burning their DVDs in protest, or a Jimi Hendrix fan pouring lighter fluid on his DVDs in honor of a legend. Before you start burning your DVDs in a technology rebellion, let me tell you what burning a DVD really means.

"Burning" is just a slang term for writing to or creating a DVD disc. A recordable DVD looks pretty plain and very similar to a regular DVD. One side has a label that can be written on with a marker. (If you prefer a more professional look, you can buy CD labeling software that will print out sticky labels to attach to your DVD.) The other side is the recordable side; it has a reflective surface that comes in a variety of colors.

If you look at the recordable side of a blank DVD, you will not notice anything special. As mentioned earlier, a laser reads a stamped pattern on the DVD. But home users can't stamp their own DVDs, so a different method was created. Instead of the two plastic discs sandwiching stamped metal foil, recordable DVDs are injected with a dye between the metal foil and one side of the disc. Data is written to the DVDs with a laser by changing the orientation of the dye. The metal foil behind the dye will allow the light to reflect back. The laser starts near the center of the disc and works out toward the edge. If you take a close look at a burned DVD, you should see a ring on it (sometimes you have to tilt the DVD in the light in order to see it). This ring marks the outside edge of the data; it's where the laser stopped writing to the DVD.

What Can I Use a DVD For?

Over the last few years I have enjoyed collecting and watching DVDs, but I've always felt that I was missing out on something. I didn't realize how much I was missing out on until my wife and I had our first child. And then it hit me. I could combine one of my existing hobbies—shooting video of my new child—with my new interest in DVD authoring. Like any other new parent, I was amazed by the amount of pictures and videos that I had collected in the months following my child's birth. I equipped myself with a DVD burner, an easy-to-use software application, and some blank DVD media. The hardest thing left to do was find stuff to put on it. In my case, it wasn't that hard.

The content possibilities of a DVD are endless. You can add videos (a wedding video, for example), still pictures (the kids at the beach), even archive your entire music collection all on one disc! Being in the DVD driver's seat, you, the author, can create a fully interactive multimedia experience that you can keep for years to come.

Consider the following scenario: Bob is fifty years old and a proud father of five. He worked very hard in his life as an investment broker. Given Bob's deep knowledge of money management, he made a few sound investments that really paid off, and he rewarded himself by retiring early. Bob's decision to retire was clinched when Bob's oldest son told him that he was going to be a grandfather.

Bob had always been interested in taking pictures and making home movies. Every Christmas he would have a camcorder on his shoulder and a camera around his neck. After his retirement, he decided it would be fun to document his new grandchild's life.

To prepare for his "home documentary," Bob bought a digital camera and a digital camcorder. Having purchased a computer just a few months earlier, Bob had only one thing left to decide. How was he going to get his movies and pictures from his brand new digital toys onto a universal medium that anyone could enjoy? Bob read a lot on the Internet about the growing popularity of DVDs. He learned that DVDs were smaller and capable of much higher video quality than VHS tapes. And he learned that unlike VHS tapes, which have a tendency to wear out over time, a DVD could last forever. Bob had found his medium of choice.

True to one of its names (Digital Versatile Disc), there are countless practical applications for DVDs, touching nearly all areas of life, from your family to your work. How cool would it be if, after his grandchild's first birthday, Bob mailed a DVD as a Christmas present to his entire family scattered throughout the world? Aside from pictures, he could also include a video of his grandchild smearing birthday cake in his hair! Let's look at a few other uses for DVDs:

▶ You just purchased a digital camcorder and digital camera. You have a child on the way, and you want to document every part of his life—including opening Christmas presents, potty training, and his first birthday. When he is old enough, you want to give him something he'll be able to share with his children.

▶ You work as a realtor for a new housing development, and you'd like to create a multimedia marketing tool that you can give to customers to take home with them. You want it to include a video tour of each house, specifications about the house, and approximate price for each upgrade to the house.

▶ You are a corporate trainer for a large company. You like to reinforce your training with electronic visual aids. Also, you would like to be able to give new employees electronic copies of things such as policies and procedures, a safety video, and a welcome message from the CEO.

▶ You are an aspiring film director, and you really like writing short films. You just graduated from college and would like to make a portfolio to hand out to potential clients. You want to leave them something that they can view on their own time.

As you can see, there are many applications for a DVD. And this list is just the beginning. For more suggested applications, please refer to Appendix B.

Why Choose DVD over Other Media?

Over the course of the personal computer's history, removable media has come and gone. I can still remember unboxing my first Commodore 64, plugging in the disk drive, and playing *Ghosts n' Goblins* until dawn. A lot has changed in terms of removable media since the Commodore 64. That antique used 5.25 inch floppy disks, which, for their time, were more than sufficient. Today, you couldn't give one of those drives away.

Removable media types that have come about since the 5.25 inch floppy disks include the 3.5 inch floppy disk, Zip disk, compact disc, and the DVD disc. Each has its advantages and disadvantages. Table 1.2 summarizes the differences among these removable media types. See samples of each media type in Figures 1.1-1.4.

Table 1.2 Differences in removable computer media

Media	Reliability	Capacity	Form	Read/Write Speed	Internal/External
Floppy	Easily Corrupted	Up to 2.0MB	Floppy disk	Slow	Mostly Internal
Zip	Very Reliable	Up to 750MB	Cartridge Disk	Fast	Internal or External
CD	Very Reliable	Up to 900MB	Compact Disc	Fast read/Slow write	Mostly Internal
DVD	Very Reliable	Up to 18GB	Compact Disc	Fast read/Slow write	Mostly Internal

Figure 1.1
5.25" Floppy disk.

Figure 1.2
3.5" Floppy disk.

Figure 1.3
Zip disk.

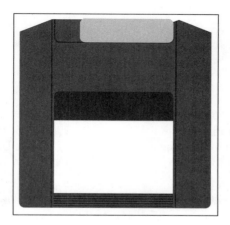

CHAPTER 1

Figure 1.4
CD/DVD disc.

In Table 1.2, *reliability* refers to the likelihood that the media will become corrupt over time. Because of the way a floppy disk is packaged, the disk has very little protecting it from the outside world. During my years in information technology support, I knew of many graduate students who lost the only copy of their thesis, because they saved it only on floppy disk. They would stuff the disk into a backpack or even paperclip it to a stack of papers. After a few days of that kind of treatment, sometimes the disk would work and sometimes it wouldn't. There was nothing I could do to help them.

SPEED AND EXTERNAL VS. INTERNAL

Read/write speed refers to how fast your computer can read or write a file to the removable media type. CDs, for instance, have extremely fast read abilities but can be cumbersome when you need to constantly edit (write) a file that is contained on the disc.

Internal/external refers to how the removable media drive is mounted. If the drive plugs into the outside of the computer, it is external. If it is mounted inside the computer, the drive is internal.

The media you choose to use depends on your purposes. If you transport files to and from work, which more and more people are doing, a zip disk may be the right choice for you. The disk can hold a fair amount of data, and the files on the disk can be easily updated. On the other hand, if you have a lot of files that you want to archive or distribute as read-only, a DVD would be the best choice.

Unfortunately, with the ability to write massive amounts of data onto a single medium comes the ability to illegally copy or distribute copyrighted material. The next section will explain the various legal concerns associated with owning a DVD burner.

What Are the Legalities of Burning DVDs?

In 1993, the first version of Mosaic, now known as Netscape, was released to the public. Mosaic was an Internet browser, and it was the first of its kind. It provided a Web surfer with a graphical interface for navigating the Internet, specifically the World Wide Web. Soon after Mosaic's release, Internet access at home became more and more common. By 1996, nearly ten million computers were online worldwide.

Think about today's high-tech society. High-speed Internet access is available in many homes throughout the world and information sharing is in its prime. Strategy Analytics, a technology research firm, forecasted that broadband sales in China would grow by 500 percent in 2002. The incredible amount of information sharing that is occurring daily has, unfortunately, brought piracy to an all-time high as well.

So what's this got to do with you? Just this: With a DVD burner, it is possible, although extremely illegal, to copy DVDs that you rent at your local video store. If you're considering piracy, try putting the shoe on the other foot: Imagine you are applying for a senior-level marketing position, and you created a DVD to show during your interview. You sent the DVD to this corporation a few days in advance to give them a chance to look at it. Unbeknownst to you, a person who currently works for the corporation also applied for the job, and he copied your DVD. In his interview, which was conveniently before yours, he ripped off your hard work and presented it as his own.

Copyright Law

With the rise of piracy, it is important that one's work is protected in case someone decides to claim it as his or her own. For example, when your band finally gets a record deal and you decide to release your first music video on DVD, you need to be sure that it is copyrighted. Some things are copyrightable and others are not. Here is a list of things that can be protected by a copyright:

► Literary works

► Musical works, including any accompanying words

► Dramatic works, including any accompanying music

► Pantomimes and dramatic works

► Pictorial, graphic, and sculptural works

► Motion pictures and other audiovisual works

► Sound recordings

► Architectural works

Any material you create is automatically copyrighted as soon as you finish working on it. For material that is copyrighted in sections, such as a book published in parts, each section is copyrighted separately when it is completed, and then copyrighted as a whole when the entire piece of material is completed. Any new material created after January 1, 1978 is copyrighted immediately upon its completion until 70 years after the creator's death. A copyright owner may transfer exclusive rights to his or her material if and only if the transfer is in writing and is signed by the copyright owner.

Copyrighting Your Own Work

Creating your own DVDs is exciting, and depending on their complexity, you may put a lot of time into their creation. You want to make sure that you are covered in the event that someone likes your work and tries to steal it.

There are two means of claiming and protecting your copyright. The first is to physically place a copyright notice on every copy that you distribute. This is free and may save you a lot of money down the road if your work is used without your permission. The second is to register the copyright with the U.S. Copyright Office. This can be done through the mail. You must send a completed application, a check for the filing fee, and a non-returnable copy of the material that you would like copyrighted. The application can be obtained from the Library of Congress' website, and the filing fee depends on the type of work that is submitted (for example, a literary work, a sound recording, a periodical, and so on). For more information, visit the U.S. Copyright Office's website (a part of the Library of Congress) at http://www.copyright.gov.

THE COPYRIGHT NOTICE

A copyright notice has a standard format, whether you are putting it on digital material or in print. Use the following syntax when attaching a copyright notice: *Copyright © <Year> by <Author>, All rights reserved.*

<Year> is the year of creation, and <Author> is the person who created the material.

Staying Legal

As the owner of material you create, you are allowed to distribute it or not, as you like. You and your band are legally allowed to hand out your CD whenever or to whomever you want. But, of course, another band's CD that you happen to own cannot be copied and handed out to whomever you like. Even though you own the CD, you did not create the music it contains, and someone else controls the copyright to it.

Here are a couple of exceptions to the preceding rules:

▶ If you purchase a movie or an audio CD, you are entitled to make one personal backup. Even though DVDs and CDs are much more reliable than their predecessors (VHS and cassette tapes, respectively), things can still happen. The DVD or CD could get scratched or even broken in half (it is possible). You are not allowed to distribute this backup to anyone else. This backup is to be used only if the original media is damaged.

▶ Music sharing has been a hot topic over the last few years. With the invention of personal MP3 players and mini-disc players, the question of "Can I copy music on to this?" is raised a lot. The answer to this question is yes. That is, as long as you purchased the original compact disc. What about making a "mix CD," taking all of your favorite tracks from a number of different CDs and putting them all on one? Again, this is legal as long as you purchased the original material.

ASK A LAWYER

This section is only the tip of the iceberg when it comes to legal issues surrounding the question of copyright infringement. For more information, please contact a lawyer trained in intellectual property and copyright.

Copy Protection Efforts

Attaching a copyright notice doesn't guarantee that DVDs will not be copied. For that, the industry has turned to technology to help prevent copyright infringement. Several groups have been active in developing technological barriers to illegal copying. The Content Protection System Architecture (CPSA), a group constructed by 4C (Intel, IBM, Toshiba, and MEI), and the Copy Protection Technical Working Group developed an initiative for the security and access control of anything that has to do with DVD technology. The goal of these DVD security groups is to eliminate mainstream DVD pirating and keep everyone honest.

Because it involves a lot of work, DVD copy protection may not appeal to every home DVD author. It is worth mentioning, though, for the DVD author who is willing to take the extra step to ensure data protection. If you are not interested in copy protecting your DVDs, feel free to move on to Chapter 2.

Let's take a look at the major copy protection technologies available:

▶ Macrovision (Analog CPS)
▶ Content Scrambling System (CSS)
▶ Region Locking
▶ Copy Guard Management System (CGMS)
▶ Content Protection for Recordable Media (CPRM)

Macrovision (Analog CPS)

Analog CPS, developed by Macrovision (http://www.macrovision.com), is one of the standard copy protection methods, and all new DVD players are required to be compatible with it. It is also referredto as Analog Protection System or Copyguard. The goal of Macrovision is to eliminate the ability to copy a DVD to a VCR. It does this by sending a series of signal bursts that the VCR cannot interpret. This burst will show up on the VCR as a color stripe or a rolling picture, seriously degrading the entertainment value of the tape. As you can probably tell from the name, Analog CPS is for analog devices only (mainly VHS tapes). It does not protect the DVD from being copied to a digital medium (a computer, another DVD, and so on). Analog CPS protects only the video on a DVD; the audio can still be copied without a problem. You have to apply to Macrovision for the right to use Analog CPS, and you have to pay royalties on each disc produced.

Content Scrambling System (CSS)

Matsushita and Toshiba developed Content Scrambling System. CSS prevents users from making a perfect digital copy of a DVD, and it is licensed through the DVD Copy Control Association (DVD CCA), a not-for-profit organization responsible for licensing CSS. The video on a CSS-protected DVD is encrypted with one of 400 standard CSS keys. Stand-alone DVD players come with CSS decrypting technology built in. When a DVD is copied, the decryption key is not copied with it, and the illegal copy will not work.

Region Locking

Region locking—sometimes known as country codes—limits *where* a DVD can be played. The reasoning behind the region code system is that movies are not released simultaneously throughout the world, and the region code allows movie manufacturers to assure that copies of their movies do not show up in homes on the other side of the world before they want them to. When the DVD is produced, it is assigned the code for the region in which it will be released. The DVD players in that region are assigned the same code. If the two codes do not match up, the DVD will not be played. There are eight regions whose codes can be assigned to a DVD and DVD player. (See Table 1.3.)

Table 1.3 Region Locking Codes

Region	Code
United States, Canada, and U.S. Territories	1
Europe, South Africa, Japan, and the Middle East	2
Southeast and Eastern Asia	3
South America, Mexico, New Zealand, Caribbean, Central America, and Australia	4
Russia, Africa, North Korea, and Mongolia	5
China	6
Reserved	7
International interests (cruise ships, airplanes, and so on)	8

It is possible, by adding a chip or entering a special command via your remote control, to modify your existing DVD player to become region-free. While this may void your warranty on the DVD player, it is not illegal in most countries.

Copy Guard Management System (CGMS)

CGMS is a system that controls how many copies can be made of a specific disc. There are three options to choose from—copy freely, copy once, or copy never. This copy control system works by setting bits contained within the video stream that tell the computer which copy option is set. Unfortunately, this standard is not widely supported and relies heavily on the software used to copy the DVD to check for the status of these bits.

Content Protection for Recordable Media (CPRM)

CPRM, developed by 4C, was designed to protect recordable DVDs from being copied. Every DVD has a section called the Burst Cutting Area (BCA) that is used to record a unique identifier. When the DVD is written, the software embeds this identifier into its encryption. Each time the DVD is played, the identifier in the BCA is matched with the identifier embedded in the DVD's encryption. If they do not match, the disc will not decrypt.

In the next chapter, we will take a look at the wide array of formats that are associated with DVDs, including disc, broadcast, recordable, and application formats.

CHAPTER 1

Chapter 2
DVD Media Formats

The number and variety of DVD formats can be confusing. And unfortunately, until manufacturers agree to settle on standards in DVD technology, these formats, and the confusion they cause, will be with us for a while. In this chapter, we'll learn about the different formats and consider issues of compatibility between them. Let's see if we can clear things up a bit.

DVD formats fall into four categories: disc formats, broadcast formats, application formats, and recordable formats. Let's define them, so you can understand the need for each one.

▶ **Disc format**—How the physical DVD disc is constructed

▶ **Broadcast format**—How the image is displayed on your television (NTSC vs. PAL)

▶ **Application format**—The *kind* of data (DVD-AUDIO, DVD-VIDEO, VCD) that is written to the DVD disc

▶ **Recordable format**—Describes the particular technology used to write the application format to the DVD

DVD Disc Formats

As you'll recall from Chapter 1, a DVD consists of two metal substrates that are bonded together. Also recall from Chapter 1 that a red laser follows the indentions on the disc and reflects the data to the decoder chip in the form of 1s and 0s. Figure 2.1 shows a cross-section of a DVD disc.

Figure 2.1
Cross-section of a DVD disc.

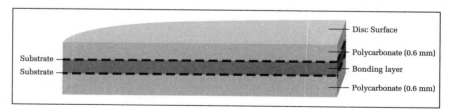

It is possible for the laser to read both substrates through one side of the disc. This is achieved by making one substrate *semi-reflective*, meaning that it reflects only a portion of the laser's light. The rest of the light passes through a transparent bonding layer and is then reflected by the next substrate layer. A DVD can be either a single- or dual-layer disc, depending on the number of substrates that can be read from one side. DVDs can also be classified as single- or double-sided, depending on whether they can be read from both sides.

Typically a DVD layer can hold 4.7 gigabytes, or two hours of compressed video. If you want to put more data (a longer movie) on one disc, there are four possibilities, referred to as disc formats, using different combinations of sides and layers—DVD-5, DVD-9, DVD-10, and DVD-18.

If you own a DVD player and a collection of DVDs, you may have examples of each of these types of DVDs. A single layer, double-sided DVD, officially called DVD-10, is nicknamed a "flipper," because you have to physically turn over the DVD after two hours of video. With some newer DVDs, manufacturers will put the normal version of the movie on one side and the widescreen version on the other. A dual layer, single-sided disc, officially named DVD-9, will have a label on one side and the data on the other. Since it is a dual layer, DVD-9 discs don't need to be flipped. Two other types of DVDs are a single layer, single-sided disc (DVD-5), and dual layer, double-sided disc (DVD-18).

Table 2.1 illustrates the different disc format combinations and their storage capacities:

Table 2.1 Capacities of Common DVD Disc Formats

Name	Layers	Sides	Logical Size (GB)	Max video (hours)
DVD-5	1	1	4.7	2.0
DVD-9	2	1	8.54	4.0
DVD-10	1	2	9.4	4.5
DVD-18	2	2	17	8

Let's take a closer look at how each of these disc formats work.

▶ **DVD-5**—This is the simplest of the DVD disc formats and is referred to as single layer, single-sided. This disc format uses only one of the substrates, leaving the other one blank. DVD-5 discs have a label on them. Alternatively, the blank substrate can be stamped with an image that will show through the poly-carbonate film, creating a more professional look. Figure 2.2 illustrates how a DVD-5 disc works; the second substrate has been omitted because it is blank.

Figure 2.2
How DVD-5 works.

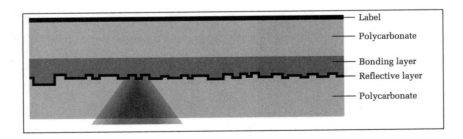

Label

Polycarbonate

Bonding layer
Reflective layer

Polycarbonate

▶ **DVD-9**—A dual layer, single-sided disc. Each layer is stamped on one substrate with the substrates being bonded by an optically transparent layer. The layer closest to the laser is a semi-transparent layer that reflects 18 to 30 percent of the laser. This partial reflection is just enough to read the first layer without reading any of the second layer. When the DVD wants to read the second layer, it can because the laser produces enough light so that the second, highly reflective layer can be read as well. Figure 2.3 illustrates how this one works.

Figure 2.3
How DVD-9 works.

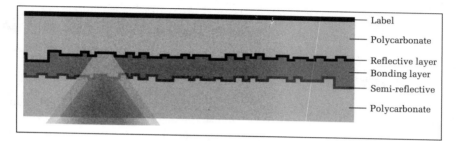

DVD-10—A single layer, double-sided disc. This format is identical to the DVD-5, except that the blank substrate is used. Figure 2.4 illustrates how DVD-10 works.

Figure 2.4
How DVD-10 works.

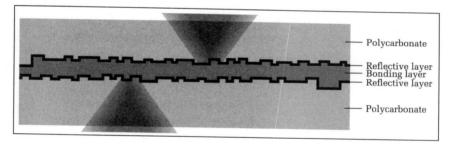

▶ **DVD-18**—A dual layer, double-sided disc. This disc format is equivalent to two DVD-9 discs bonded together. Figure 2.5 illustrates how DVD-18 works.

Figure 2.5
How DVD-18 works.

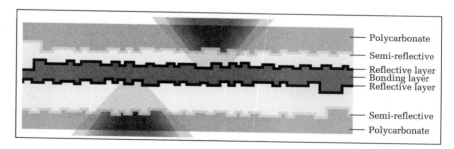

CHAPTER 2

THE DUAL LAYER, DUAL-SIDED DVD
The DVD-18 type is not widely used because of production costs and compatibility issues with some DVD players. *The Stand* was the first movie produced using this type.

Since DVD recording is still relatively new, home recording technology has not caught up with that of the commercial manufacturers. In the home and at the time of this writing, it was not possible to burn a dual layer DVD (DVD-9 and DVD-18), but it is possible to burn a double-sided disc.

DVD Broadcast Formats

When you are burning a DVD, you must take into consideration the DVD player it will be played on. It would be nice if there were an international standard broadcast format; unfortunately, there is not. The broadcast formats that you have to choose from are NTSC (National Television System Committee) and PAL (Phase Alternating Line). PAL is the dominant broadcast format in Europe, whereas NTSC is the standard in the United States, China, Japan, and many other countries. The decision to burn NTSC- or PAL-compatible DVDs is usually made according to the country that you live in—or more precisely, the country in which the DVD will be played.

There are two major differences between NTSC and PAL—frame rate and resolution. NTSC has a higher frame rate (the amount of video frames that are displayed per second) than PAL, which allows for a smoother video. On the other hand, PAL has an increased resolution, which results in a crisper image. The PAL resolution on DVD is 720 × 576 pixels (720 pixels of horizontal resolution and 576 pixels of vertical resolution), but the PAL frame rate is 25 frames per second. The DVD NTSC resolution is 720 × 480 pixels, but the frame rate for NTSC is approximately 30 frames per second.

You may need two versions of a particular DVD—NTSC and PAL. For example, you may want to send a copy to a friend in the UK. You could simply convert your NTSC discs to PAL, but the results might not be great, because when you convert from one broadcast format to the other, the videos are not re-encoded, which leads to choppiness in the video or even audio and video synchronization problems. Because of the differences in frame rate and resolution, you'll get the best results by simply burning a new disc from scratch, re-encoding the video into the intended broadcast format.

DVD Application Formats

DVD *application formats* refer to the various types of data (the content) that can be stored on the physical DVD discs. Four DVD application formats are available:

▶ **Video CD or Super Video CD**—A primitive version of the DVD that uses compact disc media.

▶ **DVD-ROM**—The primary application format for computer data.

▶ **DVD-VIDEO**—The application format we'll be focusing on in this book.

▶ **DVD-AUDIO or SACD**—The next generation of music CDs.

The term DVD-ROM can mean different things, depending on the context. It can describe the base technology that encompasses all DVD application formats and can also be used to describe the data-recording application format of choice for personal computers. In this book, we will use the latter definition.

What Is Video CD?

Many DVD burning applications give you the option to burn to VCD, or Video CD, format. Philips and Sony introduced the VCD application format in 1993, and it can be thought of as the predecessor to the DVD-ROM application format. VCD never caught on in North America because the video quality is equivalent to that of a VHS tape. On the other hand, it became a popular format in Asia.

A VCD is like a CD-ROM with moving pictures and sound that has the ability to be played in any DVD player (that supports VCD) or a regular VCD player. A VCD uses recordable CD (CD-R or CD-RW) media and can store up to eighty minutes of video, with a resolution of 352 × 240 (NTSC) and 352 × 288 (PAL). To burn a backup of a typical movie, you would need two CDs. VCD uses MPEG-1 compression, as opposed to a DVD, which uses MPEG-2 technology.

VCDs are compatible with current audio/video components. Most stand-alone DVD players will play a VCD, but to save time in troubleshooting, check with the manufacturer of your DVD player to ensure compatibility. Also, any computer with a CD or DVD drive has the ability to play a VCD as well, but you may be required to download a software decoder for this to work.

LOCATING VCD DECODERS

There are many software manufacturers out there that sell VCD playing (decoding) software. My personal choice is an application called Quick VCD Player (http://www.fwnetwork.com/description/quickvcd.html) and is free to download.

PLAYING A VCD IN A STAND-ALONE DVD PLAYER

If you burn your own VCDs and would like to play them in a stand-alone DVD player, make sure that your DVD player will play CD-R/CD-RWs. If it can handle those formats, it will more than likely be able to play a VCD. Also, some DVD players are temperamental in terms of the brand of CD-recordable media you use, so you may have to experiment until you find a brand that works. For example, I have two DVD players in my home. The older one is made by RCA and will not read CD-R/CD-RWs, whereas my newer (less expensive) APEX DVD player will play the same disc fine.

As with DVDs, you have the option of adding chapters and menus to your VCD layout and creating a photo slide show accompanied by background music.

What Is Super Video CD?

Super Video CD, released by Philips, was introduced as the new version of Video CD. SVCD offers DVD-quality video but lacks the playing time of a DVD. You can fit between 35 and 72 minutes of high-quality video on a SVCD, compared to 2 hours on a DVD.

The differences between VCD and SVCD are significant. Instead of the "VCR-like" MPEG-1 encoding that a VCD delivers, SVCD can accommodate MPEG-2 encoding (the same as a DVD). Also, SVCD has a better resolution than that of VCD—480 × 480 (NTSC) and 480 × 576 (PAL).

Like VCDs, SVCDs have not caught on in the consumer market. This is most definitely due to the superior DVD disc. It takes an average of three SVCD discs to accommodate one full-length movie, whereas one movie will fit on one DVD disc.

What Is DVD-ROM?

DVD-ROM was the first DVD application format to be introduced in the technology market and is intended to be used for "pre-recorded" or read-only content. This format has found its home with the personal computer—distributing computer games, large amounts of data, electronic encyclopedias, and so on. Since the DVD-ROM format is used for computer data, video and audio quality is usually not an issue. Some of the new DVD discs that you can buy have a DVD-ROM section that provides extra features, such as Internet access.

The DVD Forum, a collection of various hardware and software manufacturers that determine and promote each DVD standard, has a division called WG2 (Working Group 2) that is in charge of the DVD-ROM standard. They have established the following requirements for the DVD-ROM format for games and computer applications:

▶ One format for both television and computer-based applications

▶ Reliable data storage

▶ Reasonably priced drives and media

▶ Backward compatibility with existing CD-ROM drives

What Is DVD-VIDEO?

In 1996, the DVD Forum released the DVD-VIDEO application format. The goal of this format was to deliver a video quality that was much better than VHS, with surround sound that far surpassed that of the CD-Audio format, which produces stereo sound. DVD-VIDEO has been adopted by the entertainment industry as its DVD format of choice, and since the advent of DVD burners, it has become the standard application format for home DVD authors. The Studio Advisory Committee, a group that represents the Motion Picture industry, has established the following as requirements for the DVD-VIDEO application format:

- ▶ The DVD must be able to support 135 minutes of video on a single layer. This will support 99 percent of the movies currently on the market.
- ▶ The DVD must have the recording quality of a CD but with surround sound.
- ▶ The video quality must be better than that of the Laserdisc—another format, like VCD, that did not catch on in the United States.
- ▶ The DVD must incorporate copy protection.
- ▶ The manufacturing cost of the disc must be competitive with current CD manufacturing costs.
- ▶ The DVD must include parental lockout features.

With these stringent requirements, you can be assured that DVDs will usually include some pretty cool features. Here are some common ones:

- ▶ A little over two hours of high-quality MPEG-2 encoded video with the audio in surround sound.
- ▶ The choice of viewing your movie in widescreen or standard formats.
- ▶ A choice of as many as nine different camera angles that can be changed while the video is playing.
- ▶ Support for as many as eight different languages within the movie.
- ▶ Instant rewind and fast forward.
- ▶ Parental control features.

Most DVDs will also include other extras that you would not find on a VHS tape. These features can include director's commentaries, a "making of" the movie feature, interactive games, music videos that were released with the movie, and so on. These extras are the reason that some DVDs are produced in dual layer. For DVDs that would like to offer both a standard format and a widescreen format, a dual-sided DVD would be ideal, because the manufacturer could put one format of the movie on one side and the other format on the opposite side.

Keep in mind that the DVD-VIDEO format is the one you will be using when you burn your own DVDs. Of course, you will not be held to the same requirements as the entertainment industry, but depending on your software application, you will have all of these features available to you when it is time to burn a DVD.

What Is DVD-AUDIO?

The DVD Forum released the DVD-AUDIO application format in March of 1999. Whereas the DVD-VIDEO format was introduced to replace the VHS tape, the DVD-AUDIO format was released to replace the compact disc. A committee was formed, including the RIAA (Recording Industry Association of America), in 1996 to establish requirements for its release in 1999. The committee came up with the following requirements:

- ▶ DVD-AUDIO must be compatible with the current CD format.
- ▶ This application format must incorporate good copy protection technology.
- ▶ This format must include six channels of the highest-possible sound quality.

> ▶ The discs must be more durable than CDs.
> ▶ DVD-AUDIO discs must have the ability to play a slideshow while the audio is playing.
> ▶ The discs must have a minimum playing time of 74 minutes.

A DVD-AUDIO disc is far superior to the standard compact disc format. See Table 2.2 for some features you will find on a DVD-AUDIO disc that are not found on a regular CD.

Table 2.2 DVD-AUDIO vs. Standard Music CD

Specification	DVD-AUDIO	Music CD
Disc Capacity	Up to 17 gigabytes	700 megabytes
Channels	Up to 6 (surround)	2 (stereo)
Support for Video?	Yes	No
Copy Protection	Yes	No

It should be clear now why DVD-AUDIO is better than a standard compact disc. But what makes a DVD-AUDIO disc better than a DVD-VIDEO disc? Both formats can play audio, so why have two different formats? First of all, the bit rate (the speed with which data is transferred) is much higher in DVD-AUDIO than in DVD-VIDEO, resulting in better audio quality. In addition, DVD-AUDIO discs have the ability to be played in locations in which the video is not needed—in a car player, for instance, or in any mobile audio device.

Even though the two formats are different, DVD-AUDIO discs can be played in DVD-VIDEO players, if the author chooses to allow that.

PLAYING DVD-AUDIO DISCS ON A DVD-VIDEO PLAYER
When a DVD-AUDIO disc is burned to be compatible with a DVD-VIDEO player, the DVD will change the audio into the DVD-VIDEO format, since the audio playback between the two is different. This downgrades the DVD-AUDIO audio to DVD-VIDEO audio, which will not allow use of the full potential of the DVD-AUDIO disc.

What Is Super Audio CD (SACD)?

The Super Audio CD format, developed by Sony and Philips, emerged in 1999. This was conveniently around the same time that DVD-AUDIO was released. SACD and DVD-AUDIO are competing formats, and the developers of each format are convinced that theirs will replace the compact disc. The results are yet to be seen.

There are three main differences between DVD-AUDIO and SACD:

▶ SACD uses a different encoding method than DVD-AUDIO. This encoding difference gives SACD the edge over DVD-AUDIO in higher sampling and bit rates. For the true audiophile, the higher rates may give the feeling of "actually being there" more convincingly than will the DVD-AUDIO. The average listener will probably not hear a difference.

▶ SACDs cannot be played in DVD players. This can be a major snag for people interested in getting the most bang for their buck when shopping for a new component to add to their home entertainment system.

▶ Unlike DVD-AUDIO, which is burned as a hybrid disc, SACD is not capable of displaying any video on the disc.

SACD and DVD-AUDIO have one thing in common: the disc can be equipped to play in a normal CD player. These types of discs are called hybrids. Hybrid discs are achieved by putting the standard CD audio on one substrate and the DVD-AUDIO or SACD audio on the other. Figure 2.6 illustrates how the hybrid disc works:

Figure 2.6
How a hybrid disc works.

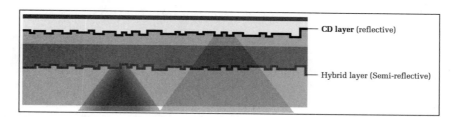

CD layer (reflective)

Hybrid layer (Semi-reflective)

DVD Recordable Formats

Application formats, with the exception of DVD-AUDIO, are pretty standard. Recordable formats—again, the way that the application format is written to the disc—are a different story. These formats include:

▶ **DVD-R**—The original recordable DVD format that can be written to once

▶ **DVD-RW**—A format similar to DVD-R, except that it can be written to and erased many times

▶ **DVD-RAM**—The recordable format of choice for data backup

▶ **DVD+R/DVD+RW**—The competing formats to DVD-R and DVD-RW, respectively

WHAT WRITES TO WHAT?
It is possible to write any application format to any recordable format, if you have the right hardware. However, it is not yet possible to burn a dual layer disc at home.

CHAPTER 2

What Is DVD-R?

DVD-R stands for DVD Recordable, and is similar to CD-R technology. DVD-R uses an organic dye that is injected between the substrate and the polycarbonate exterior. When a DVD is burned, a small portion of the dye is removed, exposing part of the substrate from which the laser will be reflected. When the laser that reads the DVD passes over the dye, it will not reflect any light, and so no data will be read. A DVD-R is based on a WORM (write once, read many) concept, which means that you can write to the DVD only once. After the burning session is complete, the DVD will be closed, and you will not be able to write anything else to it.

There are two versions of DVD-R, namely 1.0 and 2.0. DVD-R 1.0 allows for a total capacity of 3.95 gigabytes. Version 1.0 was replaced with DVD-R Version 2.0, which was split into two different categories—DVD-R General and DVD-R Authoring. Both variations of version 2.0 have a capacity of 4.7 gigabytes. DVD-R Authoring is intended for professional studios and will not be covered in this book. DVD-R General was designed for home use. You cannot write DVD-R Author level DVDs in a DVD-R General level drive, although both of these types can be read in most DVD players. The reason two DVD-R formats were developed is for purposes of content protection. Users cannot make a bit-for-bit copy of a disc that was burned in the DVD-R Author format.

CHOOSING DVD-R MEDIA

When buying media, you generally get what you pay for. Cheaper DVD-R media have a tendency to fail more consistently during the one-write session, rendering the DVD-R useless, since you can only write to it once. You will save more money in the long run if you spring for the better media.

What Is DVD-RW?

DVD-RW is an erasable DVD recording technology. Unlike DVD-R, this technology can be written to over a thousand times. DVD-RW has the same optical properties as a dual layer DVD. DVD-RW is not as compatible with DVD players as the DVD-R media. Compatibility issues with DVD-RW can be a big concern if you want to distribute your DVD to other people.

DVD-RW media is great for projects that you will add things to often—archiving pictures, converting home videos, and storing other information. For example, you could catalog your child's first year onto one DVD-RW, adding to it incrementally as he grows, without having to re-create it (and waste a disc) each time.

An advantage of DVD-RW over DVD-R is that DVD-RW supports the Content Protection for Pre-Recorded Material copy protection scheme, since it has the BCA area included on the media.

CSS PROTECTED MATERIAL
Neither DVD-RW nor DVD-R discs will allow data that has been encoded with the Content Scrambling System to be copied onto them.

What Is DVD+R and DVD+RW?

DVD+R and DVD+RW were released in October 2001 by the DVD+RW Alliance, a coalition of DVD+RW supporters including Hewlett-Packard and Dell, as competing formats to DVD-R and DVD-RW. The + formats are not supported by the DVD Forum. The + and – formats are capable of writing any of the application formats discussed in this chapter.

Unlike DVD-RW, a DVD+RW disc does not have to be finalized (closed so that it cannot be written to again) after each session. DVD+R, on the other hand, must be finalized, after which you cannot add anything else to it.

In a perfect world, a DVD burner manufacturer would produce a DVD drive that supports all of these formats. Unfortunately, nothing currently on the market has this capability. The main thing to remember in choosing a drive is to know which formats your burner will support and buy the media accordingly.

What Is DVD-RAM?

DVD-RAM, like DVD-RW and DVD+RW, is an erasable DVD recording technology. DVD-RAM is primarily used for computer data backup. It does a great job of error-checking the data, but because of this extra error-checking, it is incompatible with most DVD players, thus not making it an option for DVD video authoring. The capacity for DVD-RAM media is the same as DVD-RW discs, 4.7 gigabytes per side. At the time of this writing, DVD-RAM is the only double-sided disc usable by the home DVD author. All others use one side for burning data and the other as a label.

One drawback to the DVD-RAM drive is the required use of a caddy, a holder that the DVD must go into before being inserted into the drive.

DVD Format Compatibility

In the midst of these "format wars," you need to know which formats work with which players. DVD-R and DVD+R will work in about 85 percent of current DVD players, and DVD-RW and DVD+RW will work in approximately 65 percent of all DVD players. As time goes by, the DVD compatibility issues will diminish, as when recordable CD technology was introduced. Table 2.3 shows which formats will read/write in each type of unit.

CHAPTER 2

Table 2.3 Media and Drive Format Compatibility

Media	Standard DVD Player	DVD-R	DVD-RW	DVD+RW	DVD-RAM
DVD-ROM	Read	Read	Read	Read	Read
DVD-R	Read	Write	Write	Read	Read
DVD-RW	Most Read	Read	Write	Most Read	Most Read
DVD-RAM	No	No	No	No	Write
DVD+R	Read	Read	Read	Read	Most Write
DVD+RW	Most Read	Most Read	Read	Most Read	Write

To clarify Table 2.3, a write implies a read—for example, if the drive can write to the media, it can also read it. Second, if the value says "most read" or "most write," that means more than half of the available drives of that type are capable of that particular task.

In the next chapter, we will discuss what to consider when buying a DVD burner, and we'll walk through the process of installing a DVD burner.

Chapter 3
Installing a DVD Burner

Depending on your budget, purchasing a DVD burner can be a major decision. Once you purchase the DVD burner, you have another decision to make: Who will install it? While you may choose to have your burner installed at a local computer shop, you can save money by doing it yourself. And it's not as hard as you might think. It may seem overwhelming to open the case on the computer, mount the drive, and plug in the cables, but with a little guidance, it can be easy. If you do decide to give it a shot, this chapter should help ease your fears. We'll consider the type of DVD burner you should buy, and we'll walk through the process of installing the drive, step by step.

Choosing a DVD Burner

Just as there are many options to consider when purchasing a computer, DVD burners are available with many options as well, and you will need to consider them carefully before making your purchase decision. The options you choose will depend on your budget, your technical savvy, and your personal preferences.

Here are a few things to consider before you purchase a DVD burner:

▶ Do you prefer an internal or external DVD burner?

▶ What interface will your DVD burner use (USB, IDE, ATAPI, FireWire)? That is, what technology will the DVD burner use to communicate with the computer?

▶ What format do you want your DVD burner to support (DVD+RW, DVD-RAM, and so on)?

Internal vs. External

What are the considerations when choosing between an internal and external drive?

First, if you already have a computer and are planning to install an internal DVD burner, you need to make sure that the computer has room to accommodate it. A DVD burner will take up one available drive bay. Newer computers will have at least two drive bays. One will typically contain a CD-ROM drive, and the other one or two will be empty. Other devices that may be in the bays include additional hard drives, an internal zip drive, or a CD burner.

THE CD-ROM DRIVE CAN GO

If you have no available drive bays, consider this: All DVD burners are backwards compatible with CD-ROM drives. So you can replace your CD-ROM drive with your DVD burner and still read CDs with your new burner.

The second consideration is the ease of installation. An external DVD burner is easier to install than an internal one—all you have to do is plug it in. But an external burner will take up more desk space. If your desk is anything like mine, real estate on that desk is very valuable.

Finally, you'll need to think about the level of performance you want to achieve. Typically, most internal drive interfaces are faster than external ones. An exception is the IEEE 1394 (FireWire) interface. FireWire is a newer technology introduced by Macintosh for multimedia peripherals.

Interface Possibilities

An interface is the way that the drive communicates with the computer. Some interfaces common to DVD burners are IDE, ATAPI, FireWire, and USB 2.0. Each of these interfaces has advantages and disadvantages. For example, the FireWire interface comes standard on all new Macintosh computers. PCs do not come with this option standard, but it can be added.

Table 3.1 illustrates the differences among the common interfaces:

Table 3.1 Interface Feature Comparison

Interface	Internal/External	Transfer Speed	Widely Used
SCSI Ultra-Wide	Either	40Mbps	Not as much as IDE
IDE/ATAPI	Internal	6Mbps	All PCs and new Macs
USB 1.1	External	12Mbps	Yes
USB 2.0	External	480Mbps	No
FireWire	External	400Mbps	Mostly Macs

In the preceding table, transfer speed is the rate at which the interface can supply information to the computer. For example, an IDE CD-ROM drive can give the computer information at a maximum of 6 megabytes per second. Typically, new owners of DVD burners choose FireWire for an external interface and IDE for an internal interface. Because of its faster transfer rate, SCSI would be a better choice internally, but the computing industry has settled on IDE as the internal standard. SCSI is usually limited to older Macintosh computers and high-performance servers.

MICROSOFT WINDOWS COMPATIBILITY

DVD burners are generally not fussy about which Microsoft operating system you're using; of course, there are exceptions. Windows 95 does not support USB at all. Windows NT 4.0 has limited support for USB and FireWire. As a general rule, you're better off changing your operating system than spending a lot of time trying to get your burner to work with an old OS. I would recommend Windows 98, Windows 2000, or Windows XP, because, in my opinion, these are the most stable of the Microsoft platforms.

What Format Should My DVD Burner Support?

Since DVD burning technology is still relatively new, there are competing standards in the industry. As discussed in Chapter 2, if you purchase a new computer with a DVD burner installed, the question of formats is already answered for you.

Let's review the recordable formats and their common uses:

▶ **DVD-R**—Recordable media, created by the DVD Forum, that uses the WORM (Write Once, Read Many) concept. This format is supported by Panasonic, Toshiba, Apple, Hitachi, NEC, Pioneer, Samsung, and Sharp. This recordable format is good if the data on the DVD will not change.

▶ **DVD-RW**—Recordable media, also created by the DVD Forum, that has the ability to be written to or erased many times. DVD-RW is supported by the same manufacturers as DVD-R. This format can be used for a DVD that will have data continuously added to it—a photo album, for example.

▶ **DVD+R**—Competing recordable format to DVD-R, created by the DVD+RW Alliance, that also uses the WORM (Write Once, Read Many) concept. This recordable format is supported by Philips, Sony, Hewlett-Packard, Dell, Ricoh, Yamaha, and many others. Like DVD-R, this recordable format is good if the data on the DVD will not change.

▶ **DVD+RW**—Direct competitor to DVD-RW, also created by the DVD+RW Alliance, that can be written to or erased many times. DVD+RW has the same manufacturer support as DVD+R and is a good format to use if the data constantly changes.

▶ **DVD-RAM**—Recordable format that can be written to or erased many times, but these discs are only compatible with DVD-RAM drives. These discs typically require the use of caddies. Because of its built-in error checking, DVD-RAM is ideal for computer data backup.

You can see that the DVD "plus and minus" formats are similar. In general, I recommend purchasing the burner that uses the least expensive media. You can price media at any electronics store or on the Internet. Average prices for each media type, at the time of this writing, are listed in Table 3.2.

CHAPTER 3

Table 3.2 Recordable Media and Pricing

Media Type	Current Price per Disc (Based on 10 pack)
DVD-R	$2.50
DVD+R	$2.50
DVD-RW	$5.00
DVD+RW	$5.00
DVD-RAM	$10.00

Currently, the prices for the plus and minus formats are the same. Be advised though that media prices fluctuate frequently, so you should check for latest pricing before buying a DVD burner. The per-disc price generally goes down when you buy in bigger lots. Table 3.2 is based on a 10 pack of media, but 20 count media packs or higher are available.

PERSONAL COMPUTER COMPATIBILITY

Though most new computers will support a DVD writer, you should always check the DVD drive manufacturer's website to make sure their drive is a match for your computer. Most manufacturers will state minimum (and sometimes recommended) hardware and operating system requirements. When the manufacturer says minimum, that is exactly what they mean—it's the bare minimum required for the DVD writer to function. Performance with minimum requirements is usually less than desirable. If the manufacturer has recommended requirements, always stick with those; they will allow the DVD drive to function optimally.

Installing the DVD Burner

For the purposes of this chapter, let's assume you've purchased an internal IDE DVD+RW burner because both Dell, the leader in the retail home computer market, and Hewlett-Packard, a leader in DVD burners, support this format. It will be ideal for burning home movies on DVD, and its write-many characteristic will allow for the content to change if necessary.

Preparing the Computer for Installation

Before you install the burner, you need to make sure your computer is ready for it. First, make sure you have an available drive bay. Next, check the computer manufacturer's website for recommended requirements.

When preparing your computer for the installation:

1. Assess the number of available drive bays.
2. Remove the computer cover.
3. Make sure you have an available IDE connection.
4. Verify you have the necessary hardware for the installation.

Assessing the Number of Available Drive Bays

As stated earlier, you must have an available expansion bay in order to install an internal DVD burner. Figure 3.1 shows a computer with an available bay.

Figure 3.1
A computer case with an available drive bay.

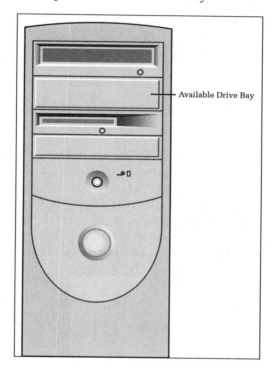

← Available Drive Bay

Removing the Computer Cover

UNPLUG THE COMPUTER!
Before opening the computer's case, you **must** unplug the computer from the wall. Failure to do so could result in serious consequences, such as receiving a major shock or even death.

Cases come in two different types—one requires a screwdriver in order to be opened and one does not. If you purchased your computer from a major computer manufacturer such as Dell or

Compaq, chances are you have a tool-less case. The best way to find out is to look at the back of the computer. If you see screws around the edge of the case, usually three on one side and three on the other, then you do not have a tool-less case, and you should grab a screwdriver.

STATIC ELECTRICITY VS. COMPUTER EQUIPMENT
Static electricity is a computer's worst enemy. Most circuit boards operate at 5 volts. A static electric discharge could cause a few thousand volts to go into the circuit, burning up the chips that make up the circuit board. It is a good idea to wear an ESD (Electrostatic Discharge) grounding strap to redirect any accidental static electricity from your finger to the grounding strap when you're working inside the computer. You can find these grounding straps at any electronics store. If you decide to brave the install without a grounding strap, the same thing can be accomplished by touching a metal surface before working with the computer, which will discharge any static electricity that may have built up.

Making Sure You Have an Available IDE Connection

IDE (Integrated Drive Electronics) is the standard controller for home computers. A controller is a connection on the main circuit board of the computer that is used to connect IDE devices. IDE (and IDE devices) is used by your computer to control things such as CD-ROM drives, zip drives, hard drives, and DVD burners. All PCs have two independent IDE controllers built in (one called the primary IDE controller and another called the secondary IDE controller). Since each controller can connect to two devices, this gives you a maximum of four connections. The hard drive that operates your computer is always the first connection on your primary IDE controller. You cannot change this; if you do, the computer will not know where to find the hard drive!

There is always a hard drive in the computer, so you can assume that you have a maximum of three available connections. Although this can be changed, a CD-ROM drive is usually the first connection on the secondary IDE controller.

IDE devices are connected to your computer's motherboard by an IDE cable (see Figure 3.2).

Figure 3.2
An IDE cable.

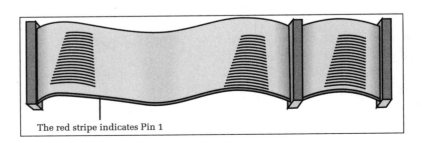

The red stripe indicates Pin 1

Verifying You Have the Necessary Hardware for the Installation

Unfortunately, a tool-less case is not truly tool-less. You will still need a screwdriver to install the DVD burner. The screwdriver is used to mount the drive rails (the mounting brackets) onto the DVD burner. The drive rails go on each side of the burner so that it mounts into the computer correctly. Some computers come with extra drive rails, but some won't. Some DVD burners will come with them as well.

Installing the Burner

Laying the groundwork for installation of the drive is the hardest part of the job, but if you do it right, the installation should be a breeze. Here are the steps for installing the DVD burner.

1. Mount the drive rails.
2. Set the drive jumpers.
3. Install the burner.
4. Verify a successful installation.

Mounting the Drive Rails

Your new drive will need a drive rail screwed onto each side of it, using the screw holes on the sides of the drive. If the holes don't line up with the holes in the rails, you will need to find another pair of drive rails that fit. There are four holes on each side. Normally you will choose the bottom set of holes, but if the drive does not line up, make sure to try the top holes before looking for a new set of rails.

Once you have located the screw holes on the DVD drive and made sure that the drive rail screw holes line up, you are now ready to install them. Figure 3.3 shows you what the DVD drive and drive rails look like, and how to mount them.

Figure 3.3
DVD drive with drive rails.

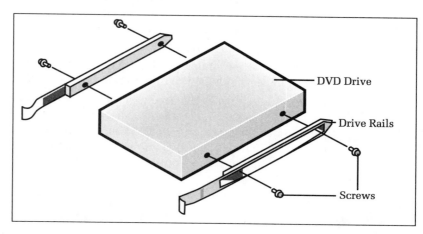

DVD Drive

Drive Rails

Screws

Setting the Drive Jumpers

Each IDE controller can control two drives. Since the two drives are controlled via *one* IDE cable, the controller must have a foolproof way of identifying and communicating with each of them. To accomplish this, one drive is designated as the master, and the other is designated the slave. The master is the "default" drive for that IDE controller, and the slave device must interrupt the master and get "permission" whenever it needs to do its thing. What does this mean for you? Simply that it's up to you to designate your new DVD drive as the master or slave drive on its controller. That might sound complicated, but it's not. Setting the slave/master mode for your drive is a simple matter of positioning a little plastic device, called a jumper, over a set of pins, called a jumper block, located on the back of the drive.

Printed on the IDE device, below the jumper block, is its appropriate drive mode. You'll see the abbreviations MA and SL printed on the IDE device; they stand for master and slave. To put the drive in master mode, simply place the jumper across the two pins directly above or below the initials MA. Similarly, if you want to put the drive in slave mode, the jumper goes over the pins designated SL. You'll also see a third set of initials: CS. That stands for cable select, a mode that allows the IDE controller to determine which drive is the master and which is the slave, based on the location of the drive on the cable.

To use the cable select mode on your IDE controller, do the following:

▶ Make sure your IDE cable supports cable select mode by checking the owner's manual or consulting the manufacturer. If you are installing a DVD burner into your computer, your computer is probably fairly new, and chances are your IDE cable will support cable select mode.

▶ Set both drives on this controller to the cable select mode by placing the plastic device over the jumper pins marked CS.

▶ Position the drives on the cable according to your preferences. The master connector is the connector at the end of the cable. The other connector is the slave.

The mode that you choose depends on the existing configuration of your computer.

▶ If the DVD burner is the only drive that you are installing on this IDE controller, you should set the jumper to cable select drive mode, since all new IDE devices are shipped in cable select mode.

▶ If you're adding the DVD burner to a controller that already has a drive connected to it, and if that previous drive is set to cable select mode, you must set the jumper on the DVD burner to cable select mode as well.

▶ If you're adding the DVD burner to a controller that already has a drive connected to it, and if that previous drive is set to either master or slave mode, you must set the jumper on the DVD burner to the opposite mode. For example, if you want to install the DVD burner on the same cable as a CD-ROM reader that's set to master mode, you should set the DVD burner to slave mode.

SHARING THE PRIMARY IDE CONTROLLER
Recall that the hard drive is required to be the master drive on the primary IDE controller. If you want to add the DVD burner to this drive, you should check the existing mode, either master or cable select, and set the DVD burner accordingly.

DOUBLE-CHECK YOUR CONFIGURATION

All new IDE drives are shipped from the factory set to cable select mode. Manufacturers have been doing this for quite a while, so if you haven't changed your existing configuration, chances are it is set to cable select mode. It's worth your while to double-check, though.

JUMPER SETTINGS FROM THE MANUFACTURER

Some older IDE devices do not have the jumper settings labeled, making it incredibly difficult to figure out which mode the drive is currently in. You can either figure it out by trial and error (hook up the DVD burner and turn on the computer) or by the preferred, much easier method: checking the manufacturer's website for a listing of the jumper settings.

Installing the Burner

The last thing to do, short of testing your installation, is slide the drive into the computer and make the physical connections. If you are installing the DVD burner on the same IDE cable as an existing device, it is best to install the DVD burner in the expansion bay closest to the drive that's on the same cable, so that you'll have enough cable length to connect both devices.

Follow these steps:

1. Remove the expansion bay cover.
2. Slide the drive into the expansion bay.
3. Make the necessary connections.

After you have removed the expansion bay cover, you will see the drive bay. It is of the same dimensions as the DVD drive. Slide the DVD drive into the expansion bay. Depending on the type of case, you may or may not have to secure the drive with screws.

Finally, you should connect the necessary cables into the back of the DVD drive. There are two required connections: the IDE interface and the power cable. Figure 3.4 shows the back of the DVD drive and the location of the power connector, IDE connector, and jumper block. Figure 3.5 shows what the power cable looks like.

Figure 3.4
Back of DVD drive.

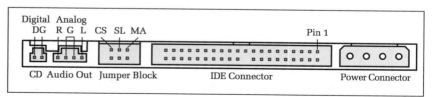

CHAPTER 3

Figure 3.5
Power connector.

Plug in the power connector—there's only one correct way to plug it in.

Next, plug in the IDE cable. The IDE connector has 40 pins, and you will notice a red line going down one side of the cable. This red line denotes pin 1 of the cable. When plugging in the IDE cable, the red stripe should be next to the power connector. Also, most IDE cables are keyed, or designed with a notch in the connector that prevents the cable from being plugged in backwards. You also have the option of hooking up the CD-Audio cable, which allows the computer to assign a default audio playback device and is connected directly to the sound card. If you have a CD-ROM already installed or you do not listen to audio CDs on your computer, this connector is not required. If the computer does not have an existing CD-ROM, or you are replacing it with a DVD burner, you should hook up the CD-Audio cable.

If you are having trouble finding the secondary IDE cable in the computer, it is best to look at the primary IDE cable that is hooked into the hard drive. Once this is located, the secondary IDE cable will look identical.

Verifying a Successful Installation

The easiest way to make sure the DVD drive is installed correctly and working is to see if Microsoft Windows recognizes it.

This check works with Windows 95 and later operating systems.

1. Turn your computer on and let Windows boot up.
2. Double-click on My Computer.
3. When you open up My Computer, you should see a new drive (designated by a new, unique drive letter). In Figure 3.6, the DVD burner is assigned the drive letter G.

Figure 3.6
DVD burner in My
Computer.

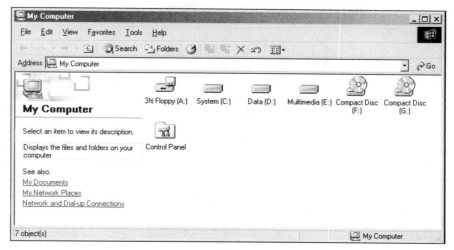

4.   If you see a new drive letter and are feeling feisty, go ahead and put a DVD in the
     player. This is the ultimate test. If it reads the DVD, you are in great shape.

A final check will be to run DVD authoring software and actually burn a DVD, but we'll cover
that in Part Two.

Installing a Macintosh DVD Burner

Although this book will focus mainly on PCs and the Windows environment, Mac owners
should know that the steps for installing the DVD burner on a Mac are identical to the steps
described above. The only difference is in testing the installation. Macintosh computers do not
have a My Computer; Mac users will look for the drive on the Macintosh desktop.

Troubleshooting

In a perfect world, everything would work right the first time. Unfortunately, we don't live in
a perfect world. Table 3.3 offers solutions for some common problems that can arise when
installing your DVD burner.

CHAPTER 3

Table 3.3 Troubleshooting a Failed Installation

Problem	Cause	Solution
Screen is blank when the computer is turned on	Pin 1 (the red stripe side of the IDE cable) is not adjacent to the power connector on the DVD burner, or the cable is not fully plugged in.	Remove the IDE cable and reseat the connection. If the problem persists, disconnect the cable from the motherboard and reseat it as well.
Screen gives an error message that prevents Windows from starting	The drive jumper settings on the drives may be conflicting. That is, both drives could be set to master or both to slave.	Verify the jumper settings for each drive on the IDE cable. Both drives need to be set to cable select or one drive set to master and one drive set to slave.
There is a yellow exclamation point next to the DVD drive within Device Manager	This means that Windows recognizes the drive, but there is a problem that is preventing it from working correctly. The IDE cable may not be fully seated into the DVD drive.	Reseat the IDE cable on the DVD burner.
I have a CD-ROM drive on the same IDE cable as my DVD burner. When I installed the DVD burner, neither of my drives worked.	The jumper settings on the two drives may be conflicting.	Verify the jumper settings for each of the drives on the IDE cable.
The DVD burner is not showing up in Device Manager (Windows 95 and Windows 98 only).	The IDE cable could not be in all the way or the DVD burner could be conflicting with another drive on the IDE cable.	Reseat the IDE cable on the DVD burner. If that does not help, try removing any other drive from the cable to eliminate any potential drive conflicts.
I cannot open the DVD drive tray.	The power cable may not be pushed in all the way.	Reseat the power cable into the DVD burner.
I cannot play music CDs on my DVD burner.	The CD-Audio cable is not hooked up correctly.	If you have a CD-ROM drive, you should use this to listen to music CDs. If you do not, then reconnect the cable to the sound card and also to the back of the DVD burner.

In the next section, we'll take a closer look at the software side of DVD burning. We will explore some of the leading software applications available. Also, we will look at the pros and cons of each, and give a brief run through on how to create a DVD.

Chapter 4
Software Considerations

Up to now, we've largely focused on the hardware side of DVD burning. From this point forward, we're going to be concerned primarily with DVD burning software. Many DVD burning software applications are available, and more are being developed and refined all the time. In this chapter, we'll consider several popular applications and help you narrow the field down to find the package that is right for your needs.

We will consider four DVD burning applications, comparing the strengths and weaknesses of each. And yes, each will have its pros and cons; there is no such thing as a perfect application. The DVD burning applications we'll be discussing in this chapter include the following (see Figures 4.1-4.4):

- ▶ Roxio Easy CD and DVD Creator 6's DVD Builder component
- ▶ Ulead DVD MovieFactory 2.1
- ▶ MyDVD 3.5
- ▶ Macintosh iDVD 3.0.

Figure 4.1
Roxio Easy CD and DVD
Creator 6.

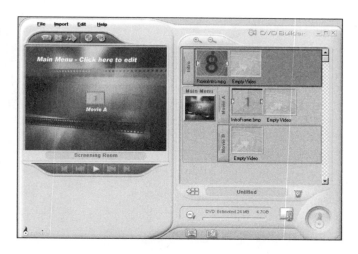

Figure 4.2
Ulead DVD
MovieFactory 2.1.

Figure 4.3
Sonic MyDVD 3.5.

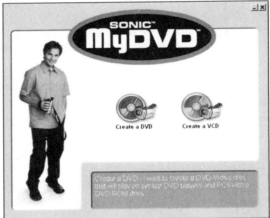

Figure 4.4
Macintosh iDVD 3.0.

This is not a complete list by any stretch of the imagination, but these four applications offer good variety in terms of user levels, features, and pricing.

Hardware Requirements

All DVD burning applications require relatively new computers; the process of encoding videos for DVD consumes enormous computer resources. It is not unusual for the encoding to take hours.

In addition to a fairly beefy computer, an abundant amount of hard disk space is also required, because you must store all of your videos on the hard drive. Once the DVD is created, you can either remove the videos or leave them on your computer for future use. Table 4.1 shows the recommended hardware requirements for each of the software applications under discussion.

Table 4.1 Minimum Hardware Requirements

	Easy DVD Creator 6	DVD MovieFactory	MyDVD 3.5	IDVD 3s
Processor	Intel Pentium III 1.5 Gigahertz	Intel Pentium III 700 Megahertz	Intel Pentium 500 Megahertz	PowerMac G4
Memory	128 Megabytes	128 Megabytes	128 Megabytes	256 Megabytes
Hard disk space required	815 Megabytes	150 Megabytes	18 Gigabytes	384 Megabytes
Video resolution	At least 1024 × 768	At least 800 × 600	At least 800 × 600	At least 640 × 480
Operating system	Windows 98SE, ME, 2000, or XP	Windows 98SE, ME, 2000, or XP	Windows 98SE, ME, 2000, or XP	MacOS 10.1 or above

The "hard drive space required" is a minimum for installation of the program; you *must* have more than the stated totals in order to operate the program. If you intend to capture and edit video on your computer, I recommend having at least ten gigabytes available for using any of the above applications. The price of hard drives has decreased drastically over the years, so you may even want to buy a hard drive that is dedicated solely to your videos.

CHAPTER 4

MORE ABOUT HARD DRIVE SPACE
In Table 4.1, the hard drive space requirement for MyDVD 3.5 is much higher than any of the other listed applications. This is because Sonic Solutions, the maker of MyDVD, figures the video capturing into its recommended requirements.

Available Features

Too many features in a DVD burning application can be overwhelming. When shopping for software, look for applications that offer the features that interest you most.

THE DVD LAYOUT
A phrase that will be used frequently throughout this book is DVD layout, or DVD project (both have the same meaning). A layout simply means the way in which all the elements of a DVD are arranged—elements such as imported videos, menus, still pictures, slideshows, and so on.

Table 4.2 lists some of the major features to consider:

Table 4.2 Feature Comparison

	Easy DVD Creator 6	DVD MovieFactory	MyDVD	IDVD 3
Flat menus	√	√	√	√
Full motion menus	√			√
Captioning	√	√		
Chapter searching	√	√	√	√
Introduction Video	√	√		
Photo slideshows	√	√		√
Transcode video	√	√	√	√
DV capture	√	√	√	
Direct burn from capture	√	√	√	
DVD preview	√	√	√	√
Create disc image	√	√		

Table 4.2 is not an exhaustive list of features. For a complete list of features, check each manufacturer's website. Most of the terms used in Table 4.2 are probably new to you. Let's go through them one by one:

► **Flat menus**—These menus are on every DVD and are the DVD's primary means of navigation. A menu on a DVD allows the author to organize the content for the viewer. For example, you can create a DVD that consists of your son's first three years of life and organize the DVD by creating a menu for each year. Every DVD-authoring application has this feature.

► **Full Motion menus**—These are identical to the Flat menus except that the menu contains moving video and audio. For example, where a Flat menu might have a picture of the sun, a Motion menu might have a video of the sun *setting*.

► **Captioning**—This feature allows the user to create various text elements, including subtitles, text that is displayed under a button when it is highlighted, and closed captioning.

► **Chapter searching**—A chapter on a DVD is similar to that of a book. This feature provides you with the ability to jump straight to an exact part in a video regardless of its location. Most DVD-authoring applications will automatically insert chapters at the beginning of each video clip included in the layout, and some applications will allow you to insert your own chapters. If, for example, you are creating a DVD of your son's first birthday party, you could create a chapter within the video that would allow viewers to jump ahead to the point at which he blows out his candle.

► **Introduction Video**—This feature gives you the ability to create a video that is shown on a DVD before the menu is displayed. Viewers will not have a choice about watching the Introduction Video; it's used for things such as the FBI warning you see at the beginning of many movies.

► **Photo slideshows**—This gives you the ability to create a slideshow displaying a group of still images for a fixed amount of time. For instance, if you have a massive collection of pictures from your last vacation, you can scan them all and create a DVD slideshow in which the pictures change every thirty seconds. Some applications will even allow you to add background music.

► **Transcode video**—As you learned in Part One, DVDs can play only MPEG files. Transcoding is a way to convert other files, such as QuickTime or AVI, to the MPEG format on the fly when the video is added to the DVD layout.

► **DV (Digital Video) capture**—This feature gives you the ability to capture, or record, something that is stored on a digital medium into a MPEG file while you are adding it to the DVD layout. For example, you can capture digital video of last Christmas from your digital camcorder to DVD. You would capture it to an MPEG file and add it to the layout from within your DVD burning application.

▶ **Direct burn from capture**—This feature will allow you to burn the DVD directly from the camcorder as the application is capturing it. You assign the layout a default Main Menu, direct it to the camcorder, and the application does the rest. As I mentioned earlier, this would eliminate the need for a lot of hard disk space, but you cannot change anything after you select your default Main Menu. This feature is great if you are limited on disk space, since you do not have to store the MPEGs on your computer.

▶ **DVD Preview**—The application will bring up a simulation of what the DVD will look like after it is burned to the disc. This will allow you to make sure that all of the menus are linked correctly and the layout looks the way you want it to. This is a good way to avoid wasting recordable media. Figure 4.5 shows exactly what the DVD will look like when it is burned to disc. The remote control in this figure is used to simulate the remote control of a stand-alone DVD player that the disc will ultimately be inserted into. If a problem is noticed during this simulation, then it will definitely show up on the final DVD as well.

Figure 4.5
Project simulation window.

▶ **Create Disc Image**—A disc image will allow you to create the DVD but save it to an image file instead of burning it to a disc. This comes in handy if you want to create the layout but not create the disc until later, or if you want to keep the layout on your hard drive so you can make more copies of the DVD later. Figure 4.6 shows the window that allows you to save a DVD layout to an image file.

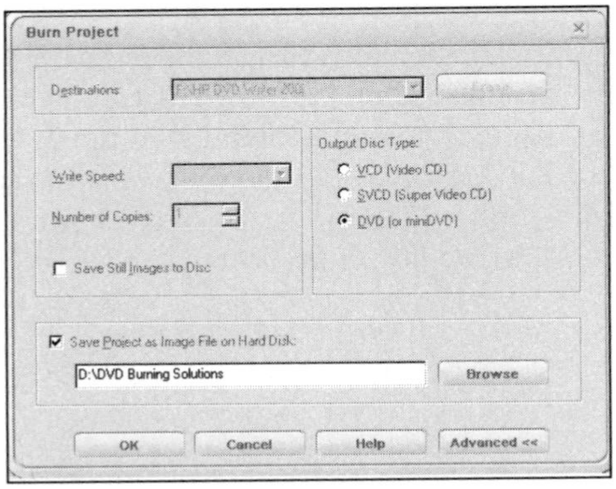

Figure 4.6
Saving a DVD layout in the Burn Project window.

As you can see from Table 4.2, DVD authoring on a Macintosh within iDVD is pretty limited. It is possible to do everything listed in the table on a Macintosh, but not within one application. If you are interested in going the Macintosh route, you can use iDVD in conjunction with iMovie to do everything listed in Table 4.2. You will see later in this chapter that price is a determining factor on the features that you get with an application.

ILIFE

Apple recently released an application suite called iLife. It consists of four applications—iDVD, iMovie, iTunes, and iPhoto. It is comparable to Roxio's Easy CD and DVD Creator 6 in that it is designed to do more than just DVD authoring.

Editing Possibilities

Video editing is a large topic, well worth an entire book in itself. It's also a broad term that can potentially be confusing. Video editing includes:

▶ Capturing the video from an external device—a digital camera or camcorder

▶ Adding text over the video—opening and closing credits, for example

▶ Cutting and pasting bits and pieces of different videos to make one video

▶ Encoding files as MPEG so they can be burned to DVD

▶ Adding transition effects—fade in/out, for example

▶ Inserting audio commentary over a video—director's commentary, for instance

I recommend that you begin with a software application that has editing functionality built in. As you become more versed at creating DVDs, you may find that the tools included in most applications are too basic, and that you would like to purchase something more advanced. At this point, you can purchase stand-alone editing applications that will give you more control over your MPEGs. After the MPEG is customized, you can add the videos to your DVD layout. Of the applications mentioned in this chapter, only Easy CD and DVD Creator 6 and DVD MovieFactory have the ability to perform basic video editing. Both DVD MovieFactory and Easy CD and DVD Creator 6 will allow you to cut a video into pieces, so you can create separate buttons for each new video. Easy CD and DVD Creator 6 goes a step further by allowing you to trim a video. Trimming is when a certain amount of video is cut to the left or right of a point of time in the video.

Formats

Chapter 3 addressed the different formats (broadcast, application, and recordable) that are available for DVDs. You should recall that not all DVD burners support the same recordable formats, meaning that one burner may be able to burn in DVD-RAM format, whereas another may not. Luckily, all DVD burning software should support all recordable formats.

Broadcast Formats

Remember that the two broadcast format options are NTSC and PAL. Every DVD burning application will ask you which broadcast format the DVD should be in. You can also globally change the setting so that the application won't ask you each time. In Easy CD and DVD Creator 6, the option to change this is within the Preferences window. To find this setting, click on the file menu in the top-left corner of the application and select the Preferences option, as shown in Figure 4.7.

Figure 4.7
Preferences window
location.

Figure 4.8 shows the corresponding dialog box in Easy CD and DVD Creator 6.

Figure 4.8
Preferences dialog box
in Easy CD and DVD
Creator 6.

Application Formats

All the DVD burning software we've talked about, with the exception of iDVD, will support the following application formats:

- ► DVD format
- ► VideoCD (VCD) format
- ► Super VideoCD (SVCD) format

At some point, before you burn the DVD or save the DVD image to your hard drive, you will be asked what application format you would like your DVD to be in. I am using the term DVD loosely here because we are in a DVD authoring application. If you choose either VCD or SVCD application format, remember you will burn these to CD recordable media instead of the DVD media, because the different VCD application formats were developed before DVD media. Figure 4.9 shows, within Easy CD and DVD Creator 6, the window that asks which format to burn in. In Easy CD and DVD Creator 6, it is the last thing that is asked before the DVD is written.

Figure 4.9
Burn Project dialog box in Easy CD and DVD Creator 6.

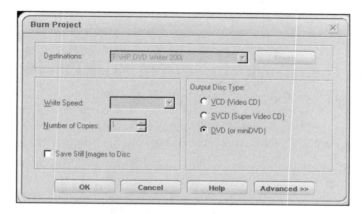

MINIDVD

In Figure 4.9, you may have noticed a MiniDVD option. A MiniDVD allows you to burn DVD quality video to CD media; the major drawback is that it only allows a maximum of 20 minutes of video.

NO VCD SUPPORT WITHIN IDVD

Macintosh did not build in VCD support for iDVD 3.0. If you are interested in using the VCD format, you must choose a different application.

SVCD COMPATIBILITY

Most stand-alone DVD players do not support the SVCD format unless it is specified within the user's manual. If you are unsure whether your DVD player supports SVCD, check your user's manual or contact the manufacturer directly.

But if the quality of VCD is similar to VHS (as you'll recall from our discussion in Chapter 2), then why even bother giving the user an option when DVD is so much better? The answer is this: Let's say that you wanted to send pictures of your Las Vegas wedding to your aunt in Alaska who could not attend. You would like to create a self-starting slideshow that she could enjoy simply by inserting the disc into her DVD player. In reality, the button on your digital camera would wear out before you could take enough pictures to fill up a DVD. With DVD media still expensive, it would be a waste of money to put one hundred megabytes worth of still images on a DVD that has over four gigabytes of free space on it. A VCD would be the format of choice in this case, because it uses less expensive CD media.

Required Knowledge Level and Pricing

All computer applications are developed with a target audience, or user level, in mind. It is a good idea to assess your current abilities and keep this in mind when you are purchasing your application. Some of the advanced applications will assume prior knowledge in DVD authoring, and the application interface will reflect this, making the interface hard to navigate.

An application's sophistication and complexity will also be mirrored, to a certain extent, in its price. Companies don't charge $500 or $600 for software that's targeted to beginners. High-level users, though, will expect to pay more for an application that offers more features. Table 4.3 lists some available applications with their intended user levels and pricing:

Table 4.3 Applications and Their Intended User Level and Price

Application	Intended User Level	Approximate Pricing
Easy CD and DVD Creator 6	Beginner to Intermediate	$100
DVD MovieFactory	Beginner to Intermediate	$50.00
DVDit MyDVD	Beginner	$80.00
iDVD	Beginner to Intermediate	Free with Mac OS that has a DVD burner

In the following chapters, we will explore in greater detail each of the applications that were discussed in this chapter; you'll learn how to burn a DVD using each of these popular programs. When you have finished Part Two, you should have a good idea of which application will suit you best.

Part Two
DVD Software Fundamentals

Chapter 5
Roxio Easy CD and DVDCreator 6

Roxio's Easy CD Creator has become a household name in CD burning. Roxio's latest version, 6.0, has added full DVD authoring support. Roxio, a spin-off corporation of Adaptec Inc., changed the name of this application to Easy CD and DVD Creator to better represent what the application does. In this chapter, you'll learn to use this product to burn your own DVDs, and we'll consider the many features of this application.

PAY CLOSE ATTENTION
This chapter is important to understand since what you learn here will be used extensively in Parts 3 and 4 of this book. In Part 3, we will explore advanced software features using this application, and Part 4 will take a real-world example and put Easy CD and DVD Creator to the test.

Before we get started, let's define a few terms that will be used frequently throughout this chapter.

▶ **DVD Builder**—The DVD authoring component of Easy CD and DVD Creator 6.

▶ **DVD project**—The entire contents and layout of the DVD you're currently authoring.

▶ **Capture vs. Import**—Capturing a video is recording it to a file from an external device—from a camcorder or VCR. Importing refers to pulling a video file from your hard drive into your DVD project.

▶ **Movie**—The term movie, used loosely by DVD Builder, consists of video clips or still images assembled in a storyboard format similar to that of a comic book. You can mix and match a movie with as many video clips or pictures as you want. We will look at different ways to organize a movie in Chapter 10.

▶ **Video clip**—When video is captured in DVD Builder, the captured results are put into video clips. You can add several video clips to a movie.

FOR MORE INFORMATION
For more information about Easy CD and DVD Creator 6 or other products
they offer for purchase, visit Roxio's website at http://www.roxio.com.

Easy CD and DVD Creator 6: In Depth

Easy CD and DVD Creator is actually a suite of applications designed to meet many multimedia-related needs. For an entry-level multimedia application, Easy CD and DVD Creator 6 seems to have it all, and at a price of under 100 bucks, you can't beat it. There are five applications included in this suite.

▶ **Disc Copier**—Gives you the ability to copy virtually any disc you own for a personal backup.

▶ **AudioCentral**—A digital jukebox packed with features that allow you to do many things related to audio: copy (rip) music CDs to your hard drive, organize your music, burn custom music CDs, and so on.

▶ **DVD Builder**—Easy CD and DVD Creator's DVD authoring application. It is the component of Easy CD and DVD Creator that we will spend the most time on.

▶ **PhotoSuite**—Allows you to manage your digital photos. Within this application, you can organize all of your digital photos into virtual albums, brighten them, remove red eye, print them out into standard photo sizes, and even e-mail them to a friend without leaving PhotoSuite.

▶ **Creator Classic**—This is the application that put Easy CD Creator on the map. Creator Classic is what Easy CD Creator once was, prior to version 6.0. Using Creator Classic, you can create data CDs, audio CDs, and jewel cases.

We will concentrate on the DVD Builder component of Easy CD and DVD Creator 6. DVD Builder is also tightly packed with its own feature set.

▶ **Built-in themes**—A DVD theme is a set of fonts, backgrounds, and pictures that create a common look, or theme, to your DVD. A beach theme could be an example, where the background may have a picture of the ocean and the menu buttons may be beach balls. DVD Builder has themes that have already been set up for your use, or you can create your own.

▶ **Motion menus**—DVD Builder allows you to add background videos to your menus if you choose. This background video will play while the viewer is making a selection on the menu.

▶ **Automatic transcoding**—If the video is not in the DVD-compliant MPEG-2 format when it is imported, DVD Builder will automatically convert it.

▶ **DVD preview**—Before the media is written, you can preview what the DVD will look like when it is burned. This is especially useful to work out any bugs that you may have missed when laying out the DVD.

▶ **Save to image**—DVD Builder can save the DVD into one compressed file, or image, on your hard drive; the image is an exact copy of the DVD. It has all of the videos, pictures, and menus compressed inside it. If you need to create another copy, you can use this image instead of creating a new DVD layout from scratch.

▶ **Create chapter markers**—This feature allows you to insert chapter markers, similar to chapters in a book, in your DVDs.

▶ **Large DVD application and recordable format support**—DVD Builder supports all recordable formats available on the market, as well as many application formats such as VCD and SVCD.

Unfortunately, DVD Builder is not perfect. Here's a short list of what I consider its drawbacks:

▶ **Per-call charge for telephone support**—In the past, Roxio has offered free telephone support if a question or problem should arise. Unfortunately, technical support via the telephone for Version 6.0 charges you for each phone call.

▶ **Six button limit**—You are limited to a maximum of six buttons per menu. If submenus are used, this button will count as one of your six.

▶ **Cluttered interface**—It may take some time to get used to the DVD Builder interface. At first, it may feel cluttered, given the amount of things that are available with DVD Builder.

As stated earlier, DVD Builder has the ability to transcode many different types of video into the DVD-compliant MPEG-2 format. Table 5.1 lists the video formats that can be transcoded in Easy CD and DVD Creator 6, with a description of each.

Table 5.1 Supported Video Formats

Format	Description
AVI	Audio Video Interlaced. A standard in some Microsoft environments.
WMV	Windows Media Video. File format used in Windows XP version of Media Player.
DAT	Video files in VCD format.
MPG	MPEG-1 encoded video.
MPEG	MPEG movie format.
M2P	MPEG-2 encoded video.
SVCD	Video files in SVCD format.
VOB	Video file in MPEG-2 encoded DVD format.
MOV	Apple QuickTime movies.
DIVX	MPEG-4, or DivX, encoded videos.

CHAPTER 5

DVD Builder will also import many different types of audio and still picture formats. The supported audio and picture formats are shown in Table 5.2.

Table 5.2 Supported Audio and Picture Formats

Format	Description
JPG	Joint Photographics Experts Group still picture format
BMP	Bitmap still picture format
MP3	MPEG-1 Audio encoded format
MP2	MPEG-2 Audio encoded format
WAV	Wave audio format
WMA	Windows Media Audio format

INSTALLING EASY CD AND DVD CREATOR 6
Since most application installs are self-explanatory, Part 2 of this book will not cover the installation of the applications. With that said, there have been some issues installing Easy CD and DVD Creator on some computers. If you have a problem with the installation, go to Roxio's support site at http://www.roxio.com/en/support/ecddvdvc/index.jhtml. This site is an invaluable tool if a problem should arise.

SOFTWARE PATCHES
At the time of this writing, Easy CD and DVD Creator had released three patches—one required and two optional. Always check the manufacturer's website for any available software updates. You can find patches for Easy CD and DVD Creator at the following website: http://www.roxio.com/en/support/ecdc/software_updatesv6.jhtml.

Using DVD Builder

There are two ways to open DVD Builder. The first is through the Windows Start Menu.

1. Click on the Start Menu.
2. Click on Programs and then Roxio Easy CD and DVD Creator 6.
3. Choose the DVD Builder icon.

The other way to open DVD Builder is through the Home menu. During the installation of Easy CD and DVD Creator, the application installed a shortcut on your desktop called Roxio Easy CD & DVD Creator 6. This desktop icon, when double-clicked, will bring up the Easy CD and DVD Creator Home. Home serves as a launchpad for all applications contained within the Roxio suite. Figure 5.1 shows this launchpad with DVD Builder as the third option from the top.

Figure 5.1
Adaptec CD and DVD
Creator Home.

One of the initial disadvantages of DVD Builder is its somewhat cluttered interface. I say initial because once you get a little practice time in with the interface, you will find that it was well thought out. DVD Builder refers to this first window as the DVD Builder Work Area, as shown in Figure 5.2.

Figure 5.2
DVD Builder interface.

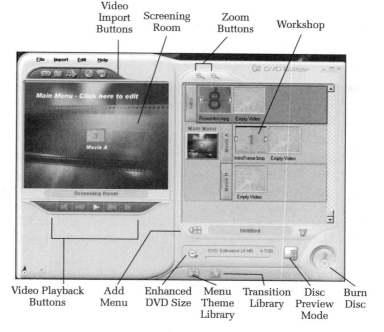

CHAPTER 5

DVD Builder's Work Area is split into two main areas—the Screening Room, on the left, and the Workshop, on the right. The Screening Room, which we will explore in great detail in this and later chapters, allows you to import, edit, and preview the videos that you would like on your DVD. There are two button clusters included in the Screening Room.

▶ Each Video Import button represents a different type of device that DVD Builder can import from. These buttons allow you to import from a digital video camcorder or VHS tape, a scanner or digital camera, or a video file that is already on your computer.

▶ Once the video is imported with the appropriate button, you can use the video playback buttons to preview, pause, or step forward or backward frame by frame.

The Workshop area is where you layout your DVD—assign themes, organize menus, and so on. Let's look at each button in the Workshop.

▶ **Zoom**—Allows you to change the size of the video clips displayed in the Workshop by zooming in or out.

▶ **Add Menu**—When selected, another menu will show up in the Workshop.

▶ **Trash can**—If you decide you don't want something in the Workshop any longer, just drag it to the Trash can.

SAVING THE TRASH

When you save a project in DVD Builder, you will be asked if the contents in the Trash can should be saved as well. If you save the Trash, you can go back later and retrieve videos that have been deleted.

There are several options that did not fall in the Screening Room or Workshop categories, but they can be used any time during the DVD authoring process.

▶ **Estimated DVD Size status bar**—Falls just below the Workshop area. It shows the approximate size of your DVD project.

▶ **Menu Theme Library**—Holds the available themes that can be incorporated into any DVD project.

▶ **Transition Library**—Use this if you want to add a cool effect during a slideshow or a transition between video clips.

▶ **Disc Preview Mode**—Simulates what the DVD will look like when played in the stand-alone DVD player. When initiated, a remote control will appear to allow you to navigate through the DVD as you would if the DVD were in a stand-alone DVD player. This is a great method to make sure all of the menus are functional before writing the project to a disc.

▶ **Burn Disc icon**—Click when you are ready to record your project to disc. You will need to choose your application format—DVD, VCD, or SVCD—and decide whether you want to burn to a blank disc or save the project to an image for later use.

Before starting your first project, it is a good idea to check your preferences and set them accordingly. This is done by clicking on the File Menu and selecting Preferences (see Figure 5.3).

Figure 5.3
Preferences window.

There are many important options in here that should be configured.

▶ Choose your appropriate broadcast format by selecting either NTSC or PAL. For more information on broadcast formats, refer to Chapter 2.

▶ If the quality of a video being imported or captured is not good enough for the DVD standard, you can have DVD Builder warn you before the video is imported; turn this on by selecting the Show Video Quality When Importing Files option.

▶ We have learned that DVD authoring takes a tremendous amount of hard disk space, because videos are imported then encoded. If you have a second hard drive in your computer, you can change the default location for these imported files, freeing up space on your primary hard drive. The location is set in the Specify a Folder for Captured Video textbox.

▶ To make sure that your hard drive has what it takes to burn a DVD, you can click on the Test Disk button. This will test the hard drive that is specified for capturing video—configured above—to ensure that the access speed is adequate to import and burn videos to a DVD.

COMPUTER HOUSEKEEPING

It is a good idea to keep your computer in an optimal state, because DVD Builder has such enormous system requirements. To that end, you should frequently defragment your hard drive, which will ensure that the video being imported is written to a continuous space on the hard drive. Consult your Windows documentation for instructions.

Choosing a Theme

Themes are comprised of several elements—motion menus, buttons, audio, and a similar font for any text on the DVD. DVD Builder has a few themes built in, but you are not forced to use them. If you feel creative, I encourage you to make your own themes.

CHAPTER 5

We will look at a built-in theme and how to add one to your DVD project.

1. Click on the Menu Theme Library button to open it (see Figure 5.2).

2. The Menu Theme Library gives you a list of themes to choose from, as shown in Figure 5.4

Figure 5.4
Menu Theme Library.

3. You can insert your desired theme in one of two ways. First, click and hold the mouse button and drag it into the Screening Room and release the mouse button. You will see the Screening Room background change. You can also add a theme by dragging it into the Workshop—the box directly below Main Menu. You can see the end result in Figure 5.5.

Figure 5.5
Main Menu with new theme.

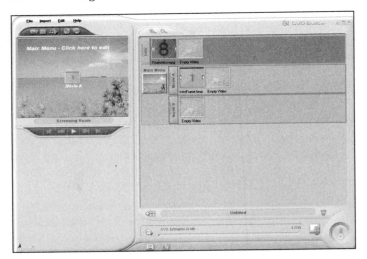

Menu themes within DVD Builder are pretty straightforward. Themes are menu specific, so you are not bound to the same theme for the entire project, although viewers may be confused if you switch themes in the middle of a project.

Adding Multimedia to Your Project

The Screening Room allows you to capture video from practically any medium, including:

▶ digital video camcorder

▶ digital camera

▶ scanner

▶ analog sources—VHS, 8mm, or beta tapes

CAPTURING ANALOG SOURCES

Capturing video from analog sources requires a video capture card. A video capture card has inputs that connect the analog source to your computer.

Capturing is accomplished with the Video Import buttons, directly above the Screening Room section of the DVD Builder Work Area. Figure 5.6 shows a close-up of this menu. In addition to capturing, importing multimedia is also accomplished using these buttons.

Figure 5.6
Video Import buttons.

Using the Video Capture Button

The first button—moving from left to right—in Figure 5.6 is the Video Capture button. This button will capture video from either a digital video camcorder or an analog source—remember you need a video capture card.

CAPTURE DEVICE

Make sure that a capture device is connected to the computer and turned on before you click the Video Capture button. If this is not done, you will receive an error message stating, "No capture device could be found."

When you click in the Video Capture button, two new buttons appear along with an elapsed time status box (see Figure 5.7).

Figure 5.7
Video Capture buttons.

▶ The Start Capture button will capture the video that is currently displaying on the selected capture device.

▶ Advanced Settings is where the capture device is selected, as shown in Figure 5.8.

▶ The elapsed time box will show exactly how long DVD Builder has been capturing.

Figure 5.8
Video Capture
Advanced Settings
window.

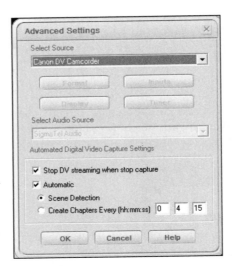

As shown in Figure 5.8, you can choose your capture source—digital camcorder, VCR, and so on. As a default, the Select Source and the Select Audio Source drop-down menus are set to the same device. If you would like to capture both the audio and video of a camcorder, for example, you need to make sure that both menus are the same.

Chapter markers can be created at given time intervals. For example, you can instruct DVD Builder to create a chapter marker every thirty seconds. DVD Builder will let you reference these markers and assign a button that will go directly to that point in time on the video.

REMAINING BUTTONS

Some of the buttons in Figure 5.8 are not addressed, because DVD Builder is smart enough to configure these for you. If you are feeling adventurous, by all means, check them out.

INSERTING CHAPTER MARKERS

DVD Builder will allow the creation of chapter markers only during the video capture, and only at certain time intervals. Once the video is captured, you must use a different application to edit or insert other chapter markers.

Now that the capture device is connected, turned on, and selected with the advanced settings, you are ready to start capturing.

1. In the Workshop area, select the menu that the captured video should be placed into. Click once on the intended menu—an orange box that indicates the current movie will appear around it. Figure 5.9 illustrates a selected menu—movie B in this figure.

Figure 5.9
Selected menu in Workshop.

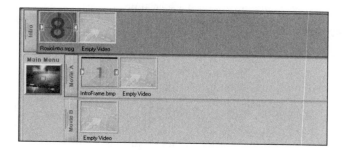

2. Press the Play button on the source device.
3. Click the Capture button. When the Capture button is clicked, the button will rename itself to Stop Capture, shown in Figure 5.10, and the video will capture from your device into a file on your computer.

Figure 5.10
Stop Capture button.

4. Once the video capture is complete, click the Stop Capture button.
5. The captured video clip will show up in the movie that was selected in Step 1.
6. Double-click on the new video clip to preview it in the Screening Room.

MULTIPLE CAPTURES
DVD Builder allows you to start and stop a capture as many times as necessary. When you stop and restart the capture, DVD Builder will automatically create a new video clip that is linked to the previous video clip in the movie.

Using the Other Sources Button

The next button included in the Video Import buttons is the Other Sources button. It is used to import from devices including scanners, digital cameras, or any other device that is TWAIN compatible.

TWAIN: A DEFINITION

TWAIN is a technology that is widely used by some digital cameras and all scanners. TWAIN allows you to take out the middleman by gaining access to a device directly within the application being used. Without TWAIN, you would have to open a special program to scan a picture, and then use DVD Builder to import the picture. Contrary to popular belief, TWAIN is not an acronym.

There are a few required steps when importing from Other Sources.

1. Verify that the device that you want to import from is connected and turned on.

2. Click the Other Sources button—the second button from the left in Figure 5.6. When the button is clicked, an Acquire Still Image button will appear, and if your computer is connected to more than one TWAIN device, a Select Source box will also appear. Figure 5.11 illustrates both buttons.

Figure 5.11
Other Sources buttons.

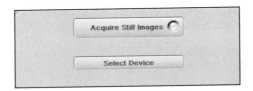

3. If applicable, select your device using the Select Source button, as shown in Figure 5.12.

Figure 5.12
Select Source window.

4. When the import is done, via a TWAIN device, DVD Builder will import the image into the selected movie within Workshop, exactly as it did when capturing from a digital video camcorder.

5. To preview the imported file, double-click on the picture within Workshop, and it will show up in the Screening Room.

DVD Builder allows you to do other things to the image once it is imported, such as adding a voice commentary. We will look at this in Chapter 9 when we explore the advanced multimedia editing abilities of Easy CD and DVD Creator 6, specifically DVD Builder.

Using the Multimedia Files Button

The third Video Import button is for importing multimedia files—videos, pictures, or audio—that are already on your computer. This button would be used if you scanned a number of pictures in the past and wanted to import them.

Importing multimedia files into DVD Builder involves a few steps.

1.   Click the Multimedia Files button—the middle button in Figure 5.6. An Import Files window will appear, as shown in Figure 5.13.

Figure 5.13
Import Files window.

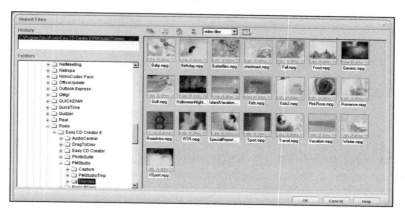

FILTER BY MULTIMEDIA TYPE

The Import Files window lets you view all supported multimedia files, or you have the option of displaying only a certain multimedia type—video, audio, or still image (pictures) files. DVD Builder can also filter by file type. Refer to Tables 5.1 and 5.2 for available file types.

2.   Select the directory that has the desired file in it. The default folder path is C:\Program Files\Roxio\Easy CD Creator 6\PMStudio\Themes. You can change the folder view by clicking on the far right icon (see Figure 5.13). You can choose from thumbnail, list, and details views. Once the directory is selected, the files will show up in the right side of the window. Only files that are available for import will show up in this pane.

3.   You can preview any file in the right pane by double-clicking on it, which will bring up a Preview window, as shown in Figure 5.14.

Figure 5.14
Multimedia File
Preview window.

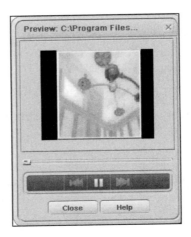

4. Click on the desired multimedia type and click the OK button. The file will be added to the selected movie.

Using the Real-Time Recording Button

The last button in Figure 5.6 is for real-time recording—capturing video "live" through a camcorder, without the intermediate hard disk step. This should only be used if you are running low on disk space, because your functionality is extremely limited. Real-time recording does not allow any video editing, since the video is taken directly from the camcorder and written to the DVD media.

Recording in real time is similar to capturing to a file. The difference is that you must use a DVD+RW burner and DVD+RW media, because it must have the ability to write to the disc many times. The number of times the disc is written to depends on the number of videos that will be captured to it. Currently, the DVD+RW format is the only recordable format that DVD Builder will recognize when using real-time recording.

CLOSE OTHER APPLICATIONS
Real-time recording uses a tremendous amount of computing power. To aid in preventing the risk of lost data while capturing from a camcorder, I suggest closing all applications while recording.

This chapter has only scratched the surface of DVD Builder's multimedia editing potential. Chapter 9 will go into greater detail on how to edit the content, and Chapter 10 will assist you in organizing this content.

Manipulating Menus

A DVD menu is the primary means of navigating the content of a DVD. An efficient DVD menu layout can make a good DVD great. You should carefully plan your menus before you burn them to disc. There are four components to a DVD Builder menu.

1. **Background**—A menu background can be either a video or a picture.

2. **Menu titles**—Each menu is given a name, or title, that describes it. For example, if you went to Las Vegas for a long weekend, your menu title could be "Our Weekend in Vegas."

3. **Menu buttons**—A DVD menu button can link the user to a slideshow, video, another menu, and so on.

4. **Menu button labels**—Menus are named with titles, and buttons are named with labels. You can change this button label to anything you want.

Creating a submenu is easy; just click on the Add Menu button, as shown in Figure 5.2. The new menu will be added directly below the Main Menu. The submenu will indent itself so that you can distinguish between the different menus. Figure 5.15 shows the Workshop with the new menu added.

Figure 5.15
A new menu has been added.

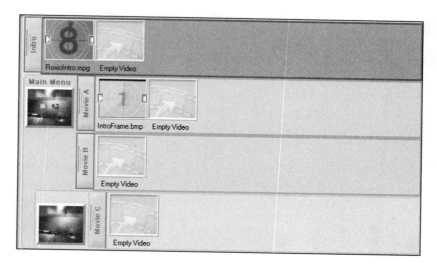

ADDING SUBMENUS

It is possible to add as many submenus as you want; just remember that DVD Builder is limited to six buttons per menu.

Any menu other than the Main Menu is considered a submenu. When a submenu is created, DVD Builder will also create a Back button—it looks like an arrow pointing to the left—so that you can go back to its parent menu. If you have only one submenu in your project, then its parent menu would be the Main Menu.

Changing Menus and Buttons

Menu customizations are done through the Screening Room. To do this, just double-click on the menu in the Workshop, and it will appear in the Screening Room. You can see in Figure 5.16 what the Main Menu looks like in the Screening Room, before customizations.

Figure 5.16
Menu in the Screening Room.

Remember that menus have titles, and buttons have labels. The method for changing either the button label or menu title is the same.

1. Put the menu into the Screening Room by either dragging the menu into the Screening Room or double-clicking on it.

2. Click once on either the menu title or button label—depending on which one you want to change.

3. Clicking on the title/button brings up a window like the one shown in Figure 5.17. Just type in the new name and click OK.

Figure 5.17
Change title/label window.

4. It is possible to change the font size, type, or style by clicking the Select Font button, which is shown in Figure 5.18.

Figure 5.18
Select Font window.

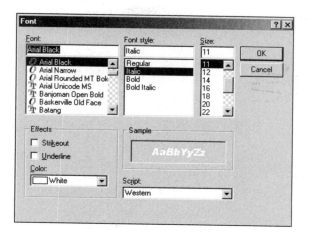

NAMING MENUS

Name the menu title or button labels as clearly and accurately as possible. You don't want to leave your viewer in the position of facing six buttons on a menu, labeled Movie A through Movie E.

RENAMING BUTTON LABELS

When you rename a button label within the Screening Room, it will also rename the movie within the Workshop and vice versa.

There may be a time when you decide that a menu or button is no longer needed. To remove a menu from your project, just drag it to the Trash can (shown in Figure 5.2), and it will be deleted from the Workshop. To remove a button, drag the movie that references that button to the Trash can.

ANOTHER WAY TO DELETE

Another way to delete, besides dragging items to the Trash can, is to right-click on either the movie or the menu and select Delete.

Finally, you can change the image shown in the button. By default, DVD Builder will show the first item in your movie. If a video clip is first, the button will use the first frame of that video clip for the image. If a still picture is first in the movie, it will use that. To change the image, just make the desired video or picture the first one in the movie.

CHAPTER 5

USING A FRAME IN A VIDEO

It is possible to use a frame in the middle of a video clip as your menu button. To do this, you must extract the frame from the video, which will create a picture, and set it first in the movie. We will cover this in more detail in Chapter 9.

Setting the Menu in Motion

A motion menu is simply a menu that has a video clip set as the background. Most built-in menu themes have motion menus. You can either use one of these or import your own video clip into your project. There are three steps involved in changing the menu background to create a motion menu.

1. Put the menu into the Screening Room by either dragging the menu into the Screening Room or double-clicking on it.
2. Click the Multimedia Files button contained within the Import Video buttons.
3. Click the mouse button once and drag a video file from the Import Files window (shown in Figure 5.13) to the Screening Room.

PREVIEWING THE MOTION

To see what the menu looks like when it is in motion, drag the menu to the Screening Room and click the Play button.

To enhance your motion menu, you can also add an audio file to it. Most built-in themes have audio included, but you can replace it if you want. You should always choose an audio file that is shorter than the video clip that is used as the menu background. If not, the audio will cut off when the video clip has finished. There are two ways to add audio to your menu.

1. Click the Multimedia Files button contained within the Import Video buttons. Click the mouse button once and drag the audio file from the Import Files window to the intended menu.
2. In the Workshop, right-click on the menu and select Attach Audio. A browse window will appear, as shown in Figure 5.19. Navigate to the folder where the audio file is stored and select it.

Figure 5.19
Browse for audio files.

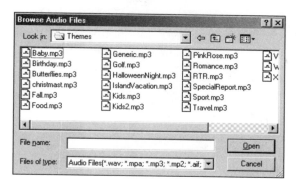

If you do not like the audio of a built-in theme, you can change it without affecting the video part of the theme. There are two ways to replace the audio contained within a theme.

1. In the Workshop, right-click on the menu and select Remove Audio. When DVD Builder asks if you are sure you want to remove this file, click Yes. Since there is no audio, add the new audio as you normally would.

2. Click the Multimedia Files button contained within the Import Video buttons. Click the mouse button once and drag the audio from the Import Files window to the intended menu. A window will pop up (see Figure 5.20) that will inform you that an audio file is already attached and ask you to confirm that you want to replace it. Click Yes.

Figure 5.20
Replace Audio window.

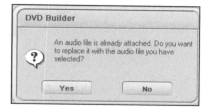

Disc Preview

DVD Builder allows you to preview what the DVD will look like before burning it to disc. This is important because it will give you a chance to work out any bugs that your DVD project may have, and you'll avoid wasting a disc.

To start DVD Builder's Preview Mode, click on the remote control icon in the bottom right-hand corner of the Work Area, as shown in Figure 5.2. When Preview Mode is started, the Work Area will disappear, and you will be left with a remote control and video window. The remote control is designed to be identical to that of a stand-alone DVD player's remote control. A picture of this remote is shown in Figure 5.21.

Figure 5.21
Preview Mode remote
control.

The buttons here are the same as those on your DVD player's remote control. Here's what they do:

▶ **Menu button**—Returns the DVD to the Main Menu.

▶ **Intro button**—Replays the Introduction Video on this DVD. We will configure an Introduction Video in Chapter 10.

▶ **Return button**—Moves the DVD up one menu if submenus exist.

▶ **Stop, Play, and Pause buttons**—The cluster of buttons in the middle of the remote control allows you to manipulate the video currently playing on the DVD Preview.

▶ **Menu navigation buttons**—The bottom cluster of buttons lets you choose a specific button on the menu and execute it.

To exit out of Preview Mode, just click the X in the top right-hand corner of the remote control. This will bring DVD Builder back up for further editing, or, if you are ready, to burn the DVD.

Burning or Saving your DVD

When the project is complete, just click the Burn button—which brings up the Burn Project window—to create your DVD, as shown in Figure 5.22.

Figure 5.22
Burn Project window.

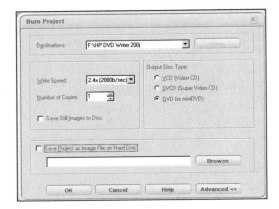

Figure 5.22 shows the window with the advanced options enabled. You can enable this by clicking the Advanced button in the lower right-hand side of the window. Let's look at the options that are available.

▶ **Destinations**—This drop-down menu allows you to select which DVD recorder you would like the project recorded to. If you are burning to VCD format, a CD recorder may also show up as a selection.

▶ **Erase**—To the right of the Destinations button is the Erase button. If you are using DVD-RW or DVD+RW media, you can click the Erase button to clear the disc's contents before recording your project.

▶ **Write Speed**—This is the speed at which the recorder—the one you chose in the Destinations drop-down menu—will write the data to the disc.

▶ **Number of Copies**—Specify the number of copies of your project you would like to burn. If you select more than one, the DVD drive will open and ask you to insert another blank disc when the previous one has completed.

▶ **Save Still Images to Disc**—Check this box if you want DVD Builder to make a DVD-ROM section on the disc, so you can open the DVD in a computer and copy the pictures from it. To find your pictures after the DVD is burned, open the DVD in a computer and look for a folder named "Images."

▶ **Output Disc Type**—Specify the application format that you will be burning to the disc. Refer to Chapter 2 for an explanation of each of these formats.

▶ **Save Project as Image File on Hard Disk**—Instead of burning the DVD project to disc, you can save it as a file on your computer. This is a compressed file that contains all of your multimedia and customized menus.

BURNING TO DISC
You must insert the DVD media into the drive before you click the Burn button; otherwise, you will only be able to save to an image file.

Saving Your Project to the Hard Drive

To save a project file for later use, check Save Project as Image File on Hard Disk in the advanced options of the Burn Project window. There are four quick steps to accomplish this.

1. Check the Save Project as Image File on Hard Disk option.
2. Click the Browse button to specify a location for the image file.
3. Choose the appropriate Output Disc Type. This is necessary so DVD Builder will encode the movies to the right standard—MPEG-1 or MPEG-2.
4. Click the OK button.

CHAPTER 5

SAVING TO IMAGE VS. SAVING PROJECT

When a project is saved to an image file, the project goes through the exact same steps as if you are burning it. The difference is that it is redirected to a file instead of a blank DVD.

Before the image file is created, DVD Builder must encode each movie included in your project. An Encode Progress window, as shown in Figure 5.23, will appear while the movies are being encoded.

Figure 5.23
Encode Progress window.

Once DVD Builder has finished encoding each movie, a Burn Progress window will show you progress of the image file (see Figure 5.24).

Figure 5.24
Burn Progress window.

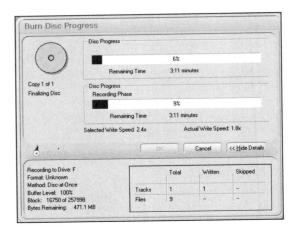

When the image is complete, DVD Builder will display "Image created successfully," as shown in Figure 5.25.

Figure 5.25
Completed image.

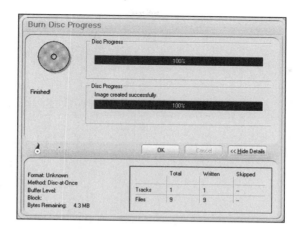

CREATING AN IMAGE FILE

To create an image file, you must remove any recordable media from the drive. If there is blank media in the drive, the project will burn to disc whether you told it to save to an image file or not.

Burning an image file to DVD is done through DVD Builder.

1. Click on the File menu in the upper left-hand corner of the window.
2. Select Burn Disc from Image File.
3. Navigate to the folder that contains the saved image.
4. Click Open and the Burn Project window will appear.

Burning Your Project to DVD

To burn your project to DVD using the Burn Project window, follow these steps.

1. If you have more than one burner, select the appropriate one.
2. If using rewritable media, click the Erase button.
3. For more than one copy, set the Number of Copies option accordingly.
4. To create a DVD-ROM section to store all of your pictures, check the Save Still Images to Disc box.
5. Select the Output Disc type.
6. Click the OK button.

The Encode and Burn Progress windows are the same as when you created a DVD image—refer to Figure 5.23 and 5.24, respectively.

Congratulations! That does it for burning a DVD with Easy CD and DVD Creator's DVD Builder. Figure 5.26 will be displayed when the disc is complete.

CHAPTER 5

Figure 5.26
Successful burn!

Chapter 6
Ulead DVD MovieFactory 2.1

Ulead Systems has been a leader in multimedia application development since its inception in 1989. DVD MovieFactory, developed by Ulead, was one of the first entry-level DVD authoring applications to reach the consumer market and has proven itself as one of the top entry-level applications available. In this chapter, the many features of DVD MovieFactory will be examined, and you will learn how to burn a DVD using the application.

ULEAD WEBSITE

You can reach Ulead's website at http://www.ulead.com. From this website, you can download a free trial of DVD MovieFactory, look for answers to any problems you may have, or check out other products that Ulead offers.

ULEAD DVD WORKSHOP

If, as you go through this chapter, you feel that DVD MovieFactory is too basic for what you want to do, I encourage you to check out Ulead's DVD Workshop. This application has more robust video editing features than DVD MovieFactory.

Ulead DVD MovieFactory: In Depth

DVD MovieFactory's features go well beyond what other applications provide in the under $50 price range. Let's look at some of its features:

▶ Over 60 built-in themes so you do not have to create your own, with the ability to customize them.

▶ Instead of using a different application to convert your QuickTime or AVI files to the DVD-compliant MPEG-2 format, DVD MovieFactory's automatic transcoding will automatically do this when the video file is added to your project.

▶ For a real-time look at your DVD before it is burned to disc, you can use DVD Preview to catch any last minute errors.

▶ You can capture video directly from any FireWire-based camcorder or analog capture card to the MPEG-2 format.

CHAPTER 6

▶ Create chapter markers manually or at certain time intervals.

▶ Easy-to-use Slideshow Editor that allows you to rearrange slides in any order that you like.

▶ Save to Image option that will let you save your completed DVD project to the hard drive in a compressed file to burn at a later date.

▶ Disc Direct allows you to capture from a video source—FireWire-based camcorder or analog source—directly to a DVD. Since the hard drive is taken out of this process, valuable hard disk space is not lost.

The advantages of DVD MovieFactory far outweigh the disadvantages, but there are still a few things to consider before buying this application.

▶ No motion menus or buttons are available in this version. With over 60 themes, you would think that at least one of them offered motion.

▶ While Ulead's website has great technical support online, you cannot e-mail with a problem. You must either call them, which if the wait is over fifteen minutes you must leave a message, or find the answer by searching their website.

▶ From a purely cosmetic standpoint, the interface may look unappealing due to its gray background.

Multimedia format support—the ability of the application to sense a certain type of still image, audio, or video file and convert it to a format that a DVD player will recognize— is a big issue when you are evaluating a software application. Typically, you should look for an application that supports many multimedia formats. Table 6.1 lists the formats that DVD MovieFactory supports.

Table 6.1 Supported Multimedia Formats

Format	Description
MPEG	MPEG movie format
AVI	Audio Video Interlaced. A Microsoft standard
MOV	Apple QuickTime movies
BMP	Bitmap still image format
GIF	Compuserve's Graphic Interchange Format for still images
JPEG	Joint Photographic Experts Group for still images
PNG	Portable Network Graphic for still images
TIF	Tagged Image File Format for still images
MPA	MPEG Audio
MP3	MPEG-1 audio encoded format
WAV	Wave audio format

Using DVD MovieFactory

DVD MovieFactory is a menu-based application, meaning that the same menus will be presented with the same steps each time you want to create a DVD. After installing DVD MovieFactory, you can start it by double-clicking the file that was created on the desktop or you can go through the Start Menu. To open it through the Start Menu, follow these steps:

1. Click on the Start Menu.
2. Click on Programs and then the DVD MovieFactory 2 folder.
3. Click once on the Ulead DVD MovieFactory 2 icon from this folder.

The question of whether the interface is unappealing—see the disadvantages section—is for you to decide. Regardless, the application is still effective. Figure 6.1 shows you the initial window that comes up when DVD MovieFactory is started.

Figure 6.1
DVD MovieFactory
interface.

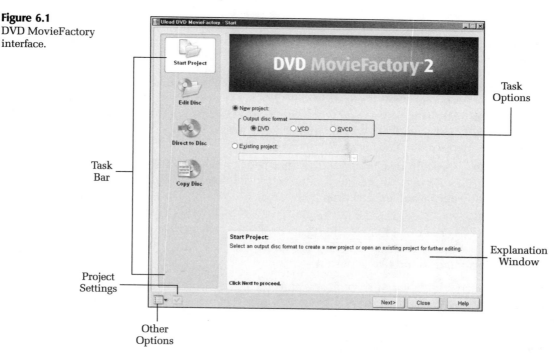

You can think of DVD MovieFactory's first window as the launchpad. Each section of this window has a specific purpose.

▶ **Task bar**—Contains four things you can do with DVD MovieFactory—Start Project, Edit Disc, Direct to Disc, and Copy Disc.

▶ **Other Options button**—You can, among other things, set preferences, visit Ulead's website, or close the application. The Other Options window is shown in Figure 6.2.

CHAPTER 6

Figure 6.2
Other Options window.

> **Project Settings button**—An advanced feature that will let you customize your video capture parameters—changing the resolution of your videos would be an example.

> **Task Options**—Depending on the task that you choose in the task bar, this area will give you the different settings for that specific task.

> **Explanation window**—Gives a brief explanation of the task options so you can better understand them.

Contained within the task bar are four tasks that will cover any DVD authoring need that may arise. This chapter will concentrate on the Start Project task, but an explanation of each task is in order.

> **Start Project task**—Used to create DVDs from scratch. This task allows you to capture video, edit menus, preview your disc, and finally burn it.

> **Edit Disc task**—Used when you have a DVD that is already created on rewritable media, and you would like to change menus or videos without having to re-create the DVD project from scratch.

> **Direct to Disc task**—Will create a DVD on-the-fly while the video is captured. It will save you precious hard drive space, since it is captured from the video device and burned right to the DVD.

> **Disc Copier task**—If you have DVDs that you previously created, you can use Disc Copier to make duplicate copies for distribution. This task is also used if you previously created a disc image—we will cover this later in the chapter—and would like to burn it.

Before you start editing your first project with DVD MovieFactory, it is always a good idea to check the preferences and set everything accordingly. Figure 6.3 shows the Preferences window, and the following list details each option.

Figure 6.3
Preferences window.

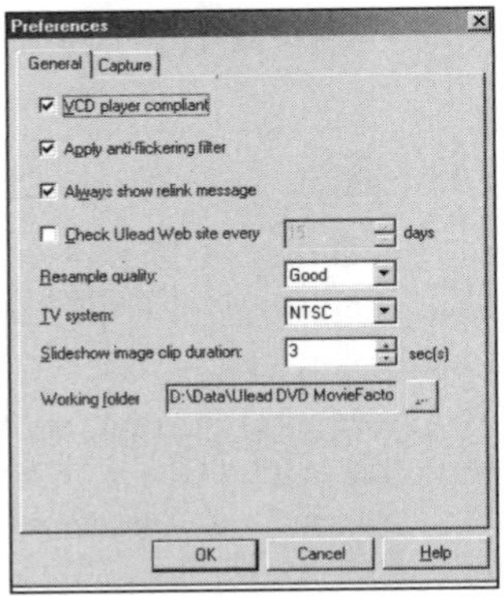

▶ **VCD player compliant check box**—If the project you are creating is in Video CD (VCD) format, you should make sure that the VCD player compliant box is checked. This ensures that the VCD project will be compatible with stand-alone DVD players that can play VCDs.

▶ **Apply Anti-flickering Filter check box**—DVD menus on some older television sets may flicker. With this option checked, DVD MovieFactory will try to reduce the amount of flicker. This will **not** work with newer progressive scan—a new projection technology—television sets.

▶ **Always Show Relink Message check box**—Will check each menu button to make sure that the movie it is linked to has not been moved. If the movie has been moved since the project was created, DVD MovieFactory will relink to its new location.

▶ **Check Ulead Web Site Every XX Days check box/drop-down menu**—XX is a time interval that defaults to 15 days—DVD MovieFactory will automatically connect to the Internet and check Ulead's website to see if an update or patch has been released for the application.

▶ **Resample Quality drop-down menu**—You can choose one of two options: Good and Best. This quality refers to the quality of the video that is included in your project. Select Best if your project requires near-perfect video reproduction.

▶ **TV System drop-down menu**—Where the broadcast format—NTSC or PAL—is configured.

▶ **Slideshow Image Clip Duration drop-down menu**—If the image is within a slideshow, this sets how long the picture will be shown before moving on to the next one. This option serves as a default within the Slideshow Editor, and can be changed.

▶ **Working Folder option**—Points DVD MovieFactory to the location where it should place its temporary files. If you have more than one hard drive, you should select a folder on the hard drive that has the largest amount of free space.

The remainder of this chapter will focus on the Start Project task. This task is organized into four major steps.

▶ **Add Multimedia**—This step includes capturing and editing your video, importing multimedia from the hard drive, and creating slideshows.

▶ **Choosing a Theme**—Menus can be customized using DVD MovieFactory's built-in items. For example, if you would like to change the way a button looks, DVD MovieFactory will ask you to choose one from a pre-defined list.

▶ **Disc Preview**—Previewing your disc will give you a real-time look at how the DVD will appear on a stand-alone DVD player. You should go through every menu to make sure the buttons point to the right place and also make sure the videos are edited correctly.

▶ **Burning or Saving your DVD**—In this step, the movies are encoded into the DVD-compliant MPEG format, and the project is either burned to a DVD or saved to a file for later use.

Adding Multimedia to Your Project

Adding multimedia, referred to as multimedia clips, is the first step involved in creating a new project with DVD MovieFactory. In this step, you can capture video from any FireWire-based camcorder or analog source (for example, VCR), import multimedia that is already on your hard drive, or create slideshows. After the multimedia has been added to your project, you can use DVD MovieFactory's video-editing toolkit to pull sections out of a video and make a new one, replace the current audio in a video, and add chapter markers. Finally, the Add/Edit Media Clip window lets you set up a First Play Video, which is a video that is shown before the Main Menu is shown—an FBI warning on a movie is an example. Figure 6.4 shows the window that will accomplish all of this for you.

Figure 6.4
Add/Edit Media Clip window.

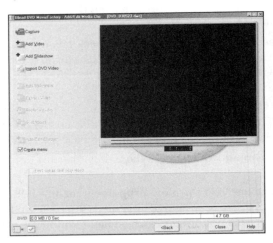

ANALOG SOURCE VIDEO CAPTURE

You must have a compatible video capture card to capture from any device other than a FireWire-based camcorder. For a list of compatible cards, check Ulead's website and http://www.ulead.com/dmf/compatibility.htm.

Capturing Video

The first button located at the top left-hand corner of the Add/Edit Media Clip window is the Capture button. Capturing video with DVD MovieFactory is easy. Figure 6.5 shows you the Capture Video window.

Figure 6.5
Capture Video window.

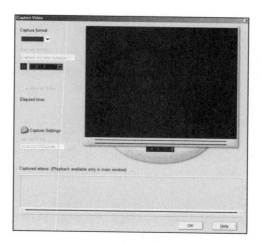

DVD MovieFactory will automatically find and configure your capture card and FireWire-based camcorder, if installed. If for some reason this does not work or you would like to re-configure the devices yourself, click on the Capture Settings button. We will not get into the advanced configuration of the capture settings since DVD MovieFactory does it automatically.

NUMEROUS CAPTURE DEVICES

If you have more than one capture device installed—a FireWire-based camcorder and a capture card, for example—you can select the device that you want to capture from by clicking on the Capture Settings button.

FIREWIRE CARDS

Although FireWire technology is the way to go, it is only slowly being adopted into the PC market. You may have to purchase a FireWire card in addition to a FireWire-based camcorder.

If DVD MovieFactory does not detect a capture device, it will display an error message, as shown in Figure 6.6.

Figure 6.6
No capture device
detected.

In addition to the Capture Settings button, there are a few other things on this window that need to be configured before the capture process is started.

▶ **Capture Format**—The format that the captured file should be saved in—DV, AVI, or MPEG. I recommend always saving to the MPEG format, because you will be able to use these clips later—even in other DVD authoring applications— if needed. Also, some video degradation will occur as you convert between formats.

▶ **Capture Mode**—Has two options—Capture by Total Duration or Capture by Marked Duration. Capture by Total Duration will capture the entire video. If you wanted to only capture a segment of the video, you would use Capture by Marked Duration.

▶ **Capture Folder**—The default folder that the captured videos will be saved to. It can be changed at any time. Similar to the temporary files path set in the preferences, I would recommend to set this path to your hard drive —if you have more than one—that has the largest available free space on it.

When everything is configured, just follow these steps for a successful capture.

1. On the right-hand side of the window, you should see a monitor window. This window will show you the scene where the capture will start. You can use the controls beneath this monitor window to get to the desired starting point on the capture source.

2. Click on the Capture Video button.

3. At this point, you can either capture the whole video and the capture will stop by itself or you can stop the capture by hitting either the Escape key or clicking the Stop Capture button—this button will appear once the video starts capturing.

4. Click the OK button to begin.

You can start and stop this process as many times as you like. Each time the process is stopped and restarted, a new video clip is created.

VIEWING THE CAPTURED VIDEO
In order to see what you have captured, you must exit out of the capture window, and preview it in the Add/Edit Media Clip window.

Importing Video

Recall that capturing is for retrieving video that is not on the hard drive, and importing is adding video or other multimedia files to the project that is on your computer. The Add Video button—located below the Capture button—is for importing videos.

When the Add Video button is clicked, you are presented with an Open Video File dialog box to locate your file, as shown in Figure 6.7. Within this dialog box, you can preview the video in a small window. In addition to previewing, you can also retrieve informational properties, such as length, file size, and other audio- and video-specific properties before the video is imported, as displayed in Figure 6.8.

Figure 6.7
Open Video File dialog
box.

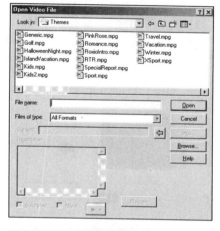

Figure 6.8
Video properties.

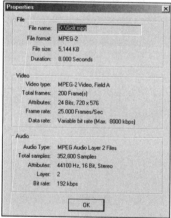

DVD MovieFactory will also let you import videos directly from another DVD. You do this by clicking on the Import DVD Video button. This button requires that the video is already in a DVD-compliant format.

IMPORTING OTHER MULTIMEDIA TYPES

Unlike other DVD authoring applications, DVD MovieFactory will not let you import audio or still image files by themselves. In fact, you cannot import audio files at all unless you replace the audio of an imported video. Still images must be imported into a slideshow, which will be covered later in this chapter.

CHAPTER 6

Editing Your Videos

DVD MovieFactory has some useful video-editing features built in that you normally do not find with a beginner-level application in this price range. These can be found on the left-hand side of the Add/Edit Media Clip window shown in Figure 6.4.

▶ **Mark-in and Mark-out**—Features that do not have buttons because they are built into the Video menu. These allow you to trim a video. When you trim a video, you specify a beginning and ending time—called Mark-in and Mark-out, respectively.

▶ **Extract Video**—Feature does the same thing as Mark-in and Mark-out, but is easier to work with, since it opens a new window. You are not forced to work in the Add/Edit Media Clip window.

▶ **Replace Audio button**—If you don't like the audio that is currently with your video, this will let you replace it.

▶ **Split Video button**—You can cut a video in half with this option.

▶ **Add/Edit Chapter button**—Gives you the ability to insert chapters manually or automatically.

▶ **First Play Video**—If you want an Introduction Video, or what DVD MovieFactory refers to as a First Play Video, just move the desired video to the left so that it is the first video in the list.

As stated earlier, trimming a video is built into the Add/Edit Media Clip window. Figure 6.9 points out the location of the different buttons that are used.

Figure 6.9
Trimming a video.

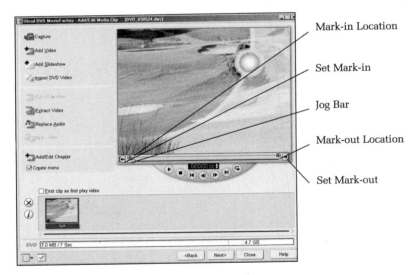

Mark-in Location

Set Mark-in

Jog Bar

Mark-out Location

Set Mark-out

As you can see from Figure 6.9, there are five items involved with trimming a video.

▶ **Mark-in Location**—Designates the beginning point for the trimmed video.

▶ **Set Mark-in**—Allows you to set the Mark-in Location.

▶ **Mark-out Location**—Designates the ending point for the trimmed video.

▶ **Set Mark-out**—Allows you to set the Mark-out Location.

▶ **Jog Bar**—Used to move the Mark-in or Mark-out Locations.

To trim a video using the above controls, you should follow these six steps.

1. Double-click the video clip that needs trimming.
2. Click and drag the Jog Bar to the place where you want the video to start.
3. Click the Set Mark-in button. Alternatively, you can press the F3 key on your keyboard.
4. Click and drag the Jog Bar to the place where you would like the video to end.
5. Click the Set Mark-out button or press the F4 key.
6. To preview your freshly trimmed video, hold down the Shift key and click the Play button. When the Shift key is held, the video will stop at the Mark-out location.

If trimming a video seems confusing, try the Extract Video button. Again, these two methods will accomplish the same thing. Figure 6.10 shows the Extract Video window that is displayed when the Extract Video button is clicked.

Figure 6.10
Extract Video window.

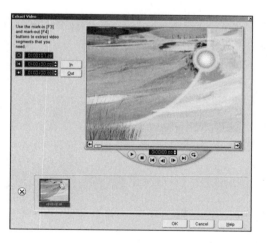

You should notice that the Set Mark-in and Mark-out locations are in this window as well. You can use the Jog Bar in here to trim your video.

You should also see three timers on the left side of the window. The first timer gives you the total running time of the trimmed video. If the video is not trimmed, this timer will give you the total running time of the video. The next two timers are where the Mark-in and Mark-out locations are set. These timers are set either by using the Jog Bar—the timers will update to the appropriate location when you set the Mark-in or Mark-out locations—or by manually typing in the desired time for each. Click the In or Out button after the respective times are entered.

PREVIEWING THE EXTRACTED VIDEO
Remember, if you want to preview the trimmed portion of the video only, make sure to hold down the Shift key while the video is playing.

The next video editing feature in DVD MovieFactory is the Replace Audio function, which is used to replace the audio associated with a video, with an audio sample that you specify. The Replace Audio window is shown in Figure 6.11.

Figure 6.11
Replace Audio window.

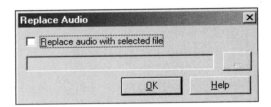

You can replace the audio by doing the following:

1. Double-click on the video in which you would like to replace the audio.
2. Click the Replace Audio button.
3. Check the Replace Audio with Selected File box.
4. Navigate to the desired audio file.
5. Click the Open button to select the audio file.
6. Click OK to replace the audio.

RESTORING THE ORIGINAL AUDIO
You can restore the original audio that came with the video file by double-clicking on the video clip, clicking the Replace Audio button, and unchecking the Replace Audio with Selected File check box.

USING AUDIO SAMPLES
Make sure the audio sample is shorter than the video it is going into. Otherwise, the audio will be cut off.

Splitting the video in half is the next video editing feature in DVD MovieFactory. This feature is useful if the video used is extremely long, and you want to split it in half and create two separate menu items. To split the video, do the following:

1. Double-click on the video that you would like to split.
2. Drag the Jog Bar to the point in the video where it should split.
3. Click the Split Video button.

Once the video is split, two new videos will show up in the video list. The default naming convention is the original video name with an underscore and the number 1 or 2, as shown in Figure 6.12. In this figure, the original file was named golf, and the two halves are golf_1 and golf_2.

Figure 6.12
Split videos.

CHOOSING THE SPLIT LOCATION

DVD MovieFactory requires that you choose a split location that is between the Mark-in and Mark-out locations.

The next video editing feature is the ability to Add or Edit Chapters in a video. Chapter markers in a video are used to index that video. DVD MovieFactory can be set to automatically add the chapters or you can add the chapters manually. There are a few things that you should know when adding chapters to a video through DVD MovieFactory.

▶ DVD MovieFactory is limited to 99 chapters per video.
▶ To have DVD MovieFactory automatically set up the chapters, the video must be at least one minute in length, or the video must include scene-change information—cues in the video that signal that the scene has changed.

CHAPTER 6

▶ If a Scene Selection menu is created—a special menu that has a button for each chapter in the video—the buttons on the menu are only links to a part within the video and do not point to new videos. This saves valuable DVD space.

The Add/Edit Chapter window is shown in Figure 6.13.

Figure 6.13
Add/Edit Chapter
window.

To manually add chapters into your video, do the following:

1. Double-click on the video in the Add/Edit Media Clip window.
2. Move the Jog Bar to the desired frame.
3. Click on Add.

If you would like DVD MovieFactory to automatically add the chapters, click the Auto button, as shown in Figure 6.13. If the video has scene change information contained in it, you can tell DVD MovieFactory to use this information to automatically create the chapters. A fixed time interval can also be set to automatically create chapters—every five seconds is an example.

When a chapter is added, either manually or automatically, the chapter will appear on the right side of the window with the first frame of the video and start time displayed. If you right-click on the chapter, you can change the thumbnail image—this is the image that is displayed as the button in the Scene Selection menu. Figure 6.14 illustrates the end result after the chapters have been added.

Figure 6.14
Video with added
chapters.

The last video editing feature within DVD MovieFactory is called a First Play Video, which is referred to as an Introduction Video in other DVD authoring applications. A First Play Video is a video that is shown before the Main Menu is displayed—an FBI warning on a movie would be an example.

You can add a First Play Video in DVD MovieFactory by checking the First Clip as First Play Video box. When this button is checked, the first video that is in the Add/Edit Media Clip window is used as the First Play Video.

SHORT AND SWEET FIRST PLAY VIDEO

The First Play Video should be relatively short, because it will be viewed each time the DVD is inserted. There is no way to cancel this.

CREATE MENU CHECK BOX

One thing that was not discussed in the Add/Edit Media Clip window was the Create Menu check box. If this button is not checked, you will not have the option to create a menu, and the videos will be shown sequentially.

Creating a Slideshow

The last buttons on the Add/Edit Media Clip window that have not been covered are the Add or Edit Slideshow buttons. These buttons, when clicked, start the DVD MovieFactory Slideshow Editor, as shown in Figure 6.15.

Figure 6.15
Slideshow Editor.

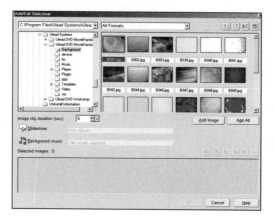

You can do the following things in the Slideshow Editor.

▶ Set the clip duration—the time that each picture in the slideshow is displayed before the slideshow moves onto the next picture.

▶ Assign a unique name to the slideshow, which will also be the name of the menu button that is created. The default name is My Album.

▶ Assign background music to the slideshow.

FILTERING YOUR IMAGES
If you have many pictures on your computer, DVD MovieFactory will let you filter them by file type. Just select the desired file type from the All Formats drop-down menu.

You can create a slideshow in a few easy steps.

1. Click on the Add Slideshow button within the Add/Edit Media Clip window to start the Slideshow Editor.

2. Navigate to the appropriate folder on your computer where your pictures are stored.

3. To add pictures one at a time, either double-click on the picture or highlight the picture and select the Add Image button.

4. To add an entire folder of pictures, navigate to the folder and select the Add All button.

5. Set the clip duration by changing the Image Clip Duration option.

6. If you want to change the slideshow name, click on the Slideshow button and type in the new name.

7. To add background music, click on the Background Music tab. You will then be asked to select the appropriate audio file.

8. Click the OK button to exit the Slideshow Editor.

Once your pictures are added to the slideshow, you can rearrange them in any order that you like. To do this, click on the far-right button shown in the toolbar in Figure 6.16. In addition to rearranging your slides from this toolbar, you can also preview your slideshow, rotate an image 90 degrees, or remove one or all of the slides in the slideshow.

Figure 6.16
Slideshow Editor
toolbar.

Choosing a Theme

The third step in the DVD creation process using DVD MovieFactory is to choose a theme and configure your menus. In DVD MovieFactory, a theme is referred to as a Menu Template, and this is what we will call it for the rest of this chapter. There is no functional difference between the two terms—only the name. As you can recall, a theme, or Menu Template, is a set of buttons and background images that give the DVD a common look.

Unlike other competing DVD authoring applications, DVD MovieFactory does not allow the DVD author the same amount of freedom when customizing the layout. For example, when you choose a Menu Template, you can customize how the buttons are laid out, but you cannot choose where the buttons are placed. If you wanted to move a button from the upper-left corner to the lower right, you would need to find a pre-defined theme that was configured this way. You cannot move the button. While this may be a disadvantage to some authors, it is ideal for an author who is happy that this part has been done for him.

To get a better idea on how the menu system is structured within DVD MovieFactory, refer to Figure 6.17. As you examine Figure 6.17, you can see that most of the multimedia is accessible on the Main Menu—slideshows, videos, and so on. If you want to create a Scene Selection menu, use a submenu. In Figure 6.17, both submenu #1 and submenu #2 are Scene Selection menus from Clip 1 and 3, respectively, on the Main Menu.

Figure 6.17
DVD MovieFactory
menu structure.

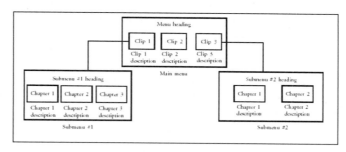

Since DVD MovieFactory automatically creates the appropriate menus for you, the theory behind how DVD MovieFactory structures its menus is important when it is time to choose your Menu Template. All you have to do is choose the Menu Template, and you are ready to go. Let's take a look at the Setup Menu window, shown in Figure 6.18, where you will be choosing your themes and customizing the menus.

Figure 6.18
Setup Menu window.

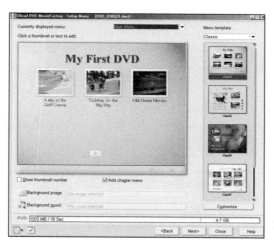

CHAPTER 6

There is a lot to take in on this window, so I will explain what each section of the Setup Menu window does.

▶ **Currently Displayed menu**—Located at the top of the window. Allows you to switch to a submenu, if one exists.

▶ **Menu Preview**—Located directly below the Currently Displayed Menu drop-down menu. This section is where you will customize your menus.

▶ **Add Chapter menu**—If this is checked, DVD MovieFactory will automatically create Scene Selection menus for any video in your project that contains chapters.

▶ **Background Image**—Located below the Add Chapter menu. You click on this if you want to add your own background image to a menu.

▶ **Background Music**—Along with the Background Image, you can also choose to add audio to your menu.

▶ **Menu Templates**—On the far right side of the Setup Menu window, you choose your Menu Template. DVD MovieFactory has organized the Menu Templates into different categories, such as Classic, Cool, Romantic, and so on. When you choose a category, the Menu Templates that are associated with it are displayed in the window below it.

▶ **Customize**—Once you have chosen a Menu Template, you have the ability to customize the way it looks using the Customize button in the lower right-hand side of the screen.

CHOOSING YOUR MENU TEMPLATE

Even though DVD MovieFactory chooses the location of the buttons on the menu, I encourage you to check out the different Menu Templates and customize them. With over 60 Menu Templates and many layouts that you can customize within this template, you should have no problem finding one that is exactly what you want.

Basic Menu Customizations

After you have chosen the Menu Template that will be used, there are a few basic things you can do customize it.

▶ Rename your menu title and button labels

▶ Select a different frame within your video to represent the Menu button

▶ Change the background image or music

Every Menu Template in DVD MovieFactory defaults to the menu title, *My Title*. To give your DVD a personal touch, you may want to customize this to better represent the purpose of your DVD. The method for changing the button label is identical to that of the menu title. You should use these four steps when changing either the menu title or a button label.

1. Click once on the My Title text area.

2. Change the My Title text to whatever you desire, as shown in Figure 6.19.

Figure 6.19
Edit Menu Heading
window.

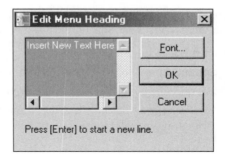

3. Before you click OK, you can change the font, font style, and font size by clicking the Font button on the Edit Menu Heading window.

4. Click the OK button, and you will see that the menu title is now whatever you changed it to.

By default, when a menu button is created, it uses the first frame in the video for the button's picture, or thumbnail. There may be a time when a certain frame, other than the first, would represent the video better. You can change the menu button's thumbnail to any frame within the video by doing the following:

1. Click on the current button's thumbnail.

2. A Change Thumbnail window will appear, as shown in Figure 6.20.

Figure 6.20
Change Thumbnail
window.

3. Use the Jog Bar to find the specific frame you would like to set as your button thumbnail.

4. Click the OK button and you should see the image change to the one that was just selected.

The Menu Templates within DVD MovieFactory are well thought out, but sometimes these templates do not capture the level of intimacy that you want with a DVD. You may want to have a DVD of your kid's first birthday. You could set the background image to a picture of him blowing out his candles, while the background music could be your family singing Happy Birthday. Follow these steps to personalize your DVD's background image.

1. Click on the Background Image button.

2. Choose Select a Background Image for this Menu from the drop-down menu.

3. Navigate to the location on your computer where the picture is stored.

4. Click Open, and you will see the background in the Menu Preview window change to the picture that you just selected.

The method for changing the background music is similar to that of the background image.

1. Click on the Background Music button.

2. Choose Select a Music Track for this Menu from the drop-down menu.

3. Navigate to the location on your computer where the audio file is stored.

4. Click the Open button.

Advanced Menu Customizations

For the adventurous DVD author, DVD MovieFactory allows you to further customize your menus. You can get to these advanced features by clicking the Customize button in the Setup Menu window. The Customize Menu window is shown in Figure 6.21.

Figure 6.21
Customize Menu window.

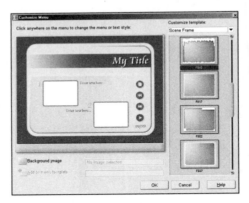

You should notice the same Menu Preview window as in the Setup Menu window. In the upper-right corner of this window, you have three options that you can customize. These allow you to do the following:

1. Change the layout of the menu buttons.

2. Customize the look of the menu navigation buttons—Home, Next, Previous, and so on.

3. Change the shape of the buttons.

If you do not like the position of either the menu buttons or title, you can change the position to another pre-defined layout in the Customize Menu.

1. Make sure the Layout option is selected from the Customize template drop-down menu; see Figure 6.21 for the location of this menu.

2. Directly below this drop-down menu is a list of the pre-defined layouts that you can choose. Browse through and find one that suits your needs.

3. Once you have found one, go ahead and double-click on it. It should show up in the Menu Preview window.

4. Click OK.

The methods for configuring the Button Image—the way that the menu navigation buttons work—and the Scene Frame are identical to changing the menu layout. Just make sure that you select the correct option in the Customize Template drop-down menu.

When you are finished customizing a Menu Template, you can save it for later use. To do this, click the Add to Menu Template button in the Customize window. This will save your new Menu Template to the Favorites category in the Setup Menu window.

Disc Preview

The third step in creating a DVD with DVD MovieFactory is Disc Preview. Using Disc Preview, you can get a real-time look at how your DVD is working. This is your last chance to find any errors that may be in your project before it is burned to DVD. Figure 6.22 illustrates what the Disc Preview window looks like.

Figure 6.22
Disc Preview window.

During this step, you are given a remote control that will simulate the remote control from your stand-alone DVD player. Make sure to check all of the menus and buttons to make sure they go to the right place. When you feel confident that your project is complete and error-free, proceed to the last step.

Burning or Saving Your DVD

Congratulations, you have made it to the Finish step of DVD MovieFactory. In this step, you can burn the DVD project to disc, save it to your hard drive in DVD format, or save it to a compressed image file for later use. Figure 6.23 shows the final step in DVD MovieFactory. An explanation of each of the main areas in this window follows.

Figure 6.23
Finish window.

▶ **Volume Name**—The name of the DVD. When you put the DVD into a computer, this Volume Name will be the name that is shown in My Computer next to the appropriate drive letter of your DVD drive.

▶ **Output Settings**—Decide what you want to do with the project—burn it to disc, create DVD folders, or create a disc image file.

▶ **Disc Burner**—Allows you to select which burner—if you have more than one—you would like to use. Remember that a VCD is burned onto recordable CDs and not DVDs, so if you are creating a VCD, make sure the burner selected in this area can burn CD recordable media.

▶ **Miscellaneous Areas**—Below the Disc Burner area, you will see various information such as how much space the project requires on both the DVD media and the hard drive, how much of the project has been burned, and an Output button that is used to start the process.

Burning Your Project to DVD

You should follow these steps to burn your project to DVD via the Finish window.

1. Name your volume appropriately using the Volume Name textbox.

2. Click the Record to Disc button.

3. If you have more than one burner, make sure the right burner is selected in the Disc Burner area.

4. Click the Output button.

When the Output button is clicked, the burn process is started. You may be warned that burning will take some time to render, as shown in Figure 6.24. This is because the videos in your project need to be encoded. Depending on the amount of video that is included in your project, it could take several hours for all of the videos to finish encoding. If you do not want to see this warning again, check the Do not show this message next time check box before clicking OK.

Figure 6.24
Render dialog box.

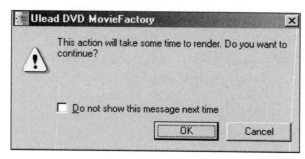

As the DVD is burning, a progress bar at the bottom of the Finish window will show you how close the DVD is to completion. Once the DVD is done, the disc will eject itself, and you will get a Completion window, as shown in Figure 6.25.

Figure 6.25
Completion window.

Saving Your DVD Project to an Image File

Instead of burning your project to disc, DVD MovieFactory gives you the option of saving it to a compressed image file. This is handy if you do not have any blank media, or if you want to save it for later use. Let's see how to save it to an image file.

1. Name your volume appropriately using the Volume Name textbox.
2. Click the Create Disc Image File button.
3. If you would like to save it to a path other than the one that is listed, click on the Folder icon and navigate to the desired location on your computer.
4. Click the Output button.

CHAPTER 6

The same things happen here as when you burned the project to disc.

▶ You will be warned that rendering may take a while; refer to Figure 6.24.

▶ The progress bar behaves in the same manner.

▶ The Completion window is also the same as burning to disc; refer to Figure 6.25.

When you are ready to burn the image file to a blank DVD, follow these steps.

1. Open DVD MovieFactory.

2. Select Copy Disc in the task area; refer to Figure 6.1.

3. Choose the Copy from Disc Image file radio button.

4. Click Next.

5. In the Copy Disc From section, click the folder icon and browse to the location of your image file.

6. Double-click on the image file.

7. Click the Output button.

In the next chapter, we will look at MyDVD 3.5, which is manufactured by Sonic Solutions.

Chapter 7
MyDVD 3.5

Sonic Solutions, created in 1986, is one of the veteran corporations with respect to DVD authoring. Sonic's MyDVD was the first home DVD authoring application to become available on the market to consumers and is bundled with many of the DVD burners that are sold today. In this chapter, you will examine ways to get the most out of MyDVD and then burn a DVD using the application.

NEWER VERSION AVAILABLE

There is a newer version of MyDVD—version 4.0—available for purchase. I chose to use version 3.5 in this chapter, because it is still shipped with many DVD burners, and there is a good chance that if you buy a DVD burner, you will get a free copy of this software.

If you need help beyond what this chapter covers, or if you would like to order the latest version of MyDVD, visit MyDVD's website at http://www.mydvd.com.

Sonic MyDVD: In Depth

MyDVD 3.5 has some features that are appealing to the DVD novice.

▶ **Extremely simple interface**—MyDVD strives on the fact that they were the first commercially available DVD authoring program, and they have made the interface as easy to use as possible.

▶ **Automatic transcoding**—MyDVD can automatically convert any AVI or QuickTime movie to the MPEG format simply by adding the movie to the project.

▶ **Direct-to-Disc technology**—MyDVD, using Direct-to-Disc, will capture a movie and burn it straight to a DVD or VCD without using the hard drive as an intermediate step.

▶ **Insert chapter markers**—You can either manually or automatically add chapter markers to your videos.

▶ **Pre-configured styles**—Also called themes; these can be imported into your project. If you don't want to use these styles, you can create your own.

Unfortunately, MyDVD 3.5 has some major shortcomings that have been addressed in version 4, but keep in mind that version 3.5 is still being shipped with many new DVD burners. Some of version 3.5's shortcomings are as follows:

▶ It does not allow motion menus.

▶ You cannot create slideshows.

▶ It is not possible to move buttons around on the built-in styles.

MyDVD was strictly designed with movies in mind. Table 7.1 will show you the multimedia types that are supported.

Table 7.1 Supported Multimedia Formats

Format	Description
AVI	Audio Video Interlaced. A Microsoft standard
MOV	Apple QuickTime Movies
MPEG	MPEG movie format
MPA	MPEG Audio
MP3	MPEG-1 audio encoded format
WAV	Wave Audio Format
AIFF	Audio Interchange File Format
BMP	Bitmap still image format
GIF	Compuserve's Graphic Interchange Format
JPEG	Joint Photographic Experts Group
PNG	Portable Network Graphic
TIF	Tagged Image File format
PICT	Macintosh Picture file
PSD	Single layer Photoshop images

FORMAT SUPPORT

As mentioned earlier, MyDVD 3.5 is geared strictly toward movies, not still images or audio. Table 7.1 shows support for audio and still images, but only for replacing audio in a video or replacing background images in a menu, respectively.

Using MyDVD

MyDVD is a template-based application, which means that the application does most of the work for you. You plug movies into a template, add a menu style to the template, and you are ready to burn the DVD. After installing MyDVD, you can get to it through the Windows Start Menu.

1. Click on the Start Menu.
2. Click on Programs and then Sonic MyDVD.
3. Click once on the Start MyDVD menu item in the Sonic MyDVD program group.

When MyDVD is started, the MyDVD Wizard will appear. The Wizard will take you through the process of choosing a disc type and then choosing a project type. The first step, which asks what type of disc to create—DVD or VCD—is shown in Figure 7.1. Refer to Chapter 2 to review the differences between the two application formats. For the purposes of this chapter, we will choose the Create a DVD option in MyDVD Wizard. The application is the same regardless of the option you choose. The only difference is that the project is customized to what you choose—MyDVD will only allow 700Mb worth of movies in a VCD project, for example.

Figure 7.1
Step 1 of MyDVD
Wizard.

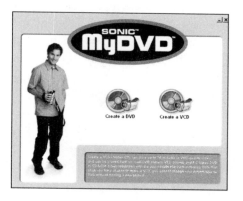

BYPASS THE MYDVD WIZARD
You can bypass the first step of the MyDVD Wizard by selecting Create VCD or Create DVD from the Sonic MyDVD Program Group accessed through the Windows Start Menu.

The next step in the MyDVD Wizard is selecting your project type, as shown in Figure 7.2.

Figure 7.2
Step 2 of MyDVD
Wizard.

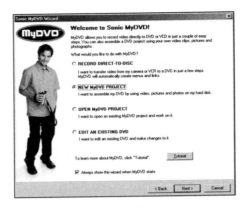

There are four project types to choose from.

▶ **Record Direct-to-Disc**—Will take videos from a capture device and record them directly to disc.

▶ **New MyDVD Project**—Will allow you to create a new DVD project from scratch. We will use this project type throughout this chapter.

▶ **Open MyDVD Project**—If there is already a saved project on your disc, you can use the Open MyDVD Project to open it and make changes.

▶ **Edit an Existing DVD**—Will take a DVD that has been previously burned on rewritable media and allow you to make changes to it. When the changes are finished, the project is burned back to the same rewritable media.

TAKING THE TUTORIAL

On the second window of the MyDVD Wizard, you should see the Tutorial button (refer to Figure 7.2). I recommend clicking this button and running through the tutorial before using MyDVD. It will give you a brief overview of the application.

When you choose to create a New MyDVD Project and click on Next, the last step of the MyDVD Wizard starts. This step is where you choose a default style, or theme, that the menus in your project will use. You can see an example of this final step in Figure 7.3.

Figure 7.3
Final step of MyDVD
Wizard.

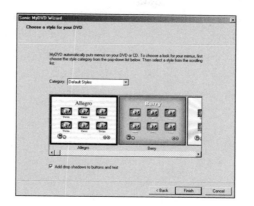

Click on the Category drop-down menu and select the default from the list that appears. Then click on the Finish button to stop the MyDVD Wizard and start the actual MyDVD program. Now that the groundwork has been laid for your DVD project, MyDVD is started. There are two parts to the MyDVD interface—the Toolbar and Menu Editor. The Toolbar is shown in Figure 7.4.

Figure 7.4
MyDVD Toolbar.

The Toolbar is the main method by which the project is edited, so you should be familiar with what each button does.

▶ **New Project button**—The same as the New MyDVD Project option in Step 2 of the MyDVD Wizard. If you do not like the current project you are in, you can start a new one with this button.

▶ **Open Project button**—Also the same as the Open MyDVD Project option in Step 2 of the MyDVD Wizard. If you started a project, or had a completed one that was previously saved, you can use this button to open it.

▶ **Save Project button**—Will save the current project to the hard drive.

▶ **Direct-to-Disc button**—Does the same thing as the Record Direct-to-Disc option in Step 2 of the MyDVD Wizard.

▶ **Get Movies button**—Will allow you to import a movie that is already on your computer.

▶ **Capture button**—If the movie is on a FireWire-based camcorder or analog capture device, you can use the Capture button to save it from the capture device to a movie file on the hard drive.

▶ **Preview button**—To start the Disc Preview mode, click the Preview button. This button will bring up a remote control interface that allows you to test your project.

▶ **Make Disc button**—When the project is complete, click this to burn it to DVD.

The other part to the MyDVD interface is the Menu Editor, located on the Main Project window. From the Menu Editor, you can add new menus or customize the current one. The Menu Editor is shown in Figure 7.5.

Figure 7.5
The Menu Editor.

The Menu Editor has a few points of interest contained within it.

▶ **Add Menu button**—Will add a new menu to your project with a link to it from its parent menu.

▶ **Change Style button**—Will change the current style that is assigned to the current project.

▶ **Status display**—In the bottom-right corner of the window, a status display will let you know how much free space you have left on your project. This amount of free space is determined by the type of project—DVD or VCD—that is being created.

▶ **Menu title**—At the top of every menu is a menu title that defaults to the name of the style that is currently in use, which can be changed at any time; we will cover this later in the chapter.

Before starting any new project, you should visit the Preferences to verify that everything is configured as it should be. To get to the MyDVD preferences, click the File menu in the Toolbar and choose Preferences. Figure 7.6 shows the General tab of the Preferences window.

Figure 7.6
The General tab of the Preferences window.

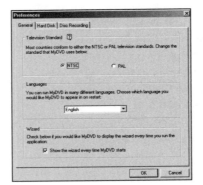

There are three options available in the General tab.

► **Television Standard**—Also known as the Broadcast Format, which is set to either NTSC or PAL. Remember to leave this as NTSC if you are distributing it within the United States.

► **Languages**—If you would prefer the application to be in a different language, choose the appropriate one from the languages drop-down menu.

► **Wizard**—By default, MyDVD Wizard will appear every time MyDVD is started. If you do not want to see this Wizard, uncheck the Show the Wizard every time MyDVD starts check box.

The Hard Disk tab, shown in Figure 7.7, is used to set the folder path for both captured and temporary files. The Temporary Files folder is used when MyDVD encodes the videos in the project. To set the path for either of these, click on Choose and browse to the appropriate folder. When you find the desired folder, click the OK button.

Figure 7.7
The Hard Disk tab of the Preferences window.

Manipulating Menus

MyDVD limits each menu to six buttons. When you add a seventh button, MyDVD will alert you that a new menu was created, as shown in Figure 7.8. The new menu is not a submenu of the Main Menu; rather, it is a continuation of the Main Menu that is chained to the first. In MyDVD, menus are chained together, which allows you to scroll through them. You can get to the chained menus by clicking on the right or left arrows, depending on the way you want to navigate. Figure 7.9 shows a chained menu—note the navigation buttons that are added automatically.

Figure 7.8
New Menu Alert window.

Figure 7.9
Chained menu.

Unfortunately, the menus in MyDVD are primitive, because you cannot change the look of the buttons (without changing the menu style) or place these buttons freely on the menu. MyDVD handles the design of the menu layout. There are a few things that can be customized, though.

▶ You can either change the menu style to one that is built into MyDVD or create a new one from scratch.

▶ The title of the menu or the labels of the buttons can be changed to anything that you desire.

▶ If you have more than one button on your menu, you can reorder these buttons any way that you like. Reordering is different from placing the buttons on the menu in that when a button is reordered, it goes to a specific area on the menu that is set by MyDVD. To switch buttons around, just click and drag the button to the place on the menu that you want and let go of the mouse button.

Menu Style Changes

The menu style is changed through the Menu Editor. If you are not interested in designing your own menu, you should choose one that comes with MyDVD.

1. Click on the Change Style button in the Menu Editor.

2. In the Select a Style window, as shown in Figure 7.10, choose the menu style that you want.

3. Click on OK to apply the new style.

Figure 7.10
Select a Style
window.

Figure 7.10 should look familiar to Step 3 in the MyDVD Wizard. These two windows are almost identical. The difference is that you can create a new menu style or import an existing one in the Select a Style window. Sonic decided to add the ability to import menu styles so you can share your creations with your friends or download more menu styles as they are created from the MyDVD website, which must be added to MyDVD manually.

By default, all styles that come with MyDVD are in the Default Styles category. If you are not pleased with any of the menu styles included with MyDVD, you can create your own in the Select a Style window, which will create a new category named Custom and put your style into it. Just click on the New Custom Style button to bring up the Custom Style Editor of the Select a Style window, as shown in Figure 7.11.

Figure 7.11
Custom Style Editor.

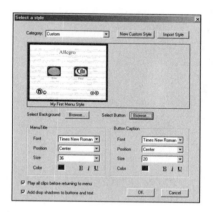

The Custom Style Editor is a bit cluttered, because a lot of controls are contained within one window. To be able to understand how to create a menu style, you should know what each item does in this editor.

▶ You can view your custom menu styles in the window that is directly below the Category drop-down menu. You should click on the custom menu style once to tell MyDVD that you want to edit it.

▶ The Select Background Browse button is used to import a supported still image and set it as the background of the menu. Refer to Table 7.1 for supported image formats.

▶ The Select Button Browse button will bring up a list of different buttons to choose from. Unfortunately, you cannot create your own, so you must select one from the list.

▶ The Menu Title section will format the text of your menu title. You can change the font type; font size; set the text to bold, underline, or italics; set the position of the text on the menu; and assign a color to the text.

▶ The Button Caption section formats the button labels. You have the same formatting options here as you did with the menu titles.

To select a custom menu style, click the Change Style button and select the Custom category. This will list all of the custom menu styles that are set up on the computer.

Changing Menu Titles and Button Labels

With MyDVD it is possible to edit the menu titles and button labels. Remember that a menu title is the name of the menu and a button label is the name of a button. The method for changing these objects is the same.

1. Click once on the desired text to edit.
2. Type in the new name of the button or label.
3. Press the Enter key. You should see the name change.

NAME PLACEHOLDERS

The text on the menu title and button labels must have a default placeholder. A menu title is set to the name of the menu style by default, whereas a button label uses the file name of the video that is captured or imported. An exception to the button label is a submenu, which uses Untitled Submenu as a placeholder.

TITLE AND BUTTON FORMATTING

In order to change the text formatting of the menu title or button label in a default style, you must create a new custom style from scratch.

DELETING BUTTONS

To delete a button from the menu, right-click on the button and select Delete Button from the pop-up menu.

One last thing that should be kept in mind when you are customizing your menus is the TV Safe Zone, which is the area of the menu that will display on every television. To ensure compatibility with all televisions, I recommend keeping all menu buttons within the TV Safe Zone. This feature is accessible through the Toolbar.

1. On the Toolbar, click the View menu.
2. Select the Show TV Safe Zone option.
3. To turn this feature off, repeat Steps 1 and 2.

When the TV Safe Zone is turned on, you will see a dotted line in the shape of a square appear on the menu, as shown in Figure 7.12. As long as your buttons are within the square, they will display on every television.

Figure 7.12
Show TV Safe Zone.

Adding Videos to Your Project

MyDVD allows you to either capture videos from a capture device or import videos that are stored on your computer. The Toolbar has two buttons that are used to get videos into your project—Capture, used to capture video, and Get Movies, which is used to import videos that already exist on your computer.

Using the Capture Button

To open the Capture to Disk window, as shown in Figure 7.13, click the Capture button on the Toolbar. MyDVD will attempt to locate a compatible capture device. You should have either a digital camcorder hooked up or a video capture card installed into your computer. If MyDVD cannot find a suitable capture device, an error message will appear, like the one in Figure 7.14.

Figure 7.13
Capture to Disk
window.

Figure 7.14
No capture device
found.

TURN CAPTURE DEVICE ON

The error message shown in Figure 7.14 may also appear if you have a digital camcorder plugged in but not turned on. Make sure to turn on all capture devices before you click the Capture to Disk button in the Toolbar.

There are three steps that are required when capturing the video—configuring the capture options, setting the starting point, and capturing the video. The first step, configuring the capture options, is done within the Capture to Disk window, shown in Figure 7.13.

Let's configure the capture options.

▶ **Record option**—Used to configure what you want to capture—audio only, video only, or both audio and video.

▶ **Quality option**—Used to specify the video quality of the captured video. The higher you set the quality, the larger your video files will be. Keep this in mind for both hard disk and DVD media space usage.

▶ **Add Clip to Menu check box**—If you do not want MyDVD to automatically add the captured video to your project, uncheck this.

▶ **Set Record Length option**—By design, MyDVD will capture until either the video has completed or the hard drive runs out of space. The Set Record Length option allows you to stop the video at a certain point. For example, you could set the record length to 5 minutes, and MyDVD will stop after 5 minutes of video has been captured.

▶ **Create Chapter Points option**—Lets MyDVD know that the video being captured should have chapter points created either manually or automatically—this will be covered later in the chapter.

Now that the capture options are set, the next step is to find the desired starting place on the capture device. For a digital video camcorder, use navigation controls that are included in the Capture to Disk window. If you are using an analog source, a VCR for example, use the buttons on the analog source to set the starting point.

CAPTURE CARDS

Analog source video capture requires a capture card that is installed into the computer. To make sure your video card is compatible, you should check MyDVD's website at http://www.mydvd.com.

Finally, you are ready to capture the video by clicking the Record button. Once the capture process is finished, MyDVD will ask you to save the new file to the hard drive. If the Add Clip to Menu option is selected, then MyDVD will add the video to your project.

ANALOG CAPTURE

Before you click the Record button to start the capture, you should first start the capture device. If a VCR is used as your capture device, press the Play button on the VCR and then click the Record button in MyDVD.

Using the Get Movies Button

The Get Movies button on the Toolbar is used to add videos that are already stored in a file on your computer. For a list of supported file types, refer to Table 7.1. When you click the Get Movies button in the Toolbar, the Add Movie(s) to Menu window will appear asking for the location of the file, as shown in Figure 7.15.

Figure 7.15
Add Movie(s) to Menu window.

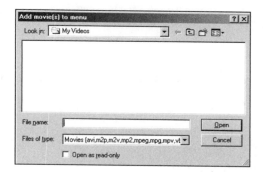

When you select the video that you want to add to your project, MyDVD will import the video into the current project and create a menu button with the button label as the name of the file. It is important to use videos that were created in the same broadcast format as the one selected in the MyDVD Preferences window. If you try to import the wrong broadcast format, MyDVD will display an error message like the one shown in Figure 7.16.

Figure 7.16
Broadcast format error message.

Editing Your Videos

Since MyDVD is a beginning-level DVD authoring application, the video editing features are not as advanced as other applications. If you would like more video editing features, you should check out Sonic's DVDit! authoring application.

There are three editing features that can be accomplished with MyDVD.

▶ Creating chapter points (also known as chapter markers) while the video is being captured.

▶ Trimming a video to a desired length.

▶ Replacing the default audio for a video.

As stated earlier, MyDVD has the ability to create chapter points either manually or automatically. To manually enter chapter points, press the spacebar while the video is capturing. You should press the spacebar once for each chapter point that should be inserted. To have MyDVD automatically create the chapter points, check the Create Chapter Points on the Capture to Disk window, and select a time interval at which the chapter points are to be created—every 1 minute would be an example. If you add a video to your MyDVD project that has chapter points, MyDVD will automatically create a different menu button for each chapter inserted.

CHAPTER MENU BUTTONS

When a chapter menu button is created, it uses the filename of the video followed by the chapter number as its label. For example, a video that has three chapter points would have three menu buttons created with labels of Filename 1, Filename 2, and Filename 3.

The second built-in video editing feature is the ability to trim videos. A video that is too long can be trimmed to an exact length. Figure 7.17 shows the Trimming window. The Trimming window shows you the starting frame, ending frame, and the total running time of the trimmed clip.

Figure 7.17
Trimming window.

There are five steps involved when trimming a video clip.

1. Double-click on the video within the Menu Editor that you would like to trim.
2. Set the Mark-in Time by sliding the green bracket on the slider bar to the left. As you slide the green bracket, the start frame will change to the Mark-in frame that is selected, and the Clip Length time will change to reflect the new total running time.
3. Set the Mark-out Time by sliding the red bracket to the right. You will see the End Frame and clip length values change as the red bracket is moved.
4. To reset the Mark-in and Mark-out positions, click the Reset button.
5. Click the OK button.

CHAPTER 7

USING THE ARROW BUTTONS

If you don't want to use the left and right brackets, you can use the left and right arrow buttons. They will do the same thing.

Another thing that you should have noticed in the Trimming window is a Thumbnail option. This option is used to set the frame that is displayed as the menu button. To change the Thumbnail value, move the thumb slider to the left or right until you find the frame to be used.

THUMBNAILS AND MYDVD

The Thumbnail option is new to MyDVD version 3.1 and above. If you have a version earlier than this, the Thumbnail option is not available in the Trimming window.

The last video editing feature included with MyDVD 3.5 is the ability to replace the original audio packaged with the video. This is useful if you do not like the video or want to use a different audio track that suits your video better. To replace the audio track, you should follow these steps.

1. Navigate to the audio file that should be added.
2. Click and drag the audio file on top of the menu button that points to the desired video.
3. To remove the audio file, right-click on the menu button and select Remove Audio.

CHOOSING THE RIGHT AUDIO

When replacing or adding an audio file to a video, you should choose an audio file that has the same approximate running time as the video. MyDVD does not have audio editing capabilities, so if you do not do this, the audio will cut off when the video is finished.

Disc Preview

With MyDVD you can preview your project at any time to make sure that all of the menus work and it looks correct. This is accomplished by running Disc Preview—accessible through the Preview button on the Toolbar. When you execute Disc Preview mode, a remote control will appear that is used to simulate exactly what the DVD will look like in the stand-alone DVD player. Figure 7.18 shows what the remote control looks like. When you are done previewing your project, close the remote control by clicking on the X in the upper-right corner.

Figure 7.18
Disc Preview remote
control.

Burning Your DVD

Now that the menus are created, the videos are imported, and the project has been previewed to work out any bugs, you are now ready to burn your DVD. MyDVD requires that you save the project before you burn the DVD. If the project is not saved, MyDVD will offer to save it for you before the disc is burned, as shown in Figure 7.19.

Figure 7.19
Save Project window.

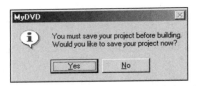

Once the project is saved, you will be prompted with a Make Disc Setup window, as shown in Figure 7.20. From this window, you can select the type of media that you used and select the burner to use, if you have more than one. Before you hit the OK button to start burning your DVD, make sure you have a blank DVD in the burner. If not, you will receive the error message shown in Figure 7.21.

Figure 7.20
Make Disc Setup
window.

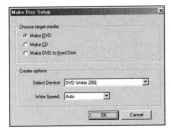

Figure 7.21
Insert media error.

SELECTING THE TARGET MEDIA
You should always select the same media in the Make Disc Setup window as you did with MyDVD Wizard.

SONIC DVDIT!

If you find that you would like more features than what is offered by MyDVD, I recommend looking at DVDit. DVDit is made by the same manufacturer and can be purchased at Sonic's website (http://www.sonic.com).

This is the last Windows-based application we will overview in this book. The next chapter will look at Macintosh's DVD authoring application, iDVD. As we did with the other applications, we will look at the different functionality of iDVD and how to burn a DVD with it.

CHAPTER 7

Chapter 8
Using Macintosh iDVD 3

Apple Computer has made a name for itself in the computing industry for its exceptional multimedia abilities. iDVD is an excellent beginner-level DVD authoring application, and, at fifty dollars, is reasonably priced. iDVD 3 combines the easy-to-use Macintosh interface with a feature set that DVD authors will find appealing. In this chapter, we will focus on the specifics of iDVD 3 by first looking at iDVD's features and then burning a DVD with it.

iDVD 3: In Depth

iDVD, with its many features, allows a novice DVD author to build fundamentals he can use well into the future. Let's look at some of its features:

▶ **Built-in themes**—If you aren't interested in creating your own menus and buttons, iDVD has pre-packaged themes from which you can choose; just drag your content into the theme and you're done.

▶ **Full Motion menus**—iDVD allows you to insert full Motion menus that give the menu a personal touch; you can add your own home movie clips as the menu background.

▶ **Integrated Slideshow Editor**—Just drag a group of still pictures to your iDVD project and iDVD will automatically create a customizable slideshow. You can add background music, order the pictures anyway you like, and choose how long each picture will show.

▶ **Automatic video transcoding**—Instead of using another application to convert your QuickTime movies to MPEG format, iDVD will automatically do this when it is added to the project.

▶ **Background MPEG encoding**—Most software applications will encode your videos when you start the actual process of burning your layout to disc. iDVD starts this encoding process, without interruption, as soon as the video is added to the project.

▶ **DVD Preview**—If you want an exact simulation of what your DVD will look like in your stand-alone DVD player, iDVD allows you to do this with Disc Preview. When the disc is previewed, a remote control, to simulate the remote control for your DVD player, will show up and allow you to navigate through your DVD project.

▶ **Seamless integration with other Apple multimedia software packages**—iLife is a suite of applications that includes all of Apple's multimedia products—iTunes, iPhoto, iMovie, and so on.

DVD LAYOUT VS. DVD PROJECT
iDVD refers to a *project* when talking about the DVD that you are authoring. This term means the same thing as a DVD *layout*, which most PC applications use. In order to avoid confusion, keep this in mind throughout this chapter.

Unfortunately, iDVD is not the be all end all DVD authoring application for the Mac OS X platform. It lacks some features that most DVD authors will deem necessary.

▶ **No VCD support**—You cannot burn into the VCD application format within iDVD 3.

▶ **No DVD-RW support**—iDVD does not support rewriteable media. You must use the DVD-R recordable format.

▶ **Cannot use native MPEG-2 files**—You cannot add previously encoded files from other DVDs to your project. The video files must be in QuickTime format for iDVD to recognize them.

▶ **Cannot create DVD image**—It is not possible to create a disc image of your DVD if you want to make another copy down the road.

Using iDVD 3

iDVD 3, like most Apple applications, has an extremely intuitive interface. Creating a DVD with iDVD is a joyful experience, because it is so easy to use. Figure 8.1 illustrates the iDVD interface we will be working from.

Figure 8.1
iDVD 3 interface.

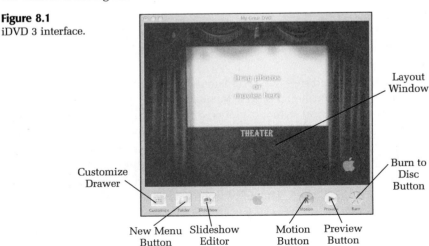

Even though the interface is rather intuitive, the buttons at the bottom of the iDVD window should be defined.

▶ **Customize button**—When you click this button, the window opens to the side like a drawer. The drawer contains the available settings that you can use to change the project to your desired result. In this drawer, you can change your menu theme, add Motion menus, check the status of the movies that are encoding, and add multimedia—movies, photos, or music.

▶ **New Menu button**—Allows you to create a new menu. iDVD is limited to six buttons per menu. If you need more than this, you must create a new menu. When a new menu is created, a Back button is automatically added to the new menu to ease the navigation. It is also possible to have a different theme for each menu.

MENUS VS. FOLDERS

iDVD refers to menus as folders. In order to stay consistent with the rest of the book, they will be referred to as menus.

▶ **Slideshow Editor**—Takes you directly into the slideshows that you added to your project.

▶ **Layout window**—Displays the current menu that you are editing. If you have more than one menu, you can click on its link within the Layout window to switch to it.

▶ **Motion button**—Allows you to turn the motion on and off. Since Motion menus take a considerable amount of computer resources, which may slow your computer down, it is a good idea to turn motion off when creating your project.

▶ **Preview button**—Allows you to switch to "simulation" mode. Remember, simulation mode will bring up the remote control to allow you to navigate through your DVD exactly as you would in a stand-alone DVD player.

▶ **Burn button**—When your DVD project is complete, click the Burn button, and you are on your way.

When you open iDVD for the first time, you should visit the General Preferences window. You can get to these preferences by clicking on the iDVD menu at the top of the screen and then selecting Preferences. In this window, you change some global settings of the application—enabling or disabling background encoding of movies, displaying an Apple watermark on each DVD that is created, and deleting the rendered files after the project is closed. The video standard section is the most important preference, because it is here that you choose the broadcast format for your DVD—NTSC or PAL. Figure 8.2 shows the General Preferences window.

Figure 8.2
General Preferences
window.

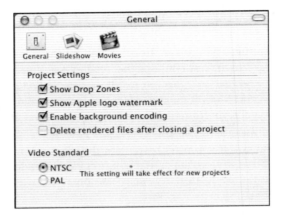

The first thing you are tasked with in iDVD is choosing a menu theme. The themes that are packaged with iDVD are really cool, but you can also create your own. Let's use the ones that are included with the application.

There are four types of themes included with iDVD 3. Each theme type included in the following list will have at least one example included in iDVD.

▶ **Drop Zone themes**—Will include at least one Drop Zone. A Drop Zone is a section of the menu where you can add pictures or movies. This theme also includes a place for adding text buttons to link to other menus. Postcard is an example of this theme type, and will be the one that is shown in the figures throughout this chapter.

▶ **Picture Only themes**—Have a still picture as the background—Green Linen Two, for instance.

▶ **Motion themes**—Incorporate short clips that loop continuously in the background, with or without sound. Global is an example of this theme type.

▶ **Picture with Audio themes**—The same as Picture Only themes, but are accompanied with background music—Claim Check is an example.

Choosing a theme is done through the Customize button, as illustrated in Figure 8.3.

Figure 8.3
Choosing a theme.

Use the scroll bars, which are the up and down arrows on the right side of the Customize drawer, to browse the many built-in themes that are available. When you click on one, it will show up in the Layout window, so you can see it in action. Make sure you have motion turned on.

SHOWING ALL THEMES
When choosing your theme, make sure you choose the All drop-down menu toward the top of the Themes window. If you don't, you may not see all of the available themes.

For the examples in this chapter, we will use the Postcard theme. It is a Drop Zone theme that will allow us to cover the basics of iDVD 3.

If you want to create your own theme or customize a built-in theme, iDVD will allow you to save these themes as a *Favorite* for future use. To do this, choose the Settings button at the top of the Customize drawer, and you will see the Save as Favorite button at the bottom of the window. (See Figure 8.4.)

Figure 8.4
Save as Favorite button.

When you click the Save as Favorite button, iDVD will ask you to give the theme a name, as shown in Figure 8.5.

CHAPTER 8

Figure 8.5
Enter name of theme.

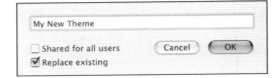

MORE THEMES

If you do not want to create your own themes, but would like more to choose from than what is packaged with iDVD, there are many third-party corporations that will sell you a bundle of themes. http://www.iDVDthemepak.com and http://www.iDVDthemes.com are examples of these.

Adding Multimedia to Your Project

Once you have decided on the theme you want to use, you are ready to add multimedia—photos, sounds clips, or movies—to your project. iDVD supports most major audio and photo formats. As mentioned earlier, iDVD will automatically transcode QuickTime movies into the native DVD MPEG format. If you have movies that are not in QuickTime format, you will need to use something other than iDVD to convert these; the professional version of QuickTime will do this.

Once you have your movies in the appropriate format, you can import them and any other multimedia that you have into iDVD. This can be done either through the Finder, comparable to the Microsoft Windows desktop, or through the appropriate iMedia browser.

There are three different iMedia browsers that you can access through the Customize drawer. The different iMedia browsers are under the Audio, Photos, and Movies buttons.

▶ **Audio button**—Will show the music that has been saved within iTunes (if you have iTunes 3 or later installed). You can click and drag this music from the iMedia browser right into your iDVD project.

▶ **Photos button**—Will display the photos that have been saved in iPhoto (if you have iPhoto 2 or later installed). Like the Audio button, you can also drag these photos directly into your project to create a slideshow.

▶ **Movies button**—Will show the movies that have been saved in iMovie (you must have iMovie 3 or later installed). This iMedia browser will only look in one place by default. If you want to access movies from any other place within iDVD, you must add a search path to the specific folder that the movies are located in. These additional search paths can be set in the Advanced Preferences window of iDVD.

ANOTHER WAY TO ADD MULTIMEDIA

If iTunes, iMovie, or iPhoto are not installed, or you decide not to use these iMedia browsers, you can use the Mac OS Finder to drag content into your project. Navigate to the folder that contains the desired content and drag and drop this into your project.

iDVD also has what is called a Scene menu, which is similar to the index of this book. Let's say you had a 20-minute video of your first fishing trip of the year. At approximately 10 minutes into the video, you catch the big one. At minute fourteen you were trying to put the fish back into the water and fell out of the boat. Instead of watching the first thirteen minutes of the video, it would be nice if you could skip right to the good stuff. This can be done within iDVD using Scene menus.

Scene menus use chapter markers—cues in the video that indicate when one scene ends and another begins—that are inserted into the video before it is imported into the project. Unfortunately, iDVD does not have this functionality built in, but chapter markers can be easily inserted using iMovie. When you import a movie into iDVD after the chapter markers are created, iDVD will automatically create a new menu with separate buttons for each chapter. You are allowed up to six chapter markers per Scene menu.

NAVIGATION BUTTONS

When a menu is created, iDVD will automatically place two buttons on the menu—a Back and Next button. A Back button is used to get to the preceding menu, and the Next button will go to the next submenu, if it exists.

Manipulating Menus

iDVD 3 is limited to six buttons per menu. These buttons can link the viewer to a slideshow, a movie, or another menu. Keep in mind when using submenus that this button counts as one of your possible six buttons, which will limit the maximum available buttons to five per menu.

When a submenu is created, you can assign it an entirely different theme than that of its parent menu. Let's create one, shall we?

1. Click the New Menu button on the main iDVD interface. The type of button that links to the new submenu depends on the type of theme that is installed. A Drop Zone theme will configure the buttons as text, whereas some of the other themes might make the button into a picture. Once the menu is created, you will see a new button that links to the submenu, as shown in Figure 8.6. (The theme used in this figure is a Drop Zone theme named Postcard.)

CHAPTER 8

Figure 8.6
New Menu button.

2. Double-click on the button that was just created to open your new menu.

3. Make sure the Customize drawer is open. Choose any theme that you would like to use.

The same holds true for a submenu as it did for a scene menu; iDVD automatically inserts a Back and Next button.

Changing Menus and Buttons

It is pretty common not to like everything about a theme. You may really like the background, but aren't too keen on the shape of the buttons. Maybe the font of the button label is not contemporary enough for the type of DVD you are creating. Apple thought about this when they were writing iDVD and gave you the capability to change them.

All menus have a title, and all buttons have a label. The menu title is the text that is at the top of the menu, and the button label is the text directly above or below the button. This is important to keep straight, because iDVD allows you to change either of these. iDVD makes this easy, because the method to change the text is the same for both. All you need to do is click the title/label once and type over what is currently there. Once you're finished typing, press the Enter key. Figure 8.7 shows the process of renaming a menu title.

Figure 8.7
Changing a menu title.

Everything that has to do with a menu title or button is changed in the Settings window within the Customize drawer. The Settings window is split into three parts—Background, Title, and Button. Figure 8.8 shows what this window looks like.

Figure 8.8
Settings window.

The Background portion of this window is covered in the next section. Now, we will concentrate on the Title and Button portions.

In the Title section, you are given four options—Position, Font, Color, and Size. The Position drop-down menu will let you determine where the menu title should be positioned on the menu. The Font drop-down menu allows you to set the font of the menu title text, and the color drop-down menu lets you change the color of this text. The Size slider bar refers to the actual dimensions of the menu title.

The Button section allows you to set the same options as you did with the Title section, but in respect to the button label not the menu title. There are two extra options in this area. The first option is the button shape. To change the shape of the desired button, just click on the Change Button box and select the button that you want. Figure 8.9 illustrates the location of the Change Button box.

Change Button Box

Figure 8.9
Change Button box.

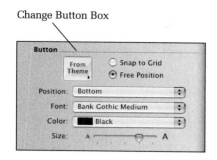

The other option is to choose Snap to Grid or Free Position with the default set to Snap to Grid. If you want three buttons in a row, iDVD will line the buttons up perfectly when Snap to Grid is selected. If you do not want the buttons in a straight line and want to hand pick where the buttons should be, click on the Free Position button.

One thing to keep in mind when creating buttons is the TV Safe Area. This is the area of the menu that is guaranteed to be visible on a television screen. When the TV Safe Area is turned on, a box will appear on your menu. Anything inside this box is safe. Since the TV Safe Area is not enabled by default, you will have to turn it on. You can do this by clicking the Advanced menu at the top of the screen and choosing Show TV Safe Area, as shown in Figure 8.10.

Figure 8.10
Finding the TV Safe Area.

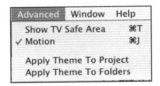

Depending on the type of theme that is selected, you may get a special button, called a Motion button, when a movie is dragged on to that theme. The button image will be the first frame of the movie that it is pointing to. When motion is turned on, you will see the button play a portion of the movie that it is pointing to, and will loop when finished. The amount of movie that is shown before looping is set by the Motion Duration slider bar in the Settings window within the Customize drawer, as shown in Figure 8.11.

Figure 8.11
The Motion Duration slider bar.

After you have decided how long you want the Motion button to play before looping, you must then set the start frame (where in the video the Motion loop should begin). You can choose any frame within the video. If you do not want to show the video—for instance, you would like the button to be a still picture of a frame within the video—you can do this as well. Clicking once on the Motion button sets these options. A window will pop up with the options. The first option is whether or not to show the movie. If this is not checked, the button will show a still image of the frame that you select. The other option is a Movie slider bar. When this bar is moved to the left or right, you can see the frame change in the button. When you find the start frame, just let go of the Mouse button, and it is set for you. Figure 8.12 shows you what this window looks like.

Figure 8.12
Setting the start frame.

Setting the Menu in Motion

Remember that Motion menus have a background video that plays as you are making your menu selection. You can set any video to be the background of your Motion menu.

iDVD gives you the ability to customize your Motion menus in a few different ways. To access this, open the Customize drawer and choose the Settings button at the top of the window.

▶ You can set the background to be a movie or a still image. There are two ways to accomplish this. First, click and drag the desired movie or image from the Mac OS finder into the box, called a well. This well is located directly above the Image/Movie text. The other way is to pull down the File menu at the top of the desktop and choose Import, then Background Video. When prompted, select your movie or image.

▶ Next to the Image/Movie well, you will see an Audio well. This well is used when you want to add your own music. A theme with a still background image and accompanying music would be a good example of this.

▶ Directly above the Image/Movie and Audio wells is the Motion Duration slider bar. This bar is used to set the length of time that is desired for the menu. Once it has reached this point, the motion, whether it is audio or video, will start over. This can be set anywhere between 1 and 30 seconds.

Creating a Slideshow

Slideshows have evolved quite a bit since the slide projector was developed. A slideshow is a generic term for showing a number of slides, either on a slide projector or digitally on a DVD. Digital slideshows are a good way to show many pictures without using a slide projector. iDVD will let you create a slideshow, set the duration that each picture will be shown on the screen, and add background music to the pictures.

With iDVD's built-in Slideshow Editor, you have the ability to organize numerous pictures on to your DVD project. Figure 8.13 shows what the iDVD Slideshow Editor looks like. Above the Slideshow Editor, you will have the pictures that are contained within the slideshow.

Figure 8.13
iDVD Slideshow Editor.

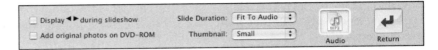

There are a few buttons in the Slideshow Editor that you need to know about.

▶ **Display <> During Slideshow**—When this option is checked, the slideshow will insert forward and back arrows on the slideshow when the DVD is playing.

▶ **Add Original Photo on DVD-ROM**—Recall from Part One that a DVD-ROM is a read-only application DVD format used mainly with computers. When this option is selected, iDVD creates a DVD-ROM section on the disc and stores the slideshow files there. You can retrieve the files the same way as you would with any other removable media (through the Mac OS Finder) without having to play the DVD. This option is useful, because you can insert the DVD into a computer and copy the slides from the DVD to your computer. You can see which pictures are in the DVD-ROM area by going to the Status window in the Customize drawer, as shown in Figure 8.14.

Figure 8.14
DVD-ROM contents.

▶ **Slide Duration**—This option sets the duration that each picture, or slide, will be displayed on the screen.

▶ **Thumbnail**—You can set the size of the Thumbnail (preview) icon displayed in the Slideshow Editor.

▶ **Audio**—This option adds background music to your slideshow. You add background music to a slideshow the same way that the background video was added for a Motion menu—just drag the audio file from the Mac OS Finder onto this audio well.

▶ **Return**—This button is used to close the Slideshow Editor and return to your DVD project.

Within the Slideshow Editor, you can rearrange the order in which the pictures are displayed. By default, the pictures in the slideshow are played from top to bottom. To rearrange the picture order, just drag one picture above or below another one, until the desired order is reached.

A Slideshow button is created on the menu when a slideshow is added to iDVD. A default icon is assigned to the Slideshow button, as shown in Figure 8.15.

Figure 8.15
Default Slideshow icon.

If you don't want to use this default icon, you can assign a picture within the slideshow as its icon. Just click on the Slideshow icon once and drag the Preview slider bar to the desired image. The same method is used for this as when you selected the start frame for a Motion button earlier in this chapter.

Using Disc Preview

You can preview your DVD at any time with iDVD's Disc Preview feature. Disc Preview mode will simulate exactly what your DVD will look like when it is burned and then played in the stand-alone DVD player. You can click the Preview button, shown in Figure 8.1, to start Disc Preview mode. When you put iDVD into Disc Preview mode, a remote control interface, shown in Figure 8.16, pops up and allows you to do everything that you could if the DVD was in a stand-alone DVD player.

Figure 8.16
Disc Preview remote control.

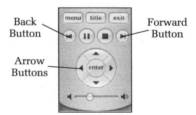

The arrow buttons in Figure 8.16 are used to select a button in the menu. Remember that you can have a maximum of six buttons per menu. Once the desired button is selected, click Enter on the remote control. The Forward and Back buttons in Figure 8.16 are used to navigate through a slideshow. The Menu button on the remote control will take you back to the Main Menu. There are two ways to exit Disc Preview mode—click Exit on the remote control or click the Preview button that you used to start Disc Preview mode.

CHAPTER 8

TURN MOTION ON

Before you go into Disc Preview mode, make sure motion is turned on. If motion is not enabled, your Motion menus or buttons will not work. To turn motion on, click the Motion button that is shown in Figure 8.1.

Burning Your DVD

Once your iDVD project is the way you want it, you can burn it to a blank DVD-R disc. Remember from Part One that you can only write to a DVD-R disc once, so when the DVD is burned, there is no way to change it.

DVD-RW AND IDVD

iDVD will not allow you to write to a DVD-RW disc. You *must* use blank DVD-R discs. At the time of this writing, Macintosh SuperDrives (their DVD burner) only supported the "-" formats.

Before you burn your DVD, make sure that motion is turned on. If it is not turned on when you try to burn the DVD, iDVD will notify you and ask if it should proceed with the burn, as shown in Figure 8.17.

Figure 8.17
Motion off warning.

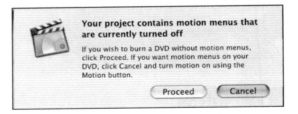

Once motion is on and you are positive that you want to burn the DVD, go ahead and click the Burn button twice. The first time will tell iDVD that you are ready to burn; the second time will confirm that you want to start the burning process. The icon will change to a radioactive symbol and will remain like this until the disc has finished burning.

Once the burning process has started, iDVD will ask you to insert a blank DVD-R disc if one is not already inserted. Figure 8.18 shows what the window looks like.

Figure 8.18
Insert blank media.

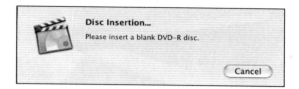

After the blank DVD-R is inserted, iDVD will verify that it is the correct media and will then start burning. The burning process consists of four stages:

▶ **Preparation**—This stage finalizes the layout and gets everything ready to burn. This stage completes quickly, so you may not see the window on your computer. Figure 8.19 shows the window.

Figure 8.19
Stage 1: Preparing.

▶ **Menu Rendering and Encoding**—This stage encodes the menus so they can be burned to the DVD. iDVD will convert the menus from their format to a universal format that stand-alone DVD players can interpret, as shown in Figure 8.20.

Figure 8.20
Stage 2: Menu
Rendering and
Encoding.

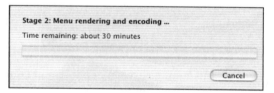

▶ **Asset Encoding**—In this stage, the assets (audio, video, and pictures) are all encoded so that they can be viewed on a stand-alone DVD player, as shown in Figure 8.21.

Figure 8.21
Stage 3: Asset Encoding.

▶ **Multiplexing and Burning**—This stage actually writes the data to the DVD. Figure 8.22 shows you the window that is displayed during this stage.

CHAPTER 8

Figure 8.22
Stage 4: Multiplexing
and Burning.

Depending on the speed of your computer, the time that it takes for iDVD to complete the four stages above varies. On average, Apple claims that it takes two to three minutes to encode and write one minute of video to a DVD.

When the DVD is finished, iDVD will display a window that it has completed, as shown in Figure 8.23.

Figure 8.23
Completed DVD.

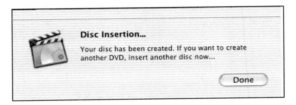

CREATING MORE THAN ONE COPY
If you would like to make more than one copy, insert another blank DVD-R into the drive before clicking done.

This wraps up Part Two of our book. In summary, we compared and contrasted four different DVD authoring applications and gave a functionality overview of each.

In Part Three, we will use our knowledge of Easy CD and DVD Creator 6 (covered in Chapter 5) and dig into the design portion of DVD authoring. We will look at such things as importing videos, organizing and creating menus, creating slideshows, and finally creating a jewel case insert.

Part Three

Creating a DVD with Easy CD and DVD Creator 6

Chapter 9

Capturing/Editing Your Content

Congratulations, you made it to Part Three. After reading everything up to this point, you are probably wondering when you will start applying it! Well, now is the time. Part Three is the design part of the DVD authoring process that will show you how to capture/edit your content, work with menus, create slideshows, and use Roxio Label Creator.

Each of the preceding items will be addressed using DVD Builder. While the same application (DVD Builder) will be shown in each item, the design fundamentals that are addressed can be applied to any DVD authoring application when it is time to design you own DVD. With that said, this chapter will focus on the first item—capturing/editing your content. Let's get started, shall we?

DVD Builder movies are defined as any combination of videos and pictures. A movie is laid out in a storyboard format so that elements—videos and pictures—are linked together. When the movie is played, it is done so sequentially. You can rearrange, add, or delete the elements within a movie through the DVD Builder Workshop. Figure 9.1 illustrates a menu with two movies assigned to it.

Figure 9.1
DVD Builder movie.

There are three required parts to a movie.

▶ **Title**—By default, movie titles are named Movie A, Movie B, and so on.

▶ **Content**—In the form of a video or still image.

▶ **Boundary color**—When a movie is selected, an orange box appears around it, serving as a visual boundary between different movies.

In addition to the required parts, transitions can be added between elements to provide a professional look to your DVD. A transition is an effect that closes an element and opens the next one—an example of this would be a fade out of a video followed by a fade in to the next video in the movie. Transitions are a nice touch in a slideshow and will be covered in Chapter 11.

DVD Builder will also accept one audio file per movie. It can accept a track directly from an audio CD, a supported audio file on your computer, or an audio commentary that is captured directly from a microphone.

Review: Importing or Capturing Multimedia

Remember from Chapter 5 that there are two ways to get multimedia into your project—capturing or importing. Capturing refers to playing the content of a capture device and saving the output of that device to a file that DVD Builder imports into the current project. Importing means that the multimedia is added to the current project from a file that is on your computer or via a TWAIN device—a scanner or digital camera.

CAPTURING VIDEO

It is important to make a distinction between capturing and importing. Capturing only refers to video on either a digital or an analog source. Pictures are imported from digital cameras or scanners.

DVD Builder has a feature called the De-noiser Filter. This filter is used to improve the picture quality of videos that were captured from analog sources that lack good picture quality—a VCR would be an example. To enable the filter, right-click on the video that needs this filter and select De-noiser; a lightning bolt will appear on the video letting you know that the filter is enabled.

VIEWING THE FILTER RESULTS

Unfortunately, when you preview a video in the Screening Room that has the De-noiser Filter enabled, you will not see a difference. The only way to see the results of the Filter is to burn the project to DVD and view the DVD in a stand-alone DVD player.

Capturing Video

Capturing video can come from one of two sources—digital or analog. A digital source would be a digital video camcorder, whereas an analog source is commonly a VCR or 8mm tape. The method for capturing from a digital or analog source is the same, with the difference being in how the source is hooked up to the computer. All sources, with the exception of FireWire digital camcorders, require a capture card that is physically installed into your computer. Let's review the method for capturing from both an analog and digital source.

CAPTURING TO A HARD DRIVE

Capturing video takes an enormous amount of hard drive space. A five-minute captured video can occupy over a gigabyte of hard drive space.

1. Verify that your capture source is connected to your computer. If you are using a VCR, make the appropriate VCR connections to the capture card, which are usually three different colored wires—red, white, and yellow, where yellow is video and the remaining are the left and right audio channels. Most capture cards use the same coloring scheme.

2. Select the Video Capture button from the Import Video toolbar (Figure 9.2). The same thing can be accomplished by using the Import menu that is located in the upper-left corner of DVD Builder, next to the File menu.

Figure 9.2
Import Video toolbar.

3. When the Video Capture button is selected, two new buttons appear below the Screening Room—Start Capture and Advanced Settings (see Figure 9.3).

Figure 9.3
Video Capture window.

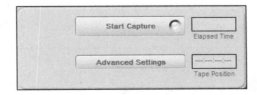

CHAPTER 9

4. If the capture device is a digital video camcorder, the playback controls below the Video window are used to find the desired starting place to capture. If capturing from an analog source, the playback controls are not available, and you should skip to Step 6.

5. Click the Play playback control to output the capture device into the Screening Room and proceed to Step 11.

6. If both a digital and analog capture device are connected to your computer, you must select the analog source using the Select Source drop-down menu from the Advanced Settings window, as shown in Figure 9.4.

Figure 9.4
Select analog source.

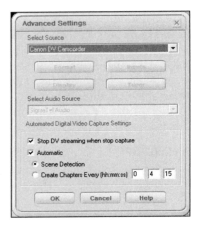

7. The ability to create chapter markers is done through the Advanced Settings window. Chapter markers are inserted automatically according to the specified time interval. For example, if you specify Create Chapters Every 0 0 30, then DVD Builder will insert a chapter marker every 30 seconds.

8. When you are finished in the Advanced Settings window, click the OK button.

9. To get the analog source to output to the Screening Room, you should press Play on the analog device—a VCR for example. Use the Rewind and Fast Forward buttons on the VCR to cue the place where the capture should start.

10. When the output is at the desired starting point, and the analog device is playing, click the Start Capture button, which records the output to a file on your computer.

11. Click the Stop Capture button when you are finished. The video that was just captured will be added to the highlighted movie in the Workshop.

12. You should repeat this process until each video is captured.

13. When you are finished, your movie will look similar to the one in Figure 9.5.

Figure 9.5
Completed movie.

DIFFERENT ANALOG VIDEO AND AUDIO

DVD Builder is able to capture from separate video and audio sources. You should press Play on both devices before the capture is started. The Advanced Settings window is used to change the audio source.

MULTIPLE VIDEO CAPTURES

You can click the Start and Stop Capture buttons as many times as you want. DVD Builder will import each of these separately into the same movie and link them as it normally does.

PREVIEWING YOUR VIDEO

If at any time you want to preview the video that you captured, double-click on the appropriate video in the Workshop, and it will show in the Screening Room.

Importing Multimedia

As mentioned earlier, DVD Builder will allow you to import from different sources. For a list of supported multimedia formats, refer to Table 9.1. Table 9.2 describes supported audio and picture formats.

Table 9.1 Supported Video Formats

Format	Description
AVI	Audio Video Interlaced. A standard in some Microsoft environments.
WMV	Windows Media Video. File format that is used in Windows XP version of Media Player.
DAT	Video files that are in VCD format
MPG	MPEG-1 encoded video
MPEG	MPEG movie format
M2P	MPEG-2 encoded video
SVCD	Video files that are in SVCD format
VOB	Video files that are in MPEG-2 encoded DVD format
MOV	Apple QuickTime Movies
DIVX	MPEG-4, or DivX, encoded videos

CHAPTER 9

Table 9.2 Supported Audio and Picture Formats

Format	Description
JPG	Joint Photographics Experts Group still picture format
BMP	Bitmap still picture format
MP3	MPEG-1 audio encoded format
MP2	MPEG-2 audio encoded format
WAV	Wave audio format
WMA	Windows Media Audio format. This is a competitor to MP3.

There are two sources that DVD Builder (and most other DVD authoring applications) can import from:

▶ **TWAIN devices**—digital camera, scanner, or webcam

▶ **Multimedia files**—most commonly videos that are stored on your computer

Importing from a TWAIN device is done through the Video Import toolbar, like so:

1. Verify that the TWAIN device to be imported from is hooked up to the computer and turned on.

2. Click the Other Sources button from the Video Import toolbar. If you have more than one device, you can use the Select Device button to choose the appropriate device (see Figure 9.6). You do not need to use this if there is only one TWAIN device attached to the computer.

3. After selecting the source, click the Acquire Still Images button, also shown in Figure 9.6, which will bring up the TWAIN Device window, as shown in Figure 9.7. The TWAIN interface shown is for a Hewlett-Packard scanner.

Figure 9.6
Select Device button.

Figure 9.7
Scanner TWAIN
interface.

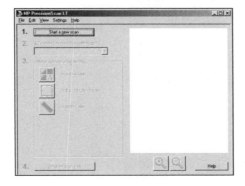

4. Scan the document as you normally would. When the scan is finished, DVD Builder will import the picture into the movie that you are working on.

You can also import multimedia files straight from your computer—the file is already stored on your computer. Again, you should consult Tables 9.1 and 9.2 for a list of supported file import types. Multimedia files already stored on your computer are also imported using the Video Import toolbar.

1. Select the Multimedia Files button in the Video Import toolbar.

2. The Import Files window will appear asking for the location of the file(s) to import (see Figure 9.8). This will only show files that are supported with DVD Builder.

Figure 9.8
Import Files window.

3. Select the file that you want to import and click the OK button.

PREVIEWING IMPORTED FILES

You can preview imported files in the same way that you previewed captured videos. Double-click on the file within the Workshop to put it in the Screening Room.

IMPORT EVERYTHING AT ONCE

Roxio recommends that multimedia is imported and captured all at once. Once everything is in DVD Builder, you can organize it into different movies and menus.

Video Editing

Although video editing is a feature that is not usually included with a beginning-level DVD authoring application, DVD Builder has a couple of basic video editing features built in.

▶ **Trimming or splitting videos**—If the video is longer than desired, DVD Builder can delete part of the video from the beginning or end. Also, if the video is too long, DVD Builder can split it into sections.

▶ **Extracting frames**—DVD Builder can extract specific frames out of a video and add them as pictures in the selected movie. This would be useful if you wanted to use a certain frame as the Menu button, since DVD Builder uses the first element in the movie as its Menu button.

ADVANCED VIDEO EDITING

To use advanced video editing, you should purchase either an advanced DVD authoring application or a third-party video editing application and import the edited videos into DVD Builder. Some advanced video editing includes splicing two videos together, adding audio to select parts of a video, and so on.

Trimming or Splitting Your Video

Trimming or splitting videos allows more flexibility when creating your DVD Builder movies. If you captured a 20-minute video, you may want to split it into two 10-minute videos, so the viewer is not forced to watch the whole movie at once. Also, if in this 20-minute video you decide not to use the last two minutes, you can trim the end of the video, or trim the video to the right, as we say.

Trimming a video can be done to the left or the right. If you trim left, DVD Builder will remove everything to the left of the current position. Similarly, trimming to the right will remove everything to the right of the current position. Let's take a look at the Trim buttons—and the Split Video button, since it is in the same window—within DVD Builder. The video editing buttons are shown in Figure 9.9.

Figure 9.9
Video editing buttons.

Let's see how to use these buttons to edit our video.

1. Make sure the video that you want to edit is in the Screening Room. Double-click on the video to put it in the Screening Room.

2. Move the slider bar—located directly above the Trim and Split buttons—to the appropriate location in the video.

3. Click one of the video editing buttons—Trim Left, Trim Right, or Split Video.

If you trimmed either left or right, the discarded portion will be deleted from the movie and moved to the Trash can. When the Split Video button is clicked, two separate videos will be created in the movie, and the original full-length video will be moved to the Trash can.

UNDO YOUR EDITS
To restore the original videos at any time, right-click on the edited video in the DVD Builder movie and select Undo Trim/Split from the menu that appears.

Frame Extraction

Extracting a frame from a video within DVD Builder is done through the Workshop.

1. Within the DVD Builder Workshop area, right-click on the video that includes the desired frame. When the menu appears, select Extract Frame.

2. When the Extract Frame window appears (see Figure 9.10), the video will start playing. You can use the slider bar to find the frame to extract. Alternatively, the playback controls can be used, which are located directly below the slider bar. The buttons on the far left and right are Frame Advance buttons.

Figure 9.10
Extract Frame window.

3. Click the OK button. The frame will be extracted and added as a picture in the selected movie.

EXTRACTED FILE TYPE
The extracted frame will be saved into the DVD Builder as a bitmap file (with a BMP extension). Luckily, this file format has great picture quality.

The Introduction Video

An Introduction Video is a video that is played on a DVD before anything else. If you choose to include an Introduction Video on your DVD, it will not be possible for the viewers to skip it and go directly to the Main Menu. DVD Builder treats the Introduction Video as a normal movie, so the same rules apply. A good example of this is the FBI warning that is shown on a DVD before the Main Menu is displayed. Another example where this would be useful is in a corporate training video. The corporation could have their company logo as an Introduction Video.

The Introduction Video is assigned through DVD Builder's Workshop area. This Introduction Video is always the top movie—assigned the name Intro, as shown in Figure 9.11.

Figure 9.11
Introduction Video.

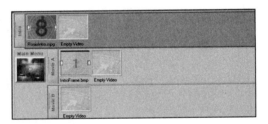

Each project created in DVD Builder is assigned a default Introduction Video that was developed by Roxio. As stated earlier, all normal movie rules apply, so it is possible to add more than one video, create a slideshow, or remove the Introduction Video all together.

REMOVING THE INTRODUCTION VIDEO
To delete the Introduction Video, remove everything from the Intro movie. In a stand-alone DVD player, the DVD will go directly to the Main Menu.

Working with Pictures

In addition to videos, DVD Builder can also import picture files into DVD Builder movies that can be grouped into slideshows—covered in Chapter 11—or shown as a single picture. Importing picture files is done the same way as importing video files, via the Video Import toolbar. Click on the Multimedia Files button and navigate to the appropriate folder that contains the picture file.

Once the picture is imported into a particular movie, DVD Builder can set how long the picture will be displayed and rotate the picture in the event that it is imported upside-down. Let's look at setting the image duration.

1. Make sure the picture file has been imported into a movie.
2. Within the DVD Builder Workshop, right-click on the picture and click the Duration item from the menu that appears.
3. Select one of the five pre-defined duration choices—1, 3, 6, 10, or 15 seconds.

STRETCHING IMAGE DURATIONS

An exception to the picture duration's pre-defined choices is when you stretch a movie to fit the length of a sound file. This requires that you have at least one picture in the movie. To stretch the movie, right-click on the movie title and choose Stretch Still Image Duration to Fit Sound Length.

When a picture is imported, there is a chance the picture may be upside-down. DVD Builder lets you rotate the image—90 degrees in either direction—after it has been imported into the Workshop.

1. Within the DVD Builder Workshop, right-click on the picture and select Rotate from the menu that appears.
2. Choose either 90° (clockwise) or −90° (counter-clockwise).

ROTATING MORE THAN 90°

To rotate the image 180° in the clockwise direction, select the 90° option twice.

Working with Audio

DVD Builder allows you to manipulate the audio that is assigned to a movie in the Workshop area. There are several possibilities available to manipulate the audio of a movie.

> ▶ Replace the original audio assigned to a video.

> ▶ Blend an audio file into the original audio assigned to the movie.

> ▶ Copy (rip) an audio track from a CD and import it directly into a movie.

> ▶ Create your own audio commentary by means of a microphone.

DVD Builder allows only one audio file per movie, picture, or video. You will be prompted to do one of two things when you add a new audio track to a video or movie that has existing audio—replace the existing audio with the new track or blend the two audio tracks together to make one file. Once the audio has been inserted in the movie, a music note symbol will appear. Always choose an audio file that is shorter than the movie; otherwise, the audio will cut off when the video is finished.

Audio files can be added in different ways.

> ▶ Use the Video Import toolbar to choose an audio file that is stored on your computer. Click and drag the file from the Browse files window to the appropriate movie.

> ▶ Use the Attach Audio option by right-clicking on the movie that needs the audio and selecting Attach Audio from the menu that appears. Use the Browse window to find the audio file.

> ▶ Insert an audio CD into your CD-ROM drive. Open the CD in My Computer and select the track that you want to add to your project. Click and drag the audio track from the CD to the desired movie. DVD Builder will automatically convert the audio track to a WAV file and import it into the project.

Audio commentary is a way to add background narration to a movie. This feature requires that a sound card and microphone be installed in your computer before the commentary starts. The recording is done via the Video Editing window that was shown in Figure 9.9.

1. If you have more than one sound card, select the appropriate one from the drop-down menu next to the microphone.

2. Click the Record button that has the microphone on it.

3. Speak clearly into your microphone.

4. When you are finished, click the Record button again.

5. To hear what the commentary sounds like after the recording is finished, double-click on the containing movie, video, or picture; this will play it in the Screening Room.

COMMENTARY PLAYBACK

The audio commentary always starts at the beginning of the movie, video, or still image. You must split the video if you want to start the commentary in a different place.

You have two choices if you no longer want the audio associated with a movie, video, or picture—right-click on the note symbol and select Remove, or right-click on the movie, video, or picture and select Remove Audio from the menu that appears.

The next chapter will show you how to create and organize the menus that will make up your DVD. Once the menu structure is created, you can add the movies that were captured and imported in this chapter into the new menu structure.

Chapter 10
Working with Menus

The next design phase that we will look at is creating a DVD''s menu structure, which can make or break a DVD. Without a well thought-out menu structure, the viewer may become discouraged. If the structure is too disorganized, this may very well take away from the viewing experience. The menu structure of a DVD is very similar to that of a website—you are presented with a main page and buttons (or links) that will take you deeper into the DVD (or website).

This chapter will help you create menus—resulting in a menu structure—using DVD Builder. As with Chapter 9, the application that is used for illustration is DVD Builder, but you can apply the fundamentals of this chapter to any DVD authoring application. Consider the following when creating your DVD menu structure.

▶ **The menus and menu buttons should be given distinct names**—This is to ensure that they can be easily identified. For example, five buttons labeled Movie 1 through Movie 5 would make it hard for the viewer to understand what each button does.

▶ **Ensure logical connections between parent and child menus**—You should make sure the menu buttons contained within the submenu are related to the menu button that contains it. For example, you would not want a menu button that linked to a video of your kid''s first birthday party in a submenu titled Our Wedding.

▶ **Don't go too deep**—Creation of submenus should be limited. The viewer may get "lost" in the DVD if there are too many menus to choose from.

▶ **Monitor running times**—The running time of the audio assigned to a motion menu should be less than or equal to the motion menu's video; otherwise, the audio will cut off when the video is done.

CHAPTER 5 REVIEW

This chapter will serve somewhat as a review to the Manipulating Menus section in Chapter 5. Whereas Chapter 5 was an overview of DVD Builder as a whole, this chapter will focus on menu creation and organization.

A DVD Builder menu consists of four parts (see Figure 10.1); each part is explained in the following list.

Figure 10.1
DVD Builder menu.

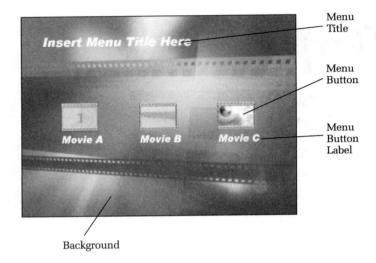

Menu Title

Menu Button

Menu Button Label

Background

▶ **Background**—The background of the menu can be either a video or a picture.

▶ **Menu titles**—The title of the menu.

▶ **Menu buttons**—Videos or submenus on your DVD are accessed via menu buttons.

▶ **Menu button labels**—Names given to the menu buttons.

To organize your movies, you can create submenus, submenus of submenus, and so on. Keep in mind though that DVD Builder will only allow a maximum of six buttons per menu. These six buttons can include links to other submenus or movies. If you exceed this limit, a window will appear (see Figure 10.2).

Figure 10.2
Menu button limit exceeded.

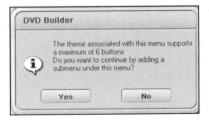

Creating a submenu is done within the DVD Builder Workshop area.

1. Click on the Create Submenu button located in the Workshop area (see Figure 10.3).

Figure 10.3
Create Submenu button.

2. A new menu is created below the Main Menu and is slightly indented so that it can be easily identified. The default title for the first submenu that is created is Submenu 1.

MENU BOUNDARY COLOR
To better distinguish the submenu from other menus, each one has its own boundary color. For example, the first submenu created has a turquoise boundary color that covers the entire menu—including the movie portion of the menu.

Menu Themes

A common feature of new DVD authoring applications is the ability to create themes. Themes visually connect each part of a menu. For example, let's say you are making a DVD of your child's first year in elementary school. Some things that may be in this theme are crayons for the menu buttons and a background image of your child's classroom. DVD Builder packages several menu themes with the application. A theme has several parts to it.

▶ **Menu background**—This can be either a menu with or without motion.

▶ **Button shapes**—The button shapes can be square, rectangular, circular, and so on.

▶ **Background audio**—This is the audio that is played while the menu is displayed.

▶ **Font options for buttons and titles**—These are used to select the font size, type, and color of buttons and titles.

Within DVD Builder, all menu themes are held in the Menu Theme Library, which can be found in the lower part of the Workshop area. The icon is shown in Figure 10.4. When this icon is clicked, the Menu Theme Library will appear (see Figure 10.5).

Figure 10.4
Menu Theme Library icon.

Figure 10.5
Menu Theme Library.

DVD Builder has two ways to apply a menu theme to a menu.

▶ Make sure the menu that the theme should be applied to is in the Screening Room. Double-click on the theme in the Menu Theme Library. The menu theme will change in the Screening Room to what was just selected.

▶ Again, make sure the menu that the theme should be applied to is in the Screening Room. Click and drag the appropriate menu theme from the library into either the Screening Room or the menu in the Workshop area.

SAVING YOUR OWN THEME
It is not possible to save your own theme. You can customize a theme for use in the current project, but you cannot save it for later use.

Menu Customizations

DVD Builder allows customization of the included pre-packaged themes. Let's look at what you can customize.

▶ Change the background image. You can set the menu in motion or leave it as a flat menu.

▶ Change the button image.

▶ Rename a button label or menu title.

▶ Add sound.

Every menu has a background image. This image can be either a video or still picture. If the background image is a video, the menu is considered to be a motion menu because the menu moves. Changing the background image is accomplished through the Import Video toolbar.

1. Make sure the menu that needs a new background image is in the Screening Room. If not, double-click on the menu in the Workshop area to put it there.

2. Select the Import Multimedia Files button from the Video Import toolbar (see Figure 10.6).

Figure 10.6
Import Multimedia Files
button.

3. Within the Import Multimedia Files window, navigate to the location of the desired video or still picture. To filter by specific multimedia type, you can use the drop-down menu located in this window; just select the type of file that you are looking for.

4. Click and drag the file from the Import Multimedia Files window to the Screening Room.

5. Click the OK button to close the Import Multimedia Files window.

USING VIDEOS AS BACKGROUNDS

DVD Builder does not allow you to capture directly into a menu background. You must capture the video first, and then import it as the background image.

A button image is the still picture that is displayed as the menu button. Unlike other DVD authoring applications, you must use a still picture, because motion buttons are not supported. The button image is always the first item in the movie that the button links to. If the movie starts with a still picture, then this picture will be the button image, and if the movie starts with a video, then the first frame of the video is used as the button image. DVD Builder does allow you to extract a frame so that you can use it as the button image, which was covered in Chapter 9.

The first menu, called the Main Menu, is always created when a new project is started. The default menu title is Main Menu - Click here to edit, as shown in Figure 10.7. You can change this default title or any button label using the same steps.

1. Make sure that the menu that needs a new title or button label is in the Screening Room. If not, double-click on the menu in the Workshop area to put it there.

2. Click once on the menu title or button label. Remember by default the Main Menu title is called Main Menu - Click here to edit.

3. A window will appear (see Figure 10.7) that allows the menu title or button label to be changed. In Figure 10.8 a menu title is shown, but remember that the procedure for a button label is the same.

Figure 10.7
Change Menu Title or
Button Label window.

4. Click the Select Font button in Figure 10.6 to change the font properties of the menu (see Figure 10.8).

Figure 10.8
Change Font Properties
window.

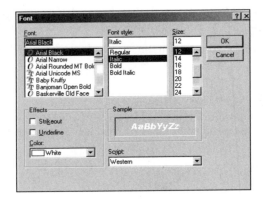

5. When finished, click the OK button.

REMOVING ITEMS
To remove a menu button or submenu, right-click on the desired item and select Delete from the menu that appears.

Audio is another thing that can be added to a menu. DVD Builder supports one audio file per menu. The steps in accomplishing this are the same as adding audio to a movie, which was done in Chapter 9. Let's review this process.

1. Within the Workshop area, right-click on the desired menu to attach audio.
2. From the menu that appears, select Attach Audio.
3. Browse to the location of the audio file.
4. Select the audio file, and click the Open button.

To remove the audio at a later time, right-click on the desired menu and select Remove Audio from the menu that appears.

Menu Preview

To get an idea of how your menu will look before it is burned to a DVD, you can preview it in the Screening Room.

1. Double-click the desired menu to put it in the Screening Room.
2. To navigate through the menus, double-click on the menu buttons.
3. If you are previewing a motion menu, click the Play button in the Screening Room to put the menu in motion.

In the next chapter, we will look at the next design phase: using the menus that were just created to add a slideshow to our DVD. As we have with this chapter and the previous one, we will use DVD Builder to illustrate how to create the slideshow.

Chapter 11
Creating Slideshows

Slideshows are a group of pictures that are shown on a DVD at a given time interval. Slideshows are useful if you have a lot of pictures that should be presented to the viewer in an unattended manner. For example, you could rent out a reception hall and throw your father a 60th birthday party. As guests arrive, a slideshow could be playing pictures of your father in various stages of his life.

Using DVD Builder, this chapter will explore the use of slideshows on a DVD. In DVD Builder, the slides, or pictures, in the slideshow are grouped together in a DVD Builder movie. In addition to grouping pictures together, a slideshow can have other features added to it, which are listed next. The additional features will be discussed in more detail later in this chapter.

▶ **Transitions**—Effects that are added between slides. DVD Builder comes standard with many transitions, such as fade out then fade in—the current slide in the slideshow gradually fades out, while the next slide fades in.

▶ **Background music**—The background music file can be anything that is supported by DVD Builder.

There are three steps required when creating a slideshow.

1. Import your slides into a DVD Builder movie.

2. Customize your slideshow—set the time interval between slides, add background music, rearrange the order of the slides, and delete slides that are no longer needed.

3. Add transitions between slides.

NEW SLIDESHOW: SAME METHODS

With the exception of transitions, the methods used to import slides and then customize your slideshow have been covered to some degree in previous chapters.

Importing Slides

Slides are imported into a DVD Builder movie in the same way as video—via the Video Import toolbar using either the Import Multimedia or the Other Sources button. The Import Multimedia button (see Figure 11.1) is used for files that are already on your computer, whereas the Other Sources button (see Figure 11.2) is used when importing from a TWAIN device. To import slides, do the following:

Figure 11.1
Import Multimedia
button.

Figure 11.2
Other Sources button.

1. If you are acquiring from a TWAIN source, skip to Step 4. Otherwise, click on the Import Multimedia button and navigate to the folder that contains the slides that should be added to the slideshow.

2. To make things easier, you can filter the results to pictures only by clicking on the Still Image Files Filter button (see Figure 11.3).

Figure 11.3
Still Image files Filter
button.

FILTER OPTIONS
In addition to filtering by slides, you can also filter by video or audio.

3. Click and drag the slides from the Import Files window into the movie where the slideshow is being created. If you are not importing pictures from a TWAIN device, then you are finished. Otherwise, proceed to the next step.

4. When clicked, the Other Sources button will bring up the default TWAIN interface (see Figure 11.4). If you have more than one TWAIN device installed on the computer, the Select Source button is used to specify which TWAIN device will be used for the import (see Figure 11.5). If there is no TWAIN device installed on the computer, the error message in Figure 11.6 will appear.

Figure 11.4
HP TWAIN interface.

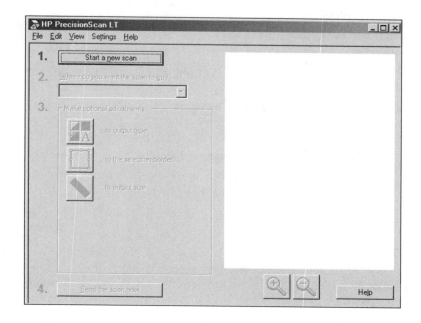

Figure 11.5
Select Source button.

Figure 11.6
No TWAIN device
detected.

5. The picture will import, via the TWAIN device, into the highlighted movie in the DVD Builder Workshop area.

Once the slides are imported into the specific movie that is designated as the slideshow, it will look similar to Figure 11.7.

Figure 11.7
Imported slideshow.

Baby.bmp   Birthday.bmp   Butterflies.bmp   Christmas.bmp   Empty Video

Customizing Slideshows

There are many ways to customize your slideshow once it is in a movie.

▶ Slides can be rearranged or deleted.

▶ Slide duration can be changed. This is how long the slide will display on the screen before advancing to the next one.

▶ Background music can be played during a slideshow.

Moving or Deleting Slides

The ability to rearrange slideshows is important. If this ability didn't exist, you would be stuck with the order in which slides were imported! When the slides are rearranged, you are changing the order in which the stand-alone DVD player displays them. To rearrange a slide, do the following.

1. Click and drag the target slide—the slide that you want to move—from its current location to its desired location.

2. Once the target slide is over the location, release the mouse button.

3. The original slide will be replaced with the target slide, and the remaining slides to the right of the target slide (including the slide that was replaced) will move over one location.

To delete a slide, click and drag the slide from the DVD Builder into the Trash can.

Setting the Slide Duration

The slide duration is assigned one of the time intervals built into DVD Builder. These intervals are 1, 3, 6, 10, or 15 seconds with a default duration of 10 seconds per slide. The slide duration is set at the individual slide or slideshow level. I recommend setting the slide duration at the slideshow level so that all slides have the same duration; otherwise, the viewer may think that the DVD is malfunctioning because of the apparent choppiness of the slides. Let's see how to set the slide duration in DVD Builder.

SETTING DURATION
The procedure is the same whether the slide duration is set at the slideshow or slide level. The only procedural difference is where the duration is assigned. You will see in the next numbered list where to set each one.

1. To set at the slideshow level, right-click on the movie handle. This is the left-most part of the movie (usually denoted by Movie A, Movie B, and so on). A typical movie handle is shown in Figure 11.8. The slide level duration is set by right-clicking on the individual slide.

Figure 11.8
Movie handle.

2. Select Still Images Duration from the menu that appears.
3. Another submenu (see Figure 11.9) appears from the Still Images Duration menu with the available duration times.

Figure 11.9
Still images duration.

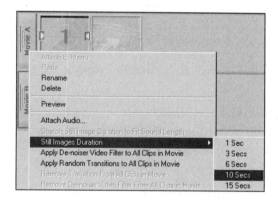

4. Select the desired slide duration.

VIEWING THE SLIDE DURATION
DVD Builder will not display the current slide duration at the slideshow level, meaning that if you assign a certain duration to a slideshow, then go back in to see what it is, the setting will be blank. This does not happen when setting at the slide level. Also, setting a slide duration at the slideshow level will override any slide durations set at the slide level.

SETTING AT THE SLIDE LEVEL
When the slideshow image duration is set at the slide level, you must right-click on each slide in the slideshow and set each one individually, which can be time-consuming.

Adding Background Music

Background music is audio that is played during a slideshow. Remember from Chapter 10 that DVD Builder allows one audio file per movie, which means that a slideshow is also limited to one audio file. Once the background music has finished, it will restart and continue to loop until the slideshow has finished. DVD Builder supports many different audio file types. Table 11.1 shows the most common formats that DVD Builder supports.

Table 11.1 Supported Audio Formats

Format	Description
MP3	MPEG-1 Audio-encoded format
MP2	MPEG-2 Audio-encoded format
WAV	Wave audio format
WMA	Windows Media Audio format

Background music is added in DVD Builder within the Workshop area, like so:

1. Right-click on the movie handle containing the slideshow.

2. Select Attach Audio from the menu that appears (see Figure 11.10). This will bring up the Browse Audio Files window.

Figure 11.10
Attach Audio menu.

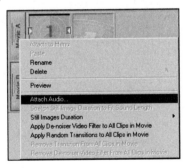

3. In the Browse Audio Files window (see Figure 11.11), navigate to the audio file to be set as the background music.

Figure 11.11
Browse Audio Files window.

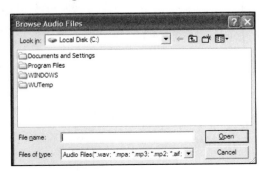

4. Click Open to assign the background music.

5. To confirm that the audio has been attached, a musical note will appear in the movie handle.

Even though DVD Builder is limited to one audio file per movie, it is possible to combine more than one together. Each time an audio file is added, a warning will appear asking what DVD Builder should do, as shown in Figure 11.12.

FIGURE 11.12

Attach audio warning.

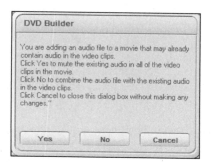

▶ The Yes button will mute any video already associated with the movie and only play the assigned audio file.

▶ The No button joins the two audio files so that they will be played sequentially.

▶ The Cancel button will not make any changes to the movie.

AUDIO FILE LENGTH

Always make sure the background music is either shorter or the same length as the slideshow to avoid cutting the background music off when the slideshow is finished.

There are two ways to remove the background music from the slideshow.

▶ Right-click on the movie handle and select Delete from the menu that appears. Click the Yes button to confirm the deletion.

▶ Right-click on the musical note located within the movie handle and select Remove. Click Yes to confirm its deletion.

Adding Transitions

Transitions are effects that are added to slideshows in order to transition between slides. A transition can look a number of different ways. One way, for example, is for the current slide—that is, the slide being displayed—to fade out as the next slide is fading in. DVD Builder comes standard with many transitions, and, unfortunately, it is not possible to add your own. Luckily, there are enough transitions built in that you should find what you are looking for.

To use transitions, open the Transition Library, which is found at the bottom of the DVD Builder Workshop area (immediately to the right of the Menu Theme icon). A picture of its icon is shown in Figure 11.13. When this icon is clicked, the Transition Library (see Figure 11.14) appears from the bottom of the DVD Builder window—below the Transition Library icon.

Figure 11.13
Transition Library icon.

Figure 11.14
Transition Library.

Looking at each transition, you will notice part of the letters A and B. The letter A represents the current slide, and B represents the next slide in the slideshow. As the mouse is moved over each transition, the transition will come to life. This motion is a preview of what the transition will do when it is added to the slideshow. For example, when you put your mouse over the first transition, A will appear first. B will then slide in from left to right. This is exactly what will happen when the transition is added to a slideshow. The current slide will display until it is time to advance to the next one. Upon advancing, the next slide will come into the picture from the left-hand side.

In DVD Builder, transitions are added between each slide in the Workshop area, like so:

1. Make sure that the Transition Library is open. If not, click on the Transition Library icon to open it.

2. Click and drag the desired transition from the Transition Library to the link between the slides in the Workshop area. The link (see Figure 11.15) looks like two arrows that are pointing away from each other.

3. To confirm that the transition is installed, the link arrows will turn from blue to gold.

Figure 11.15
Slide link arrows.

USING TRANSITIONS

Transitions are an easy way to spice up a slideshow, and I recommend using them often. If you cannot decide which transition to use, DVD Builder lets you randomize the transitions between all clips in a DVD Builder movie. To do this, right-click on the DVD Builder movie and select Apply Random Transitions To All Clips in Movie from the menu that appears.

The next chapter is the last design part of this book. It covers how to create jewel cases, DVD covers, and disc labels that are packaged with your DVD.

Chapter 12
Creating a Jewel Case

Until this point, we have focused on the actual DVD disc itself, including how to add videos, create slideshows, and design an effective menu system. Once all of this hard work is complete, you will want to package and distribute your new DVD to friends, family members, potential clients, or employees. Roxio's Label Creator was designed for just this task. In this chapter, we will examine how to use Roxio Label Creator to create attractive DVD and jewel case labels.

Before we get into the specifics on how to use Label Creator, you should familiarize yourself with some terms that are used in this chapter and in the application itself.

► A jewel case is the plastic case that stores the DVD. The purpose of the jewel case is to give the DVD a safe home and reduce the risk of it scratching or cracking.

► A DVD case is a special type of jewel case designed specifically for DVDs. These cases are usually larger than a normal jewel case. Most commercially produced DVD movies are packaged in these cases.

► Labels are paper cut in the circular shape of a DVD. They have an adhesive backing, which allows them to stick to the label side of a DVD. A label can contain anything—the DVD title, the date the DVD was created, and so on.

► Covers are paper inserts that are designed to fit into a jewel case. There are a few different types of covers that will be covered in this chapter—front, booklet, back, and DVD case. Typically, covers contain specific information about what is on the DVD. For example, a back cover may list the different videos or slideshow names contained on the disc.

► Within Label Creator, a layout includes all of the design elements of a cover or label. There are six layouts to choose from in Label Creator: Disc Label, Front Cover, Booklet, Back Cover, Mini Disc Label, and DVD Case Cover. Each of these layouts will be covered later in this chapter.

There are two ways to open Label Creator—through the Start Menu or via the Roxio Home Menu. Let's discuss the Start Menu first.

1. Click on the Start Menu.
2. Click on the Programs folder and then Roxio Easy CD and DVD Creator 6.
3. Choose Label Creator from the Program menu that appears (see Figure 12.1).

Figure 12.1
Roxio Easy CD and DVD
Creator 6 Program
menu.

The Roxio Home Menu way of starting the application involves less mouse clicks and (because of this) is my preferred method!

1.   Double-click on the Roxio Easy CD and DVD Creator 6 icon located on the desktop. This will bring up the Roxio Home Menu.

2.   From the Roxio Home Menu (see Figure 12.2), click the Label Creator icon (see Figure 12.3).

Figure 12.2
Roxio Home Menu.

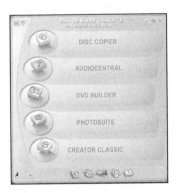

Figure 12.3
Label Creator icon.

When Label Creator starts, you are presented with its main interface, shown in Figure 12.4.

Figure 12.4
Label Creator interface.

Project Buttons

Properties toolbar

Layout Toolbar

Theme Library

Project Layout

Print Project

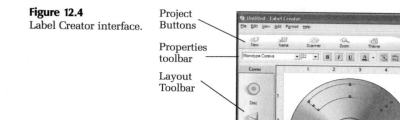

There are several default components to the Label Creator interface.

▶ The Project Layout area is where the project is edited.

▶ The Project buttons assist you in managing your project. There are a few buttons to choose from in this part of the interface; these will be explained later in this chapter.

▶ The Properties toolbar allows you to change the style of the text in your project. You can set font type and size, change the type of text (bold, underline), and change the alignment of the text within its text box.

▶ The Layout toolbar will switch from one layout to another.

▶ Similar to themes in DVD Builder or other DVD authoring applications, Label Creator has a theme library built in for customizing the look of the covers and labels.

▶ When your project is complete, use the Print Project button to print one or all of the layouts contained within a project.

In addition to the default components, there are also two optional components that can be added—the Objects and Alignment toolbars. These toolbars are added through the View menu, as shown in Figure 12.5. To make the toolbars visible, click on the appropriate toolbar in the View menu; a checkmark will appear next to it. To hide the toolbars, uncheck them.

CHAPTER 12

Figure 12.5
Adding optional
toolbars.

PROPERTIES TOOLBAR

The Properties toolbar is made visible and invisible in the same View menu as the Objects and Alignment toolbars. To hide the Properties toolbar, uncheck the Properties Toolbar option in the View menu.

These toolbars are used to manage the content of your layout. The use of these toolbars will be covered later in this chapter.

▶ **Objects toolbar**—Add pictures and text to your layout; shown in Figure 12.6.

▶ **Alignment toolbar**—Tools that will assist you in rearranging objects that were created with the Objects toolbar; shown in Figure 12.7.

▶ **Properties toolbar**—Format the text contained within the objects; shown in Figure 12.8.

Figure 12.6
Objects toolbar.

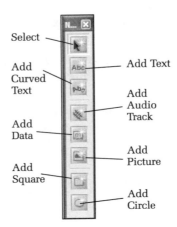

Figure 12.7
Alignment toolbar.

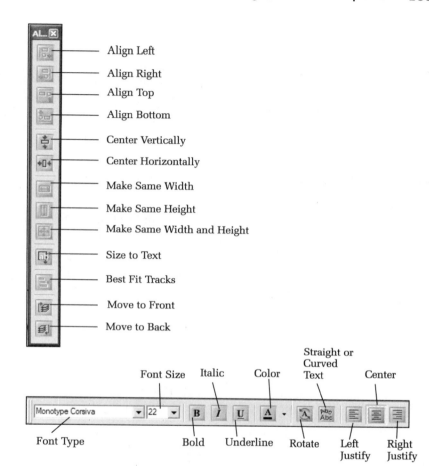

Figure 12.8
Properties toolbar.

Let's say you were making a DVD of a trip to Hawaii. The view from your hotel room balcony was stunning, so you took a picture of it. You decide that this picture would go great on the front cover of the jewel case. You would use the Objects toolbar to add the picture to the Front Cover layout, and you would use the Alignment toolbar to center the object. With these toolbars, you can create objects—adding textboxes and pictures—and then orient the text within these textboxes in many different ways—left or right text alignment within the textbox is an example.

Understanding Layouts

Label Creator has six layouts—two label layouts and four cover layouts—built into the application. Click on the appropriate layout in the Layout toolbar to bring it into the layout area. From here, you can design and print each layout.

CHAPTER 12

DVD LAYOUTS

With the exception of the Mini Disc layout, any of the layouts discussed in this section will work for a DVD. The layout that is used depends on the case that will hold the disc—a standard jewel case or DVD case. A DVD case will use the DVD Case Cover layout, whereas a standard jewel case can use any combination of the other layouts.

Disc Label Layout

Disc Label layout is used to design the label that is attached to the DVD media itself, and is the default layout when the application is started. Figure 12.9 shows an example of the layout area with the Disc Label layout.

Figure 12.9
Disc Label layout.

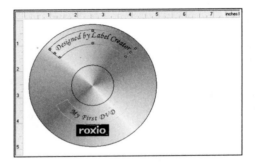

USING LABELS

Disc labels can be found at any office supply store.

Front Cover Layout

The Front Cover layout (see Figure 12.10) is used to design the front jewel case insert. Label Creator assumes that this cover is one-sided. When you open the jewel case, the back side of the front cover insert will be blank.

Figure 12.10
Front Cover layout.

Booklet Layout

The Booklet layout (shown in Figure 12.11) is a variation of the Front Cover layout. However, this layout has a front and back side to it, whereas the Front Cover layout had only a front side. The two sides are made by printing the layout and then folding the printout in half.

Figure 12.11
Booklet layout.

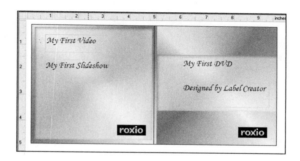

Back Cover Layout

If you have ever examined a jewel case, you know that it splits into three sections—the front cover, the disc tray, and the back cover. The Back Cover layout (shown in Figure 12.12) is one-sided and is inserted between the disc tray and the back cover of the jewel case. Typically, the back cover contains the same information as the back side of the booklet cover.

Figure 12.12
Back Cover layout.

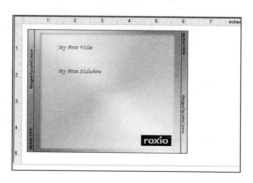

Mini Disc Label Layout

The Mini Disc Label layout (see Figure 12.13) is the other label layout built into Label Creator. Mini Discs are CDs that are physically smaller than regular CDs, thus requiring a different size label.

Figure 12.13
Mini Disc Label layout.

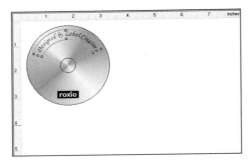

MINI DISC DVD
Mini Discs do not come in DVD format, so this layout will not be used when authoring DVDs.

DVD Case Cover Layout

As you learned earlier in this chapter, a DVD case is a special case that is larger than a normal jewel case. A DVD Case Cover (displayed in Figure 12.14) is a single-sided cover that requires folding, because both the front and back cover are included on the same piece of paper.

Figure 12.14
DVD Case Cover layout.

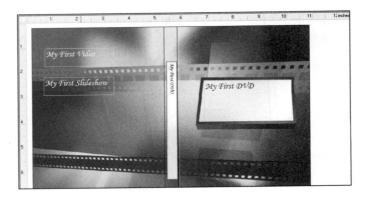

Creating a Project

A layout project consists of the layouts we've discussed. Label Creator gives you the option of using all of them or choosing certain ones. To start a new project, click on the New button in the Project Buttons area of Label Creator. If a project has already been started, Label Creator will ask if you want to save or discard the current project.

There are three steps involved in creating a project.

1. **Applying a theme**—A theme is applied to the project and includes background graphics, text style, and object placement.

2. **Adding layout content**—Once the theme has been applied, text and pictures are added to the layouts.

3. **Customizing the layout**—The layout is customized by moving objects and formatting the text within the objects. If you are satisfied with the text style and placement provided by the theme, this step may not be required.

Applying a Theme

When a theme is applied to a project, every layout within that project, except for the DVD Case Cover, is assigned the same theme. Themes include background images, fonts and colors that coordinate with the background image, and text placement that has been designed specifically with the theme in mind.

Label Creator has three types of themes.

► **Generic theme**—Can be used for either an audio or data CD or DVD.

► **Audio theme**—Designed specifically for an audio CD.

► **Data theme**—Similar to an Audio theme; designed for the rest of the media— data CDs or regular DVD-ROMs.

DVD CASE COVER THEMES

The only theme type that is available when working with the DVD Case Cover layout is a generic theme. Because of this, certain themes may look different when switching from the DVD Case Cover layout to other layouts.

Each theme has textboxes that are pre-configured to streamline the process of creating labels and covers. Tables 12.1 and 12.2 list the textboxes for both audio and data themes. Textboxes and their uses will be discussed later in this chapter.

CHAPTER 12

Table 12.1 Data Theme Textboxes

Textbox Name	Description
Title	Title of the data CD
Contents	The files and folders that are contained on the media
VolumeID	With Label Creator, this textbox is the date and time the media was created
Date	The date the media was created

Table 12.2 Audio Theme Textboxes

Textbox Name	Description
Title	Audio-CD title
Artist	Artist name
Tracks	Audio track information

GENERIC THEME TEXTBOXES
The Title textbox (available in the data theme type) is the only one that is available in a generic theme.

There are two ways to assign a theme to a project. The first way is through the Theme Library located at the bottom of the main Label Creator interface, shown in Figure 12.4. On either side of the Theme Library are arrows that allow you to scroll through the many available themes. If you are interested in a theme, hold your mouse over it until a bubble appears telling you the name and type of the theme, as shown in Figure 12.15. When you have found a theme, either double-click on it or click and drag the theme into the Project Layout area. A window will appear that says, "Updating Theme…". Once the Update window has disappeared, the theme you chose will be assigned to all of the layouts in your project.

Figure 12.15
Theme information.

The other way to assign a theme to a project is through the Change Theme window, shown in Figure 12.16. To bring up the Change Theme window, click on the Theme button located in the Project Buttons area of the main Label Creator interface.

The left side of the Change Theme window shows the available themes. You can filter the results by deselecting either the Show Audio Themes or Show Data Themes check box. If at any time you want to preview the theme, click the theme once and it will preview on the right side of the window. When you have found the theme that you want to use, click the OK button, and the layout will update with the new theme assigned to it.

Figure 12.16
Change Theme window.

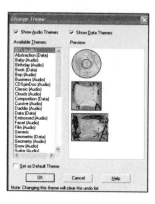

THE FORMAT MENU
Another way to open the Change Theme window is to click the Format menu and select Change Theme from the menu that appears.

PREVIEWING VIA THE CHANGE THEME WINDOW
An advantage to using the Change Theme window is that Label Creator previews the Front, Back, and Disc layouts simultaneously, whereas the Theme Library only previews the Disc layout.

Adding Layout Content

There are two ways to add content to a project. Label Creator can read information from either an audio or data disc and automatically add the information to the appropriate textboxes in the layouts. If the disc hasn't been created yet or Label Creator cannot read the disc, you can add content manually.

Adding Content Automatically

One of the coolest features of Label Creator is its ability to automatically add information from your disc to your project. To add the information from a disc, click on the Name button in the project buttons area. The selected theme type will determine whether Label Creator looks for an audio CD or other media. If there is no disc inserted, the disc cannot be read, or if the wrong type of media is inserted, an error message will be displayed, as shown in Figure 12.17.

Figure 12.17
Problems with disc.

DATA ERROR MESSAGE
Figure 12.17 shows the error message when an audio theme is assigned. A similar error message will appear when a data theme is assigned.

Another built-in feature is Label Creator's ability to download track and artist information from the Internet. Label Creator can double-check the audio CD information against an online database to make sure that it is correct. Additionally, Label Creator will attempt to find any missing information from the Internet as well. By default, Label Creator is configured to always attempt to download audio CD information from the Internet without asking for permission, but this option can be changed in the Internet area of the Preferences window as follows:

1. From the main Label Creator interface, click on the Edit menu (shown in Figure 12.18) and select Preferences from the menu that appears.

Figure 12.18
Edit menu.

2. Click the Internet tab from the available choices, as shown in Figure 12.19.

Figure 12.19
Internet tab of the
Preferences menu.

3. If you want Label Creator to warn you before it downloads anything from the Internet, check the Prompt Me Before Attempting Download check box.

4. Click the OK button.

Adding Content Manually

If the information cannot be retrieved automatically from the disc, you will have to type in some disc information by hand. Fortunately, Label Creator will update all layouts at once when the information is entered into a textbox. To enter information into a textbox, double-click on the textbox in the Layout Area and enter the appropriate information.

ADDING NEW LINES IN TEXTBOXES
In order to have more than one line in a textbox, you must hold down the Control key while pressing the Enter key. Otherwise, pressing the Enter key by itself will close the Edit Textbox window.

If you tried to enter track information into a textbox before reading this, you probably could not find a Tracks textbox. You must add track information by means of the Add New Track window, shown in Figure 12.20. To add a new track, click the Add menu and select Track from the menu that appears. When a new track is added through this window, the layouts will update and display this information. You can add as many tracks as needed through the Add New Track window.

Figure 12.20
Add New Track
window.

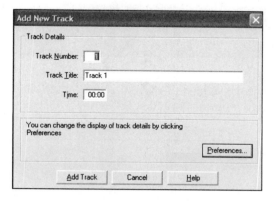

Customizing the Layout

The layout can be customized after the theme is assigned. This is done through the Objects, Alignment, and Properties toolbars described earlier in this chapter. Since a DVD Case Cover is required to use a generic theme, you will want to customize this layout.

Figure 12.14 showed the DVD Case Cover layout. The two objects labeled My First Video and My First Slideshow were customized after the theme was assigned. These objects were added using the Objects toolbar. Let's see how the DVD case cover was customized—adding a textbox then customizing the text within it.

1. Make sure the Objects and Alignment toolbars are visible.

2. Click the Add Text button in the Objects toolbar.

3. In the Layout area, position the mouse over the desired location of the textbox and click the mouse button. A textbox will appear with a value of New Text.

4. Double-click anywhere within the new textbox. The inside of the square will turn white and the text in the textbox will turn blue.

5. Type **My First Slideshow** in the textbox for this example.

6. Press the Enter key.

7. If the entire text is not visible, click the Size to Text button in the Alignment toolbar (refer to Figure 12.7). The Size to Text button will resize the textbox so that the entire text can be seen.

In addition to adding textboxes, Label Creator can add other things as well.

▶ From the Objects toolbar, Label Creator can add squares and circles to a layout, which then can have other objects added on top of them (see Figure 12.21).

Figure 12.21
Shapes example.

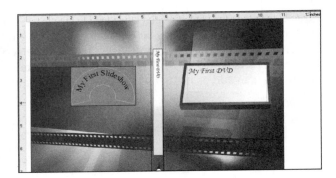

▶ Pictures can also be added to a layout. Figure 12.22 shows a picture of a mountain range with the "My First Slideshow" textbox added on top of it.

Figure 12.22
Picture example.

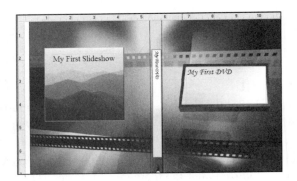

What I have shown here is just a couple of examples of what is possible when customizing the layout. I would recommend experimenting with the Objects, Alignment, and Properties toolbars to see what they have to offer.

Printing the Project

Once the project is complete, you are ready to print it out. There are a few things that need to be done when printing your project.

▶ Select the appropriate paper type for each layout.

▶ Set each layout's printing preferences.

▶ Print the layout.

The type of paper or label that is used is important when preparing to print your project. Generic paper is less durable than higher-quality paper that can be purchased at any office supply store. Also, disc labels must be purchased if you want the label to stick to the media. Once you choose the paper and label type, Label Creator needs to know about it. This is done through the Page Setup window shown in Figure 12.23. To access the Page Setup window, click the File menu and select Page Setup from the menu that appears. Within the Page Setup window, each layout has its own menu that needs to be configured separately.

Figure 12.23
Page Setup window.

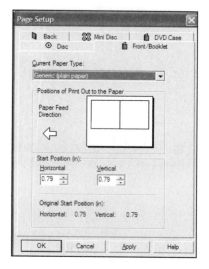

PAPER TYPE
Even though there are a lot of paper types to choose from in Label Creator, you should be able to find the type of paper or label that you intend to use. Most paper types in the Page Setup list are organized by brand.

The next thing to do before printing the project is to set the layout's printing preferences. These preferences consist of two items that are set to be visible or invisible when the project is printed. Similar to the paper type, these preferences are also set per layout in the application's Preferences window. In the main Label Creator interface, click on the Edit menu and select Preferences from the menu that appears. This will bring up the Preferences window, as shown in Figure 12.24.

▶ When the outline box is selected, your layout will have a solid outline around it on the printout.

▶ To assist you in assembling your project after it has been printed, you can show cutting and folding lines on each layout, which will appear as dotted lines on the printout.

Figure 12.24
Preferences window.

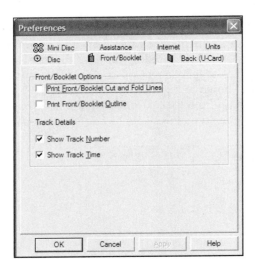

Now that the preferences have been set, you are ready to print your project. To open the Print window, click on the File menu and select the print option (see Figure 12.25).

PRINT PREVIEW
To see what the printout will look like without physically printing it out, you can use the Print Preview option. This will show you exactly what the project will look like when it is printed. Print Preview is accessed through the File menu in the main Label Creator interface.

Figure 12.25
Print window.

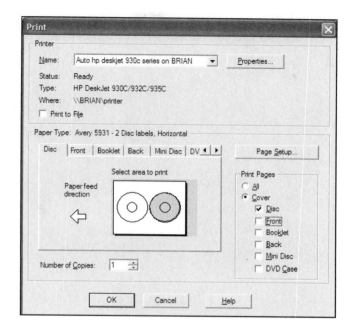

PAGE SETUP

Roxio recommends printing each layout on plain paper first to make sure that everything looks good and to avoid wasting potentially expensive paper. Because of this, you may notice that the paper type resets to plain paper the first time the project is printed. You can either print it on plain paper or use the Page Setup button that is located in the Print window to change it.

To print out a cover or label, follow these steps:

1. If you have more than one printer hooked up to your computer, select the one that you want to print to from the Name list.

2. In the Print Pages section, check the layouts that you want to print.

3. Some label makers put more than one label on a sheet. If this is the case, you can print the same layout on all labels included on the sheet or print to one label leaving the other one blank for later use. The labels that will be printed on will show up in blue in the Print window. Click on the label to turn it blue. If you change your mind, just click on it again.

4. If you want more than one copy, specify it using the up and down arrows next to Number of Copies box.

5. Click the OK button.

This concludes the design part of this book. The final part of this book will introduce two case studies—Bart and Lili. As you will see, each of these case studies will have very different uses for a DVD.

Part Four
Putting it All Together

Chapter 13
Preparing Your Project

We've looked at many aspects regarding DVDs, and more specifically DVD authoring. While the first two parts of this book served as a high-level overview of DVDs (with Part One concentrating on the hardware side and Part Two comparing and contrasting competing DVD authoring applications), Part Three used DVD Builder to demonstrate some of the different features that were available to a DVD author. Combining the three parts together, three DVD authoring components can be derived.

▶ **Preparing your project**—This component of DVD authoring—covered in Chapters 1 through 9—includes preparing your computer and then capturing video as needed.

▶ **Laying out the DVD**—The design component of DVD authoring—covered in Chapters 9 through 11—that includes importing and editing your videos, creating an efficient menu structure, and adding pictures either singly or in the form of a slideshow.

▶ **Completing the project**—The last design component includes either burning your DVD project or saving it to a disc image and creating the covers and labels that are inserted into a jewel case.

COMPONENT OVERLAP

You may notice some chapter overlap—specifically with Chapter 9 because it discussed video capturing, importing, and editing—when looking at the first two DVD authoring components. Since video editing is considered part of the design process—that is after the video has been inserted into the project—it will be discussed in the second component, whereas video capturing will be discussed in the first component.

This brings us to Part Four of the book, which ties the first three parts together. In this chapter, two real-world examples will explore each of the DVD authoring components. The two case studies are extremely different in regard to the requirements of the user. In order to follow the case studies better, Part Four is split into (you guessed it) three chapters that will address each of these components.

Case Study Introduction

In the first case study, you will be introduced to Bart, whose technology and usage requirements are low. Our second case study subject, Lili, needs a professional DVD to hand out to potential clients. The two case studies will be explained simultaneously within each of the DVD authoring components. The goal of this side-by-side case study approach is to let you (the reader) quickly compare the two without having to constantly flip back and forth between different sections of the book. Let's meet the two case studies.

Case Study One: Bart

Bart is sixty-five years old and has lived his entire life in the small rural town of Rock Ridge. This is your typical small town where everyone knows everyone, and life is pretty simple. Bart's wife passed away some years ago, so he has become pretty independent. His kids are grown and out of the house.

Bart worked for the Rock Ridge Police Department for many years until he retired. Upon his retirement, Bart decided to hang up his independent lifestyle and move into a place—cleverly named the Rock Ridge Retirement Village—where he would spend his remaining years having someone else take care of him. The staff at the retirement village is always helpful and attentive to his needs. In addition to the staff, Bart really enjoys the company of his fellow residents with whom he engages in several weekly social activities. He has even taken an active role in many of the village-sponsored festivities. His latest coordinated effort was a trip to Las Vegas for a night on the town.

With a family and a demanding career, he did not have a lot of free time for hobbies, but now that he is retired, he kicks around a few hobbies to occupy this newfound free time. He tried to learn how to play the guitar, but the arthritis in his hands was too bad, and playing shuffleboard did not provide enough stimulation. Unfortunately, he could not find a hobby that sparked his interest—that is until he got a camcorder for Christmas from one of his children. Bart decided to start recording videos and taking pictures of the different functions that took place at the retirement village. Hedley, Bart's father, had been an avid photographer as well as a movie buff, so Bart has been exposed to multimedia his entire life. It was out of these good childhood experiences that his love for multimedia grew.

With his new camcorder, Bart was asked to videotape as much of the Las Vegas excursion as possible. In order to get the full effect, the retirement village chipped in and bought him a camera to take still pictures—in addition to the videos. As you can imagine, Bart was really excited about his new project and wanted to take full advantage of it. He bought several videotapes and rolls of film to take with him on their charter bus.

To begin the documentary, Bart interviewed some of the residents as they were loading the bus. He also conducted on-the-spot interviews with some other residents during the four-hour bus ride to Las Vegas. As the day progressed, he took several hours of video and shot many rolls of film.

The big premiere night arrived, and the presentation was a hit. Everyone in the retirement village loved it so much they wanted a copy of their own. He agreed to make copies for everyone, but, given the target audience, Bart had a few requirements that he had to keep in mind when thinking of its distribution.

- ▶ The media must be easy to operate, with little user intervention.
- ▶ Since everyone in the retirement village does not own a computer, the distribution media must not require a computer.
- ▶ Bart has a lot of video coverage on his trip to Las Vegas, so the distribution media must be able to handle a couple of hours of video.

Taking all things into consideration, Bart decided to use a DVD for means of distributing his videos and pictures. He thought about using a VHS tape, but it would take a considerable amount of editing time—not to mention editing experience that he did not have—to put together a slideshow on a VHS tape. Editing time for the slideshows does not even take into account the time that it takes to edit the videos. A DVD would allow him to layout all of his multimedia and organize it before burning it to disc.

Case Study Two: Lili

Lili has been on Broadway most of her life. She got her start in a production of Annie when she was just eight years old and has since starred in many Broadway productions. Lili, now 35 years old, is getting tired of the entertainment industry. While she loves being involved in the theater, Lili has grown weary of the rat-race involved with getting a part, not to mention the long hours involved when a production is in full swing.

Lili has been married for several years and just recently had her first child. Once her child was born, she realized that she needed to settle down into a more structured work environment and start planning her future as a mother. Thinking for a while that it was time to get out of the fast-paced Broadway lifestyle, she decided to try her hand at starting her own business. Currently, Lili is performing in one Broadway production but has started informing people that this will be her last.

To give back to the entertainment industry that has been so good to her from an early age, she decided to start a children's talent agency. Lili wants to attempt to help children make it in "the business" by providing good ethical practices, insight, and advice from decisions she has made—right or wrong—in the past. The business, named Twue to You, will start out small, with Lili as the only employee, and will be based out of her studio attached to her house located in New York.

Because she is starting a business that will rely heavily on videos and pictures to get her young talent signed, Lili will depend heavily on technology to aid her in presenting her clients' material the most effective way possible. While Lili does not have a lot of multimedia or computer experience, she is eager to learn. She purchased a computer a few months ago in order to manage her finances and electronically trade on the stock market.

Lili needs to figure out a way to get clients for her new business. She wants to hand something out to potential clients so they can take it and look at it when it is convenient for them. She thought about a brochure, but didn't think that it would capture the type of personal atmosphere she wanted to achieve with Twue to You. She has a few requirements that should be met when she distributes this advertisement to people.

▶ The advertisement must be personal.

▶ It must be easy to use by anyone, including the children that she would like to represent.

▶ The advertisement must be robust enough to change over time. For example, if in a year she wants to add a portfolio of one of her clients, the means of advertisement must be able to accommodate.

After looking into many different ways to distribute advertisements within her requirements, she settled on a DVD. By adding an Introduction Video to the DVD, Lili can give her clients the personal feel that she is after. The Introduction Video will pan around the office until it reaches her. Then the camera will stop, and Lili will say "Twue to You welcomes you and your family." In addition to being personal, a DVD is easy enough for anyone to use—even children. Lili will design her DVD so that when it is inserted into a DVD player, the personal Introduction Video will appear, followed by the Main Menu. The final requirement is met because of the DVD media's storage capacity of 4.7 gigabytes. In the beginning, this DVD will have an abundant amount of free space, but as the company grows, Lili will be able to put many client portfolios on there. If this advertisement works out for her, she plans on using this as a template for designing portfolios for her clients so that they can take these into auditions with them.

Checking Your Connections

The first step involved when preparing for your project is to make sure that you have all of the required hardware and software. Once you confirm that, you should make sure it works! First, make a list of everything you have, and then compare this with what you need. Sounds easy, huh? For the most part it is.

The second step—hooking everything up and making sure that it works—can be more involved. An unfortunate fact of life is that computers are temperamental. The best piece of advice that I can give you—to minimize the amount of problems that you may have—is to be selective with your hardware and software. Pay the extra bucks for good hardware, and you will not regret it.

Bart: Checking the Connections

A few months prior to the Las Vegas trip, Bart purchased a new computer. Being his first computer, he decided to go all out with a large hard drive, flat panel monitor, and a DVD burner. Other than his computer, Bart's technology is pretty "low-tech," so to speak. In order to get an accurate assessment of the hardware that is required, let's take an inventory of what Bart has.

▶ An analog (non-DV) camcorder that he used to record their trip.

▶ An analog camera (purchased by the Village) to take still pictures.

▶ A brand-new computer that far surpasses the recommended hardware requirements required to burn a DVD.

Since Bart already has a new computer and DVD burner, half of his requirements have already been met. There are still a few things that he will need to buy, though.

▶ Bart's camcorder is not digital, so he must buy a video capture card in order to transfer his video tapes to a digital video on his computer.

CHOOSING A CAPTURE CARD

Most analog camcorders use RCA-style cables, so when purchasing a capture card, make sure it has appropriate inputs on it.

▶ A scanner is required to convert the developed film into digital pictures.

CHOOSING A SCANNER

When choosing a scanner, you should confirm that it is compatible with the operating system installed on your computer. Make sure that your computer supports the interface that you purchase; also, verify there is a free port on your computer for this interface. Before you go to the store to purchase the scanner, make sure you know what operating system you have and what interfaces are available on your computer. Once in the store, the box should say which operating systems the scanner is compatible with. If it doesn't, make sure to ask a salesperson.

▶ Even though Bart's computer came with a DVD burner installed, it did not ship with DVD burning software. He must purchase an authoring application before burning any DVDs. For this case study, we will use Roxio Easy CD and DVD Creator 6 (specifically DVD Builder).

▶ As you learned from earlier chapters, the computing industry has not yet settled on a recordable format standard. This means—at least for the time being—you should consult the manufacturer of your DVD burner to find out which recordable format is compatible. Bart's DVD burner is manufactured by Hewlett-Packard, so he will be using DVD+R and DVD+RW media.

CHAPTER 13

BUYING MEDIA

Depending on how many residents want a copy of Bart's DVD, the price for the media could get expensive. He may need to pass around a "media collection plate" or make each resident buy his or her own blank disc.

▶ To create inserts for each DVD to be distributed, Bart will need to purchase jewel case covers and disc labels.

So far we've looked at the usage requirements that Bart had to consider when choosing the type of media that the Las Vegas night will be distributed on. Once Bart made his distribution media decision, he inventoried what he had and figured out what he needed. Now that Bart has everything required to burn a DVD, he is ready to get started.

There is some groundwork that Bart needs to do before he starts capturing video.

1. Open the case on the computer and install the video capture card in an open PCI slot. Most PCI cards are packaged with excellent installation instructions, so definitely check them out. Once the card is installed and working, hook up the camcorder to the capture card using the RCA cables that were supplied with the camcorder.

CHECK FOR NEW DRIVERS

You should always check the manufacturer's website for any updated drivers that may have been released after the card was shipped.

2. Insert the installation CD-ROM for Easy CD and DVD Creator 6 and run the setup program from the CD.

PATCHING EASY CD AND DVD CREATOR

Don't forget to connect to the Internet and download the latest patches for Easy CD and DVD Creator before using it. The early release versions of Easy CD and DVD Creator can be unstable depending on the software environment that it is being installed into.

3. Install the scanner. Most new scanners manufactured today are installed via the USB port and are automatically detected when the scanner is connected. When prompted, insert the CD that was shipped with your scanner and let Windows install the drivers from it.

POWER OFF COMPUTER

Some scanners require that the computer is off when the scanner is physically installed. As a general rule, I always install a scanner with the computer powered off, whether it is required or not.

Proceeding with the case study, the next step for Bart is to capture all videos and import his pictures from his TWAIN device, which in this case is the scanner. Before we move on to Bart's next step, let's check on Lili to see what her requirements are and make sure she has everything ready to go.

Lili: Checking the Connections

Recall from the introduction that Lili bought a new computer to manage her finances and trade electronically on the stock market. Unfortunately, when she bought the computer, a DVD burner upgrade was too expensive. Why would she need a DVD burner to help her manage her finances anyway? As we did with Bart, let's take an inventory of what Lili currently has so we can figure out what she needs.

▶ A brand-new computer that exceeds the hardware requirements (with the exception of a DVD burner).

▶ Some great ideas and strong motivation to start her business off on the right foot.

As you can tell from this list, Lili has quite a bit left to buy. Preparing for this, Lili got a small business loan that would cover the technology costs along with any other expenses that may/will come up. Let's look at what she needs:

▶ First and foremost, Lili needs a DVD burner to burn DVDs! Nowadays, these can be purchased online or at any computer retail store. Lili purchased an internal DVD player online, and it was shipped the same day.

▶ In order to take pictures and videos, she will need some multimedia recording devices, specifically a camcorder and camera. Since Lili got a small business loan, she decided to go digital on both of these devices. If she would have gone with an analog camcorder, the price of this type of camcorder plus the video capture card would have been equal to the price of one digital camcorder.

▶ Most after-market DVD burners do not ship with software. In the off-chance that it does, the software is usually outdated and lacks the newest bells and whistles. For this reason, Lili decided to purchase Roxio Easy CD and DVD Creator 6 in order to lay out her projects and burn them to DVD.

▶ Lili will need to buy blank DVD media for her new Hewlett-Packard DVD burner. As you learned from Bart and earlier in this book, the type of media depends on the type of DVD burner that is purchased. In Lili's case, she will be purchasing DVD+R and DVD+RW media.

CHAPTER 13

► When Lili distributes this advertisement DVD, she wants to make her company logo and contact information available. She can put it on the DVD, but the potential client will have to insert the DVD into a DVD player and write down the desired information. To Lili, that seems like a lot of unnecessary work. To make the clients' lives easier, she bought disc labels and jewel case inserts that she will put this information on as well.

Lili assessed what she needed and purchased it. Let's take a look at how each item will be installed.

1. To install an internal DVD burner (as we discussed in Chapter 3), Lili should check for an available drive bay, install the DVD burner into an open drive bay, and make the necessary connections—power cable, IDE cable, and optional CD-Audio cable. This listing sums up Chapter 3 in a few sentences. If you are not yet comfortable with installing a DVD burner—if this is your first install, you probably are not—you should revisit Chapter 3.

2. The next thing on the list to install is a digital camcorder. Installing a FireWire-based camcorder—the preferred digital camcorder interface—is just a matter of plugging the camera into the FireWire port and powering on the camera.

FIREWIRE OPERATING SYSTEM COMPATIBILITY

Make sure the operating system installed on your computer supports the IEEE 1394 (FireWire) standard. At the time of this writing, all Microsoft operating systems—Windows 98 and later—support FireWire. Also, FireWire is widely supported on Macintosh computers—they were the ones that designed it. Regardless of what technology you choose—FireWire or analog capture— you should always consult the computer manufacturer's website to confirm that the technology works with your computer.

3. Digital cameras are installed by plugging them into the computer. Software is provided with the camera that will assist you in moving the pictures from the camera to the computer. Although DVD Builder will allow you to acquire images directly from your digital camera, it has been my experience that it is best to use the software provided with the camera to copy the pictures and then import them with DVD Builder later.

DIGITAL CAMERA RESOLUTION

When shopping for a digital camera, you will get what you pay for. Always look for a high-resolution and a high-megapixel setting. You will be happy that you did.

4. Now, insert the installation CD-ROM for Easy CD and DVD Creator 6 and run the setup program from the CD. Make sure to revisit the Caution in Bart's section on patching Easy CD and DVD Creator.

5. You should consult the manufacturer of your DVD burner to find out which recordable format is compatible. Lili's DVD burner is manufactured by Hewlett-Packard, so she will be using DVD+R and DVD+RW media.

BUYING MEDIA IN BULK

Unlike Bart's situation, Lili will need to buy all of the media. With that said, DVD media is much cheaper when it is bought in bulk from either the Internet or retail consumer electronics stores.

Assembling the Data

Assembling the data is the last step involved in "Preparing for Your Project." It is important to get all of your data in one central place so that it is easy to organize. For our purposes, the central place we are referring to is DVD Builder. So, what is involved with this data assembly step?

▶ Capture any video—whether it is stored on an analog or digital camcorder—to a file stored on your computer. We will capture our videos via DVD Builder and store them in a project.

▶ If pictures must be scanned, you should scan each picture in DVD Builder. When the pictures are imported this way, they will be automatically imported into a DVD Builder project. Remember if the pictures were taken with a digital camera, they should be transferred to the computer and then imported into DVD Builder.

▶ If your multimedia—videos, pictures, or sound—is already stored on your computer, then you should directly import into your DVD Builder project.

In the case of Bart's DVD, his recording devices are strictly analog so he will not need to worry about the third step in the assembly process. If another resident who went with them had a digital camera, or if Bart had his own, he would have to import those files. With Lili, her recording devices are digital so she will use the third step above to retrieve her pictures. Let's start by looking at how Bart assembles his data.

Bart: Assembling the Data

Because of Bart's relatively "low-tech" recording devices, such as his camcorder and camera, he has his work cut out for him now that it is time to move the multimedia from an analog medium to a digital one. As you learned earlier, Bart recorded a lot of video from the Las Vegas trip. He will not want to use all of the video for the following reasons.

▶ Since everyone who wants a copy attended the trip, he doesn't want to show everything that transpired, but rather highlight the most memorable moments.

▶ Even though the storage capacity of a DVD is large at 4.7 gigabytes, it will only allow for two hours of high-quality video. Knowing that Bart took almost four hours of video, he will have to cut some out.

▶ Bart has several pictures that he wants to put into a slideshow that will take up quite a bit of space. He needs to plan for this space and make sure that his DVD can accommodate it.

Capturing Bart's Videos

In order for Bart to capture his video, he must first decide how the video will be presented on the DVD. He does not need to be extremely detailed with the layout yet, but a general idea will make it easier for him to figure out how the videos will relate to the project and each other. For example, he wants one long video of the group walking down the strip. But he also wants many short videos that will make up a blooper stage. He has decided split his trip into four different stages.

1. The first stage is used to show what the residents were doing before they got on the bus. This stage includes any last-minute packing, the exciting chatter that took place in the dining hall during breakfast, and some impromptu interviews of the residents as they loaded on the bus.

2. The second stage consists of the bus ride to Las Vegas.

3. The last stage shows the residents from the time they unloaded from the bus until they got back on the bus for their departure home. The video in this stage includes filming the group as they walked down the strip, videos of the many attractions that are outside of the different casinos, and more resident interviews throughout the night.

4. A bonus stage will show a series of bloopers. This stage consists of many short videos that captured the funny things that happened during the trip.

Now that Bart has organized a layout in his mind, he is ready to start capturing the different videos. It helps some people to sketch out on paper how the DVD should be organized. Recall from Chapter 9 that DVD Builder captures video through the Screening Room.

1. Turn on the camcorder and set it to VCR or Play mode.

2. Open DVD Builder via the Windows Start Menu, as shown in Figure 13.1.

Figure 13.1
Open DVD Builder.

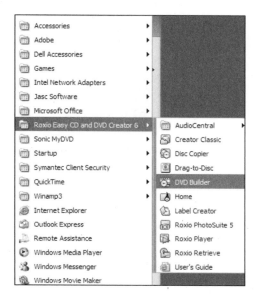

3.   Click the Capture Video button, shown in Figure 13.2.

Figure 13.2
Capture Video button.

CONNECTIVITY PROBLEMS

If there is a communication problem between your computer and the capture
device, DVD Builder will return an error message (see Figure 13.3).

Figure 13.3
No Capture Device
Found error message.

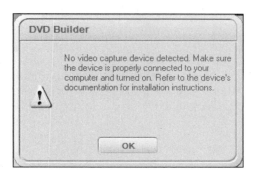

4. Use the camcorder's Cue buttons to retrieve the starting position of the portion of the video to be captured.

USING AN ANALOG CAMCORDER

Since Bart is using an analog camcorder, he must use the buttons on the camcorder to cue the starting position.

5. Click on the Start Capture button, shown in Figure 13.4.

Figure 13.4
Start Capture button.

6. When the video has reached the point where you want the video file to end, click the Stop Capture button (see Figure 13.5).

Figure 13.5
Stop Capture button.

START AND END VIDEO POSITIONS

It is not critical to start and end the video exactly as it should be in the finished project. With that said, it is a good idea to start and end with a few seconds on each side, especially in the case of an analog camcorder, because it takes a few moments for the video to start. You can always trim the video at a later time, but you cannot add video to the file without recapturing it within DVD Builder.

Bart should repeat this process for each separate video file that he wants in his project. Once Bart has captured and imported all of his videos into his DVD Builder project, he will put them into different menus and movies. We will look at the organization of his captured videos in the next chapter.

Scanning Bart's Pictures

As stated earlier, Bart has several photos that he would like to add to his project as a slideshow. Using the same layout—the morning of the trip, the bus ride to Las Vegas, the time in Las Vegas, and a bloopers section—that he used for capturing videos, Bart is going to create a slideshow that represents each stage of the trip.

Because Bart does not have a digital camera, he must scan each picture and then import it into his DVD Builder project. Fortunately for Bart, DVD Builder combines these steps into one; you can use DVD Builder to acquire an image (not taken by a digital camera) from a scanner which will add it to the project. As you can recall from Chapter 9, pictures are imported from the Screening Room.

1. If it is not already open, start DVD Builder from the Windows Start Menu

2. Click on the Other Sources button, shown in Figure 13.6. As with the video capture devices, if DVD Builder does not find a TWAIN device, it will display the error message shown in Figure 13.7.

Figure 13.6
Other Sources button.

Figure 13.7
No TWAIN device found error message.

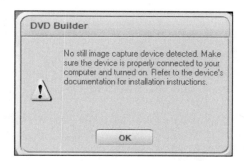

3. The Other Sources button brings up the window shown in Figure 13.8. From this window, you can either choose a source or start the scan.

Figure 13.8
Select source or scan.

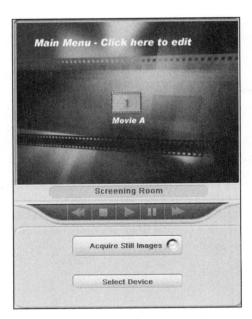

4. If you have more than one TWAIN device, click the Select Device button and choose the appropriate source.

5. Once the source has been selected, click the Acquire Still Images button.

6. The Acquire Still Images button brings up the appropriate TWAIN interface for your device, as shown in 13.9.

Figure 13.9
HP TWAIN interface.

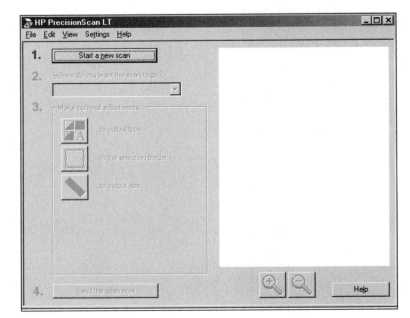

7.   As you did in Chapter 9, scan the document using the TWAIN interface. Once the document is scanned, DVD Builder will automatically add it to the selected DVD Builder movie.

Bart will scan each picture using DVD Builder. Once the scanning is complete, he can organize the pictures into slideshows or make them icons for menu buttons—more on that in the next chapter. Right now, let's check back in with Lili to see how she is going to assemble her data.

Lili: Assembling the Data

Unlike Bart, Lili has all digital multimedia devices. This will make it easier for her to assemble her data. Although she will still have to capture videos from her FireWire camcorder, it will be much easier since the use of a capture card is not required; she can use the playback controls in DVD Builder to cue up the desired tape position. Not only does a totally digitized setup make capturing videos easier, it also takes out a huge step—scanning each picture—when assembling the data. A digital camera and its associated retrieval software will transfer the photo from the camera to the computer into a file that is supported by DVD Builder. Lili will still need to import each file, but the time involved in doing this is much less.

Capturing Lili's Videos

In Twue to You's initial stage of business, Lili's DVD will be relatively small compared to other DVD possibilities. Remember from earlier though, one of Lili's requirements is that her DVD must be robust enough so that she can add large videos or slideshows as she gets more clients.

Lili plans on the first version of her marketing video to use an Introduction Video—the one that was discussed earlier—and a few videos of her latest (not to mention last) Broadway performance. She had a friend who works as a cameraman at a local television station film her Introduction Video. Let's capture this video for her.

1.   Plug in the camcorder to an available FireWire port and turn it on. Make sure it is set to camera or Play mode.

2.   Open DVD Builder from the Windows Start Menu.

POWER ON CAMCORDER FIRST

Make sure the camcorder is powered on and set to camera or Play mode before DVD Builder is started. If not, you could receive an error message that a capture device could not be located.

3.   Click on the Capture Video button from the Import Video toolbar, as shown in Figure 13.10.

Figure 13.10
Capture Video button.

4. Using the playback controls in the Screening Room, find the position that should be used as the starting point of the video clip. The playback controls are shown in Figure 13.11.

SCREENING ROOM PLAYBACK CONTROLS
When Bart imported from an analog source, he had to use the cue buttons on the device itself, not the playback controls in the Screening Room. If a FireWire-based camcorder is not used, the playback controls in the Screening Room will not be available.

Figure 13.11
Playback controls.

5. Click the Start Capture button, shown in Figure 13.12.

Figure 13.12
Start Capture button.

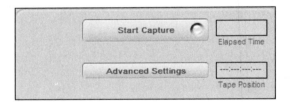

6. When the captured video is at the desired ending point, click the Stop Capture button, as shown in Figure 13.13.

Figure 13.13
Stop Capture button.

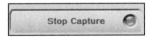

7. Repeat steps 3 through 7 for each video that needs to be captured.

Now that Lili has captured her videos that will be included in the first version of her marketing DVD—the Introduction Video and a couple of short video clips from her latest Broadway role—she needs to import the pictures that were taken with her digital camera.

Importing Lili's Multimedia Files

Since purchasing her new digital camera, Lili has taken many pictures of her office, her final role in a Broadway play, and of course her new baby. Lili would like to incorporate all of these pictures into her marketing DVD. As mentioned earlier, it is best to use the software that comes with your digital camera to transfer the pictures to your computer. Don't forget that with a regular, non-digital camera, you should use DVD Builder to scan and import your pictures in one step. Once all of the pictures have been transferred to the computer, Lili is ready to start importing them into her DVD Builder layout.

1. Make sure the pictures have been transferred from the digital camera to the computer.

DIGITAL CAMERA SOFTWARE PICTURE PLACEMENT
When transferring your pictures from a digital camera to your computer, make sure to put everything in the same folder on your computer. In addition to this, you should also use a naming convention that can be easily identified. This will make it very easy when it is time to import the files into DVD Builder.

2. Click on the Import Multimedia Files button located in the Video Import toolbar. This icon is shown in Figure 13.14.

Figure 13.14
Import Multimedia Files button.

3. When the Import Multimedia Files button is clicked, the Import Files window appears, as shown in Figure 13.15. To filter by file type, click on the Still Images filter icon (shown in Figure 13.16).

Figure 13.15
Import Files window.

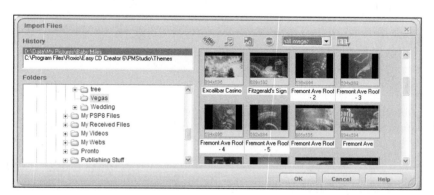

Figure 13.16
Still Images filter icon.

4. Within the Import Files window, navigate to the folder that contains the pictures that should be added to the project.

5. Once you are there, click and drag the pictures that should be added to the desired DVD Builder movie. The end result is shown in Figure 13.17. Looks a lot like a slideshow, doesn't it? In fact, importing files into the same DVD Builder movie creates a slideshow by default.

CTRL+CLICK PICTURES

If you have a lot of pictures to import into a DVD Builder movie, dragging each one singly can be a daunting task. By pressing and holding the Ctrl key on the keyboard, you can select as many files as you want. Then click and drag the group into a DVD Builder movie.

Figure 13.17
DVD Builder with
pictures.

Summary

This chapter had two primary goals: to introduce our case studies and to help each of our case studies prepare for their DVD projects. Preparing for our project is the first component required when authoring a DVD. This component involves taking an inventory of what you currently have and checking it against a list of items you need; you should then install what you do not have. After everything is installed and working, you need to capture and import all multimedia that will be included in your project.

As we progress through Part Four of this book, we will further look at both Bart's and Lili's projects. We will examine the remaining DVD authoring components and see how Bart and Lili apply their own situations to the components.

Chapter 14
Laying out Your DVD

In this second DVD authoring step, your DVD project transforms from a bunch of miscellaneous videos and pictures into a powerful, organized multimedia tool that can be used for business, pleasure, or both. The first step laid the groundwork, and this second step is where all of the design work will be done. Because all the content is organized within this step, it is essential that it be well thought out to ensure that the DVD viewer's needs are met. Three steps are included in this chapter:

▶ **Menu structure**—In this step, a menu structure is created and multimedia is added to the menu, as we did in Chapter 10. To avoid confusion, a well-structured menu will help the viewer find items of interest in a reliable and efficient manner. In my opinion, this is the single most important step of the design process.

▶ **Video editing**—In this step, the videos that were captured in the previous chapter have the final touches put on them.

▶ **Creating slideshows**—As you should recall from Chapter 11, slideshows are groups of slides (still pictures) that are organized within a DVD Builder movie. Once the slides are organized, they are assigned a specific time duration between slides and optional background music.

As we go through this chapter, we will look at some of the design considerations—some that have been addressed in earlier chapters and some that haven't—that were encountered by Bart and Lili. We will also look at the way they were handled, to be of assistance to you when it is time to lay out your own DVD.

Creating a Menu Structure

Being the primary means of DVD navigation, it is important that the DVD's menu structure is planned out in the most effective way possible. Before we look at how Bart and Lili organized their menu structures, there are a few general considerations.

▶ Try to keep the menu structure as flat as possible. A flat menu structure is one where the number of submenus is kept to a minimum. Think of a menu structure in terms of an apple tree, where the trunk is the Main Menu and each limb on the tree—directly connected to the trunk—is a menu button on the Main Menu. These limbs can either have other limbs (submenus) or apples (videos and slideshows). Now imagine trying to climb a tree with many limbs to get an apple; the more limbs on the tree, the harder it is to get the apple. This analogy holds true for a DVD menu structure as well. A DVD containing many submenus will make it more difficult for the viewer to get to the desired video.

▶ Make sure to use font sizes that are easy to read from a reasonable distance away. The viewers will not want to walk up to the TV to read the menu button labels each time they want to select a menu.

▶ In addition to font sizes, font color is another thing to consider. Make sure the font color coordinates with the background image. Blue text on a blue background would make it extremely hard to read, as shown in Figure 14.1.

Figure 14.1
Blue text on a blue background is difficult to read.

▶ The button image should represent what is contained within it. For example, a button label of Our Honeymoon with a button image of the Eiffel Tower would not make sense if your honeymoon was in Hawaii.

Bart: Menu Structure

The preceding chapter introduced Bart, our retired police officer. You learned that he was asked to document a trip to Las Vegas with his retirement village. Bart had some of the hardware and software requirements—a new computer, a DVD burner, and multimedia devices—but had to purchase some additional items as well. Given the amount of video he had from a full day in Las Vegas, Bart decided to break his project up into four stages. These four stages will be essential when we create the menu structure, so let's review them now.

▶ The first stage covers the time until everyone loaded on the bus, which includes video of the residents in the dining hall having breakfast and some impromptu videos of the residents packing in their rooms.

▶ The next stage covers the four-hour bus ride to Las Vegas. Given everyone on the bus was excited for the day out, this stage contained a lot of conversation and some great video of the desert.

▶ The third stage captured everything from when the residents unloaded from the bus until they got back on the bus to go home.

▶ The fourth stage is a bonus blooper stage that Bart decided to add for comic relief. Some of the bloopers include a resident snoring loud enough to wake everyone else up on the way home and a resident who got too excited when she hit the jackpot on a slot machine and tripped over her chair and fell into a group of onlookers.

Bart wanted to make a button on the Main Menu of the DVD for each of the four stages. Figure 14.2 illustrates the Main Menu that Bart created. This figure is shown in DVD Builder Preview Mode. As you can see from Figure 14.2, he used a still picture looking up at one of the towers of the MGM Grand Casino as the background image.

Figure 14.2
Bart's Main Menu.

In addition to the general considerations we covered in this chapter's introduction, Bart had to keep a few things in mind to achieve his desired menu structure.

▶ Since Bart decided to use a color-rich background, he had to make sure the font selection on both the menu button labels and title were pleasing to the eyes.

CHOOSING A BACKGROUND

Background images that are "busy" can make it difficult to find a color scheme and font size that coordinate. Make sure to keep this in mind when organizing your menus.

► Because there is a finite amount of television screen available, Bart needed to make sure his menu button labels were not too long; otherwise, they would cut off. Figure 14.3 shows DVD Builder in Preview Mode. In this case, you can see that the lower two menu labels are too long, which made them blend together.

Figure 14.3
Menu button labels can blend together.

SCREENING ROOM VS. PREVIEW MODE

The Screening Room will cut off menu button labels that are actually fine in length, but when DVD Builder is in Project Mode, this will not happen. The reason is because there is less space available in the Screening Room than in Preview Mode. To get an accurate assessment of the button labels, you should always check it in Preview Mode, regardless of what the Screening Room displays.

MENUS IN PREVIEW MODE

For a menu to appear in Preview Mode, either a picture or video must be assigned to a movie. As your project develops, this will not be an issue (because you will have multimedia in your project), but you may run into this when you are checking your menu button label lengths in the beginning.

Now that Bart has the Main Menu laid out, he is ready to move on to the submenus. In the first stage, Bart did not use his regular camera, so he will not add any slideshows. Instead, three menu buttons are included in this submenu. Each button links directly to a video that was recorded before the residents got on the bus. Figure 14.4 shows Bart's first stage submenu structure in DVD Builder Preview Mode.

▶ **Breakfast Time**—This video was taken in the dining hall during breakfast. Bart walked around talking to some of the residents as they ate, trying to catch the excitement and anticipation that filled the air.

▶ **Interviewing Bill**—Bill is one of the youngest residents in the village. He has a great sense of humor and likes to crack jokes. As you can imagine, Bart's interview of Bill was pretty amusing, so Bart decided to make this interview its own menu button.

▶ **Last-minute Packing**—It seems like everyone waits until the last minute to pack for a trip. Bart walked around the village before everyone loaded on the bus and caught some of the procrastinators' last minute frenzy.

Figure 14.4
Before the Trip submenu.

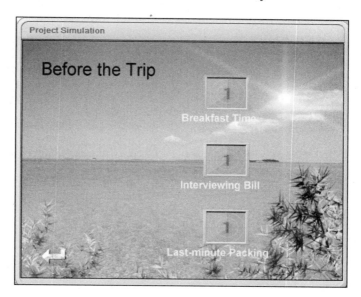

DON'T OVERCROWD
DVD Builder will allow for a maximum of six buttons per menu (plus menu button labels). While this is possible, it is not always advisable. In order to avoid viewer confusion, be careful not to overcrowd your menu.

The next stage is organized under the Bus Ride submenu. In this stage, Bart took video as well as still pictures. Bart took some great still pictures as they were driving in the desert. He also conducted a video interview with one of the residents and shot video of both Lake Meade and the Hoover Dam in action. The submenu of the second stage is shown in Figure 14.5 and includes a menu button that links to both slideshows and videos.

▶ **Desert Slides**—As the bus made its way to Las Vegas via the desert, Bart took many still pictures of the different landscapes. He compiled them into this slideshow with a slide duration of six seconds, and he also added accompanying background music.

▶ **Lake Meade**—If you have ever flown into Las Vegas, you probably saw Lake Meade. It is an awesome site to have a crystal clear blue lake in the middle of such desolation. Bart's bus made a stop at a gas station by Lake Meade. Bart went out to the lake and recorded the sights and sounds of this beautiful place.

▶ **Hoover Dam**—The residents asked the bus driver to stop again when they reached the Hoover Dam. Although they couldn't stay long because of their tight schedule, Bart managed to get some good video of it to put on his DVD.

▶ **Talking to Howard Johnson**—Howard Johnson is regarded as the wise one of the village. He gained this wisdom from opening a chain of ice cream parlors. It was strange it did so well since they only sold one flavor! Bart held an interview with him and put it into this menu button.

Figure 14.5
Bus Ride submenu.

MENU BUTTON PLACEMENT
It is not possible to change the location of the menu buttons. There is a way to get around this by choosing a different menu theme. Depending on the menu theme, the menu buttons can display horizontally or vertically—Figure 14.5 shows a horizontal placement and Figure 14.6 illustrates a vertical placement. In addition to horizontal and vertical placement, menu buttons may line up in different places on the menu as well—left side, right side, or center. You should experiment with the different menu themes to find one that works for the specific menu you are working on.

The next stage can be accessed through the On the Town menu button on the Main Menu. This stage is similar to the first one in that it contains both pictures—grouped in slideshows—and videos. A majority of this menu is devoted to the time spent in Vegas, with a video of the group walking down the strip, pictures of the different casinos that they passed, and interviews with some of the more serious gamblers on the trip to see how they came out. Figure 14.6 shows the DVD Builder in Preview Mode for the On the Town menu.

▶ **Cruising the Strip**—Not everyone wanted to gamble the entire time they were there, including Bart. This group of residents walked down the strip to check out the different attractions, such as the water show at the Bellagio. Bart recorded the different casinos and the reactions of some of the residents that had not been to Las Vegas in the past.

▶ **Casino Slideshow**—Bart recorded as he was walked down the strip, but he also took still image pictures of each casino that they passed. He compiled these pictures and put them into a slideshow accessible through this button.

▶ **Counting our Riches**—As everyone started to file back into the bus to go home, Bart interviewed the big gamblers of the bunch to see how they ended up. Some reports from the residents were good, while others were not so good.

Figure 14.6
On the Town submenu.

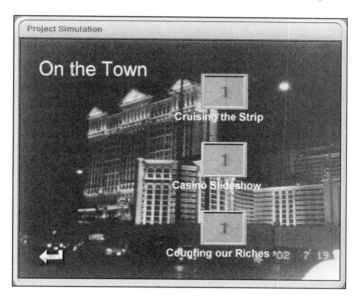

REPLACING THE BACKGROUND WITHOUT REPLACING THE MENU THEME

Remember that DVD Builder will not let you move the menu button's placement. If you find a menu theme that has the menu buttons placed where you want them, you can change the background image without changing the icon placement. Also, changing the background image will not change the associated audio either.

The last stage is an extra stage that includes some of the funny things that happened during the trip. It is accessed through the Bloopers menu button located on the Main Menu. Regarding content, this stage is short, but is worth putting in there for its comedic value. Two videos are accessible through this menu using the two menu buttons. Figure 14.7 illustrates the menu that Bart created for this bonus stage.

▶ **Snoring Taggert**—Taggert is another resident of Rock Ridge Retirement Village. He has a bit of a snoring problem—that is an understatement—that kept everyone else up on the way home. Bart had the idea of a bloopers section before the trip started, so when he saw this, it was too hard to pass up.

▶ **Betty is too Excited!**—Betty is yet another resident who went on this trip. Betty is not a big gambler—rather, a lucky gambler. She was the big winner out of the group when a slot machine hit for $1,000. When she won the big jackpot, she jumped around so much that she fell into a group of onlookers. Luckily, Bart was there with his camcorder to capture this precious moment.

Figure 14.7
Bloopers submenu.

Now that we've looked at how Bart organized his menu structure, let's switch gears and look at Lili's menu structure. Her user requirements are much different.

Lili: Menu Structure

Remember Lili from the preceding chapter? She is a Broadway actress planning on changing careers soon, which was reinforced when she had her child. A Broadway schedule is not easy with children. To give back to the entertainment industry, she wants to start her own children's talent agency, named Twue to You, which emphasizes high moral and ethical values. Lili wants to make a DVD that she can distribute to potential clients and eventually create video portfolios for her clients on DVD.

In the beginning, Lili's DVD will be pretty basic. She envisions her DVD as a constant work-in-progress; she will eventually add more testimonials of her clients on the DVD that she will hand out to potential clients. She has decided on the following layout.

1. **History**—This section will give some background on the company and the people that are employed there. For the time being, Lili will be the only employee, so she will have pictures and videos of what she has done both professionally and personally.

2. **Testimonials**—This section will have videos of her clients praising Twue to You. Lili has a few clients that are ready to sign up when she starts the business, so she will use one or two of these clients to kick off her testimonial section. While this section will be small in the beginning, it will grow quickly as more clients are signed.

3. **Contact Us**—This section will include basic contact information for the business. For example, this section will include mailing address, website, and contact phone number.

In order to stay simple, Lili decided to use default options for most of her DVD—she used a built-in theme without any customizations, for example. With that said, let's take a look at what Lili has designed for her Main Menu (see Figure 14.8).

Figure 14.8
Lili's Main Menu.

Similar to Bart, Lili had some specific considerations when laying out the DVD.

▶ For a professional-looking DVD, she wanted to use a motion menu. Lili decided to use one that is built into DVD Builder.

USING MOTION MENUS

Most of the menu themes included with DVD Builder are motion menus. If you want to create your own motion menu, just drag a video on the menu background. I would recommend keeping them as short as possible.

▶ Recall from the preceding chapter that Lili has an Introduction Video she would like to use. She would like to add audio commentary to it as well, which will be covered later in the chapter.

CREATING AUDIO COMMENTARY

To add audio commentary with DVD Builder, you must have a microphone plugged into your computer.

The first submenu is accessed by clicking the History menu button. Initially, this menu will contain the most content. As time goes by and Lili's business matures, the Testimonials submenu will have more information in it. There are three menu buttons that each link to videos. A picture of the menu is shown in Figure 14.9.

▶ **About Twue to You**—This button is a video about the company's history. It will contain some trivia about where the company started (out of Lili's house) among other things.

▶ **Lili's Professional Accomplishments**—This button is used to show potential clients that Lili is qualified, since she has been in the "business" for so long and to let potential clients get to know her. This video will contain an interview with Lili reflecting on her career, as well as clips from her latest production.

▶ **Lili's Personal Life**—The purpose of this button is to show potential clients that Lili is a real person with a real life. And of course, contained within this video will be several shots of her new child.

Figure 14.9
History submenu.

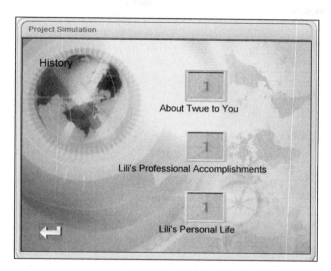

The second menu, Testimonials, is pretty self-explanatory. This submenu is accessed through the Main Menu via the Testimonials button. This menu will grow exponentially as Lili's business grows. In the beginning, she thought it would be a neat effect to have the kids that are shown in these videos think of a nickname for their menu button label. Needless to say, she had some pretty creative kids. Figure 14.10 shows what the Testimonials menu looks like.

▶ **Waco Kid**—The Waco Kid, with his real name being Gene, dreams of being a cowboy. This video is an interview with Gene talking about himself and explaining some of the productions he has been in since he signed up with Twue to You.

▶ **Mongo**—Mongo, with his real name being Alex, wants to be a football player when he grows up. This video is another testimonial about the way that Twue to You has opened up many doors of opportunity for his childhood career.

Figure 14.10
Testimonials submenu.

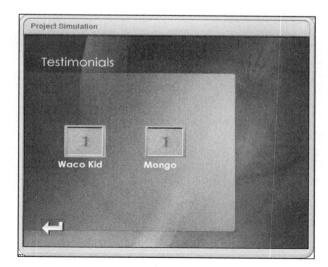

ORGANIZING THE TESTIMONIALS

In the beginning, Lili will be able to have all of her testimonials on one page, but remember that DVD Builder is limited to six buttons to a menu. Eventually, she may want to split them into other submenus.

The last menu, called Contact Us, is accessed through the Contact Us submenu on the Main Menu. This menu contains two menus that will link to slideshows with contact information. A picture of this menu is shown in Figure 14.11.

▶ **Mailing Address**—This menu button will link to a slideshow with the company's mailing address, phone number, fax number, and so on.

▶ **Internet Contact**—The purpose of this menu button is to link to a slideshow that will show pertinent information regarding Twue to You on the Internet. Some included items are the company's website address and an e-mail address for Lili.

Figure 14.11
Contact Us submenu.

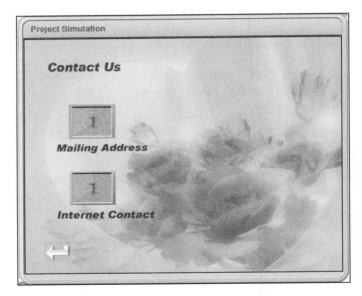

ADDING CONTACT INFORMATION

Adding contact information to a DVD is a great way to get your name and address out. You need to make sure it will not change anytime soon, though. Otherwise, you will need to send out new DVDs.

Video Editing

The last part of Chapter 9 focused on how to edit your videos once they have been either captured or imported into DVD Builder. The editing possibilities are pretty minimal in a beginner-level DVD authoring application, which includes DVD Builder. For more advanced functionality, you should look into purchasing a separate video editing application to edit your videos and then import them in DVD Builder. Keeping DVD Builder's editing limitations in mind, remember that there are a couple ways to manipulate your videos within DVD Builder.

▶ If a video is longer than desired, the video can be split in half, or trimmed. Trimming is done to the left or right of a certain point.

▶ If you don't like the audio that is currently in the video—or the video doesn't have audio—you can replace it.

VIDEO VS. MOVIE

Remember that DVD Builder refers to videos and movies as two different things. Videos are captured or imported and then inserted into a movie—DVD Builder movies can contain videos or pictures.

Since we are in the design component of our DVD project, there are a few general considerations that need to be addressed before editing any video.

▶ Your videos should be kept at a reasonable length. This is more of a courtesy to the viewer than anything. The viewer must watch the whole video or manually stop the video to get back to the menu.

▶ Try not to upstage your own video with excessive background audio. This simply means that background audio is just that, in the background. Too much audio can distract the viewer from the video.

▶ Your audio running time should be less than or equal to the length of your video. If the audio is longer, it will cut off when the video has finished.

Both Bart and Lili will be using video in their projects. Bart's DVD is not meant to be changed often, whereas Lili's DVD will change frequently as she gets more clients. For the purposes of this book, you will notice that Bart has quite a bit more work to do than Lili. Bart's video editing work will be intensive in the beginning, but once the DVD is complete, he's finished. Since Lili's DVD is a constant work-in-progress, her time spent on video editing will be spread out.

Bart: Video Editing

Bart used DVD Builder's maximum potential for his video editing. He trimmed all of his videos in order to get the start and end point exactly where he wanted it. Because he didn't want to lose the interest of his viewers, Bart split a few videos with DVD Builder. Once he did this though, he decided that he didn't need one of the halves and discarded it. Last, in the Bloopers section, Bart replaced the audio of Betty celebrating her victory over the slot machine with something that better fit her tripping over her chair.

CHAPTER 14

Instead of trying to capture the video at the exact starting point of the video, Bart captured a few seconds before the actual starting point and also left a few extra seconds on the end. This design technique is used to assist the DVD author by adding a video buffer at the beginning and end. Since capturing is done in real-time, it is hard to start the video capture at the exact desired starting point. Not only do you have to hit the button at the exact starting time, you also have to account for the delay that it takes for the computer to recognize your instruction to start the capture and then send it to DVD Builder. Keep in mind, this is all done while the video is playing. Using the video buffer that he gave himself, Bart was able to trim the extra material from the beginning and end of the captured video. Because of the amount of video that Bart had captured, he has a lot of trimming to do.

VIDEO TRIMMING DEMONSTRATION
Instead of showing how Bart trimmed each video, we will look at how he trimmed one video. Keep in mind, the same method applies for each video, as well as each video that you will trim when you create your first DVD.

The first video that Bart wants to trim is the Cruising the Strip video located in the On the Town submenu. Let's see how Bart trimmed this video. Bart should repeat these steps for each video that he wants to trim.

1. If DVD Builder is not already started, from the Windows Start Menu, click Programs then Roxio Easy CD and DVD Creator 6. From the menu that appears, click on DVD Builder, as shown in Figure 14.12.

WINDOWS XP
In Windows XP, the Windows Start Menu is organized slightly different. To get to DVD Builder, choose All Programs and then Roxio CD and DVD Creator 6.

Figure 14.12
Initiate DVD Builder from the Start Menu.

2. Load the video clip into the Screening Room by double-clicking on the video clip in the DVD Workshop area. The result is shown in Figure 14.13.

Figure 14.13
Loaded DVD Builder
movie.

3. Using the mouse, click and drag the slider bar to the position that should be trimmed. If you are setting the start position, you will always trim left. Likewise, if you want to set the end position, always trim right. The slider bar and trim buttons are shown in Figure 14.14.

Figure 14.14
Slider bar and trim
buttons.

SPLIT VIDEO BUTTON
The Split Video button, shown in Figure 14.14, will be covered later in this section.

UNDOING A TRIM
If you want to restore the movie back to its original state, just right-click on it in the DVD Workshop area and choose Undo Trim from the menu that appears.

The next video editing tool built into DVD Builder is the ability to split a video. Bart had to do this with one of his videos, specifically the video of the residents walking down the strip. If you have ever been to Vegas, you know that it can take a couple of hours to get from one end to the other during a busy weekend night. Once Bart had his menu structure and started to finalize his videos, he decided that the video was way too long. While the video may be interesting to the residents, I don't know if any of them would want to watch it for two hours straight. It was then that Bart decided to split the video, like so:

1. If DVD Builder has not been started, open it via the Windows Start Menu. as shown in Figure 14.12.
2. Load the video clip into the Screening Room by double-clicking on it in the Workshop area (see Figure 14.15). The Screening Room will show the video clip.

Figure 14.15
Open the video clip in the Workshop area.

3. Position the slider bar (shown in Figure 14.12) to the place where the video clip should split.
4. Click the Split Video button, shown in Figure 14.16.

UNDOING A VIDEO SPLIT

Similar to undoing a trimmed clip, you can undo a split video by right-clicking on one of the split clips and selecting Undo Split from the menu that appears.

5. When the video clip is split, DVD Builder will create two video clips in the same DVD Builder movie.

Figure 14.16
Split Video button and slider bar.

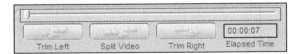

DELETING A VIDEO CLIP

If you decide that you do not want to include one of the split video clips, just click and drag it to the Trash can.

The last video editing tool that Bart will use is the ability to replace audio on a video clip. Bart wanted to enhance his Bloopers section a bit by adding an audio track to Betty's video. Bart decided to add Frank Sinatra's version of "I Get a Kick Out of You" as background music while the video is playing. Let's see how he did it.

1. If DVD Builder has not been started, open it using the Windows Start Menu, as shown in Figure 14.12.

2. Right-click on the movie that needs the audio attached.

3. Select Attach Audio from the menu that appears.

4. When Attach Audio is selected, a Browse Audio Files (see Figure 14.17) window appears. Navigate to the location of the audio file and select it.

5. Click on OK.

Figure 14.17
Browse Audio Files window.

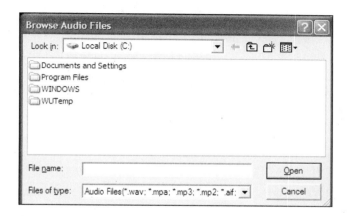

6. If audio already exists on the video, the window shown in Figure 14.18 will present you with three options: Choose Yes to replace the existing audio, Choose No to blend the two audio files together, and Choose Cancel to leave the movie as is.

Figure 14.18
Replace Audio window.

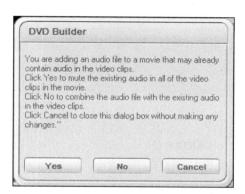

As you can see, Bart has a lot of video editing work ahead of him. Let's check on Lili and see what she has decided to do with her business DVD.

Lili: Video Editing

In many ways, a business DVD is the same as any other DVD. The methods of importing and editing the video are the same. With that said, instead of rehashing what Bart did earlier in this chapter, I will only cover what Lili is doing differently.

▶ Bart did not want to use an Introduction Video. He didn't feel that the target viewer would care either way. On the other hand, Lili thinks that an Introduction Video is a great attention grabber for her target viewers and is going to use it as a hook to excite the viewer into checking out everything on the DVD.

▶ The other thing that Lili would like to do is add an audio commentary over the Introduction Video to further reel her viewers in. The goal of the audio commentary is to show the potential client that she has high moral and ethical values. She feels that if she doesn't have her own voice in the Introduction Video, her goal may not be achieved.

The Introduction Video—introduced in Chapter 9—is a video that will play before the Main Menu is started. It cannot be stopped or skipped over. An FBI warning is a great example of this. Recall from Chapter 13 that Lili had a friend videotape her Introduction Video, and then she captured it from her FireWire-based camcorder. As with all videos, she will have to trim it to set the start and end point exactly as she wants it. The Introduction Video is added through the Workshop area on the main DVD Builder interface. Let's see how she added it to her DVD.

1. If DVD Builder is not started, go ahead and start it via the Windows Start Menu, as shown in Figure 14.12.

2. In the DVD Builder Workshop area, you will see a movie named Intro, which is in all projects and cannot be deleted. Click on the Import Multimedia files from the Video Import toolbar.

3. Click and drag the desired video clip from the Import Multimedia Files window into the Intro DVD Builder movie, as shown in Figure 14.19.

Figure 14.19
Intro movie.

4. Remove the default Introduction Video clip—called RoxioIntro.mpg—from the Intro DVD Builder movie. Just click and drag the video clip into the Trash can.

ROXIO'S INTRODUCTION VIDEO

Each project created with DVD Builder has the default Roxio Introduction video. You must remove it if you do not want it to run.

Adding an audio commentary can be very useful. I am sure you have rented DVDs that had a special feature—Director's Commentary—where the audio in the movie is muted and the director talks throughout the whole movie, letting the viewer know what he was trying to accomplish with a particular scene. Lili wanted to add an audio commentary to her Introduction Video to give it a personal touch. Adding audio commentary is done through the Screening Room—remember, a microphone is required.

1. If DVD Builder has not been started, go ahead and start it from the Windows Start Menu, as shown in Figure 14.12.

2. Double-click on the video clip that needs the audio commentary added to it. This will add the video clip to the Screening Room.

3. At the bottom of the Screening Room, you will see a Record button (see Figure 14.20) and an option to select a sound card. If you have more than one sound card, choose the appropriate one from the list.

Figure 14.20
Record audio
commentary.

4. Once the clip is loaded and the sound card selected, click on the Record button.

5. A window (see Figure 14.21) will appear—just like it did when Bart replaced the audio—asking if you want to mute the current audio (click the Yes button), blend the two audio files together (click the No button), or do nothing (click the Cancel button).

Figure 14.21
Replace Audio
Commentary window.

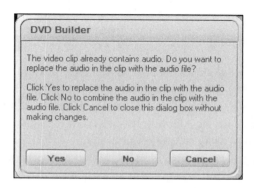

CHAPTER 14

COMMENTARY IS NOT AUDIBLE

If your commentary is silent when playing it back, check the Sounds and Multimedia (Sounds and Audio Devices in Windows XP) control panel to make sure the microphone input is turned up.

Creating a Slideshow

As you remember from Chapter 11, slideshows are just a collection of pictures that are grouped together in a DVD Builder movie. To review from Chapter 11, there are a few things that are possible with slideshows in DVD Builder.

▶ You can rearrange the slides within a slideshow any way you like. Just click and drag the slide on top of the slide to be replaced. When you let go of the mouse button, the two slides involved will switch places.

▶ Slide duration is the time that the slide will appear on the screen before the slideshow advances to the next one. Remember that the slide duration can be set at the slide or the slideshow level. The slideshow level is a global setting that applies to all slides in the slideshow unless it is overridden on a particular slide itself.

▶ Unlike video, pictures do not have sound embedded in them. Fortunately, DVD Builder allows you to assign background music to a slideshow.

▶ A cool video effect—that can be added to more than just slideshows—is called a transition. Transitions are added between the slides in order to pleasantly advance from one slide to another. Some transition examples include dissolve out of one slide while dissolving into the next or spin out of one slide while spinning in the next slide.

As with anything related to DVD authoring, there are a few things to consider when creating your DVD.

▶ Don't set the slide duration too small or the viewer will not be able to enjoy the slide.

▶ Make sure the background music is shorter than the slideshow. Otherwise, the background music will cut off prematurely.

▶ Try not to let your transitions upstage your slideshow. While transitions are an easy way to spice up your slideshow, use them with caution; otherwise, it may distract the viewer from the slideshow.

Slideshows are pretty cut and dry, so the context that each case study will use them in may seem similar, but the target audience is much different. With that said, as we go through the different case studies, keep the target audience in mind and how each one may relate to what you may use your own DVD burner for.

Bart: Creating Slideshows

Although Bart did not take an enormous number of still pictures, he did take enough to make two slideshows. The first one is a slideshow of pictures that were taken in the desert, and the other slideshow contains pictures of each of the casinos that the residents passed as they were walking down the strip.

Similar to video trimming, we will look at only one of the slideshows. The slideshow we will look at is the Casino slideshow that is accessible in the On the Town submenu. The method is exactly the same to create the other (or any slideshow for that matter); just repeat the following instructions for each slideshow.

1.   If DVD Builder has not started, open it using the Windows Start Menu, as shown in Figure 14.12.

2.   In the DVD Workshop area, click and drag the pictures into the movie that will be used as a slideshow. If the pictures are not imported into the layout, go ahead and import them now using the Import Multimedia button contained on the Video Import toolbar. The movie that contains the Las Vegas slideshow is shown in Figure 14.22.

Figure 14.22
Las Vegas Strip
slideshow.

KEEPING SLIDESHOWS SEPARATE
It is a good idea to keep each slideshow in its own DVD Builder movie. If a video clip is added into the movie that contains your slideshow, it will play wherever it resides in the movie.

3.   Once the slides are imported, arrange them in the order you would like to see them displayed.

4.   Right-click on the DVD Builder movie that contains the slideshow. Choose Still Images Duration from the menu that appears (see Figure 14.23).

Figure 14.23
Setting slide duration.

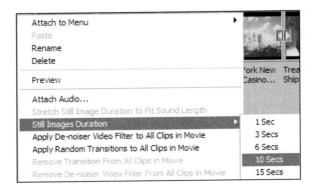

Attach to Menu	▶
Paste	
Rename	
Delete	
Preview	
Attach Audio...	
Stretch Still Image Duration to Fit Sound Length	
Still Images Duration	▶
Apply De-noiser Video Filter to All Clips in Movie	
Apply Random Transitions to All Clips in Movie	
Remove Transition From All Clips in Movie	
Remove De-noiser Video Filter From All Clips in Movie	

1 Sec	
3 Secs	
6 Secs	
10 Secs	
15 Secs	

5. Choose 10 Seconds, also shown in Figure 14.23.

6. Add the desired transition by clicking on the Transition Library button (see Figure 14.24), and then choose a transition from the Transition Library, as shown in Figure 14.25. Click and drag the transition from the Transition Library to the two arrows between the slides and release the mouse button.

Figure 14.24
Transition Library icon.

Figure 14.25
Transition Library.

ADDING TRANSITIONS

You must add a transition between each slide. Unlike slide duration, you cannot set a transition at the slideshow level—only at the slide level.

PREVIEWING THE SLIDESHOW

If at any time you want to preview the slideshow that you are working on, either double-click on the movie to put it in the Screening Room or run DVD Builder in Disc Preview Mode and navigate to the slideshow from there.

Lili: Creating Slideshows

Compared to Bart, Lili's slideshow needs are pretty limited, at least for right now. She would like to create two slideshows that will be attached to menu buttons in the Contact Us submenu of her DVD. The first slideshow—connected to the Mailing Address button—will show contact information, such as telephone number and mailing address, and the second slideshow—connected to the Internet Information button—will show any Internet information that she has, such as her company's website address and e-mail address.

Before Lili will be able to create any slideshows, she will need to create the slides. The next two figures show examples of slides that will be included in each of the slideshows. Figure 14.26 is an example of the first slideshow, and Figure 14.27 is an example of the second.

Figure 14.26
Example slide in
Mailing Address.

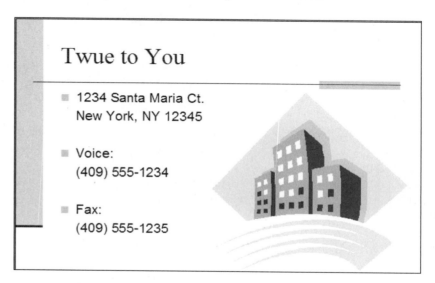

Figure 14.27
Example slide in
Internet Contact.

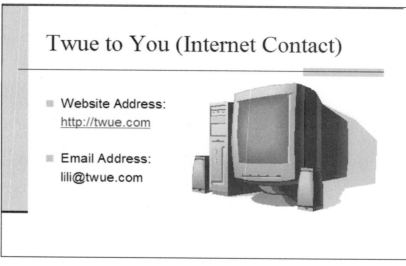

CREATING SLIDES

Slides can be created in any photo editing application. I recommend Photoshop or PaintShop Pro.

Summary

This chapter concentrated on the design process of DVD authoring. There were three things that were covered in this chapter: creating a menu structure, editing the videos, and creating slideshows. Creating a menu structure is, in my opinion, the most important step in the whole DVD authoring process. The menu structure should be well thought out and logically structured, so that the viewer will not get confused and frustrated. The second step has to do with editing the videos. While DVD Builder is pretty limited in its video editing abilities, it will do the job for most novices. If you find yourself wanting to do more than what is allowed in DVD Builder, you should capture your videos into a third-party application, such as Adobe Premiere, and edit them from there. The last thing covered in this chapter was creating slideshows. Slideshows are a grouping of pictures that have a specific slide duration and optional background music.

With each concept that was discussed, we looked at how each case study confronted and worked through them. The next chapter is the last chapter in our case study. We will look at how both Lili and Bart completed their projects and distributed them. This distribution includes creating a jewel case insert for each of the DVDs.

Chapter 15
Completing the Project

So far we've looked at importing your multimedia from different multimedia devices, such as a camcorder or camera, and these can be either analog or digital. Next, we designed our DVD layout by creating a menu structure. Then we edited our videos and finally created the various slideshows that we wanted to include.

This brings us to the last chapter of the case study—and consequentially the last chapter of the book—which concentrates on packaging and burning your DVD. After having read Chapter 14, you will probably think this chapter is a breeze. There are two parts to be addressed when you are ready to distribute your DVD.

▶ **Creating jewel case covers**—If you recall from Chapter 12, jewel case covers are pieces of paper that you insert into a jewel case. The purpose of these covers is to give information about the DVD that is contained in the jewel case.

▶ **Burning your disc**—Saving the DVD includes either burning the project to disc or saving it to an image file for later use.

This chapter is intended to be more straightforward than the previous two in that there are fewer decisions that need to be made. For example, there is only one way to burn a DVD with DVD Builder. Before we burn our DVD to disc, let's look at how Bart and Lili created their jewel case covers.

Creating Jewel Case Covers

Remember that DVD Builder is only one component of a bigger suite of applications called Roxio Easy CD and DVD Creator. Another application included in this suite is Label Creator, which you learned how to use in Chapter 12. To understand this section, we should review some terminology that is used.

▶ Jewel case layouts are similar to a DVD layout, but in this case, text—instead of video and pictures—is organized in a certain way to present information to the viewer.

▶ Labels are used to adhere to the DVD media itself. Label Creator is used to print the title of the disc—or anything you want, for that matter—and the other side has adhesive that will stick to the media.

▶ Covers are paper inserts that are used in a jewel case. You should remember from Chapter 12 that a jewel case is the plastic case used to store the DVD. The covers are slid into the front and placed between the disc tray and back of the jewel case. Whereas the label is used to display the title of the DVD, the covers are used to display what is on the disc.

Now that you understand the terminology, let's review the six different layouts that are possible with Roxio Label Creator.

▶ **Disc Label layout**—Used to create the label that will stick directly to the DVD disc itself.

▶ **Booklet layout**—The cover that is inserted into the front of the jewel case. Normally, the front cover is double-sided with the title of the DVD on the front side and the contents of the disc on the back side.

▶ **Front Cover layout**—A one-sided version of the Booklet layout. The front side holds the DVD title, and the back side is blank.

▶ **Back Cover layout**—The cover that is sandwiched between the disc tray (the plastic tray that holds the disc) and the back of the jewel case. The back cover is comprised of the left and right spine that show the title of the DVD and the back cover that displays the contents of the DVD.

▶ **Mini Disc layout**—Similar to the Disc Label layout, this is a label layout that is used to stick to a mini disc instead of full-size media. This layout is used for CD and not DVD media.

▶ **DVD Case Cover layout**—Used for a jewel case made especially for DVDs. It is longer than a regular jewel case. This layout's functionality is pretty limited in Label Creator because only one theme can be applied to it.

There are a few steps involved in opening Label Creator.

1. From the Start Menu, click on Programs and then Roxio Easy CD and DVD Creator 6.

2. Choose Label Creator from the menu that appears, as shown in Figure 15.1.

Figure 15.1
Label Creator via
Windows Start Menu.

3. Alternatively, Label Creator can be accessed through the Roxio Home Menu, as shown in Figure 15.2.

Figure 15.2
Label Creator via Roxio
Home Menu.

Both Bart and Lili will need to use labels and covers to distribute their jewel cases. Bart's covers will not be as involved as Lili's, since Bart only plans on distributing DVDs to his fellow residents. Lili wants her covers to look as professional as possible, without having to pay someone to do it for her.

CUSTOMIZING EACH LAYOUT

We will customize each layout for both of the case studies. If at any time you feel that this chapter is moving too fast, don't hesitate to refer back to Chapter 12 for a more detailed explanation.

Bart: Creating Jewel Case Covers

Bart wanted to create a basic jewel case cover and disc label that he could distribute with his project. He needed to keep his target viewer in mind, as well as provide labels and covers that are pleasing to the eye. Bart made a few decisions in order to create the covers and labels for his DVD.

▶ Because of the limited functionality that Label Creator has with DVD case covers, Bart decided to use a jewel case instead of a DVD cover.

▶ In the interest of time—the residents were really excited to get their new DVD—Bart decided to use a cover and label theme that was built into Label Creator.

▶ The text on the covers and labels must be large enough that all of the residents can read it.

▶ Knowing that his target viewer would never use the back side of the Booklet layout, Bart decided to use a Front Cover layout in conjunction with the Back Cover layout.

There are a lot of parts that go into creating jewel case covers and disc labels—a lot more than you would think. In order to organize everything in the most efficient way possible, Bart's label has been split into several sections.

▶ **Choosing a Theme**—Similar to DVD Builder, Label Creator allows you to assign themes to your covers and labels. There are two themes to choose from: data (the theme that will be covered in this chapter) and audio.

▶ **Creating the Disc Label and Front Cover layouts**—Remember from Chapter 12 that textboxes are used throughout each layout. They can be added either manually or automatically. The Disc Label and Front Cover layouts use the same textboxes, so these will be grouped together for discussion purposes.

▶ **Creating the Back Cover layout**—The layout has an additional textbox—the Contents textbox—that is not contained on the Disc Label and Front Cover layouts. We will configure the Contents textbox in this section.

▶ **Printing the layout**—When the layouts that you want to include on your DVD are complete, Label Creator will print them all at once.

Choosing a theme is the first thing that Bart should do to create his labels and covers. To shorten the list he has to choose from, Bart filtered out the audio themes. After looking over the available data themes, Bart decided to go with the Book data theme. Now that the theme is chosen, let's see how he assigned it to the layout he is working on.

1. If Label Creator is not open, start it from the Windows Start Menu, as shown in Figure 15.1.

2. Click the Theme project button. The window that appears is shown in Figure 15.3.

Figure 15.3
Change Theme window.

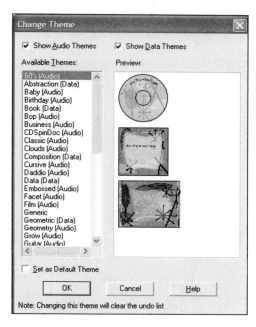

3. In order to narrow down Bart's search, uncheck the Show Audio Themes check box. Removing the checkmark will filter out the audio themes and display only the data themes. The result is shown in Figure 15.4.

Figure 15.4
Filter out audio themes.

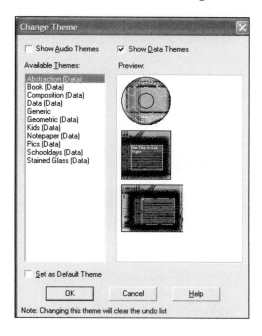

4. From the remaining list, choose the theme that you want to assign to your layout. The assigned theme is shown in Figure 15.5.

Figure 15.5
Bart's assigned theme.

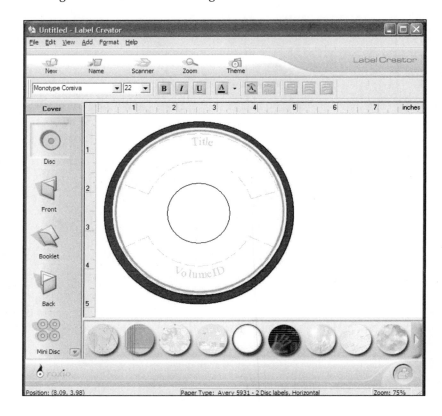

5. Click the OK button.

After the theme is assigned, the next thing to do is customize the layout. Recall from Chapter 12, that Label Creator uses global textboxes to enter data. Once the textboxes are populated with data, Label Creator will allow you to change the look of them by changing the font size, type, and formatting. Bart decided to bold all text and use the Twentieth Century Poster1 font type.

Because both the Disc Label and Front Cover layouts contain the same textboxes—when you update one, it updates the other—we will look at both of these layouts at the same time.

1. If Label Creator is not open, start it from the Windows Start Menu, as shown in Figure 15.1.

2. The first layout that is shown is the Disc Label layout. Enter the appropriate text into the Title and VolumeID textboxes. The Title textbox is at the top, and the VolumeID textbox is at the bottom.

3. Select the Twentieth Century Poster1 font type and bold each textbox. The formatted Disc Label layout is shown in Figure 15.6.

THE LAYOUT FIGURES
The following layout figures have been cropped to show only the project layout area.

Figure 15.6
Bart's Disc Label layout.

4. Switch to the Front Cover layout by clicking on the Front button on the left side of the main Label Creator interface.

5. You should notice that the text that was entered into the Title textbox on the Disc Label layout shows up in the Front Cover layout.

6. Format the text in the Front Cover layout as you did with the Disc Label layout. This consists of bolding the textbox and setting the font type to Twentieth Century Poster1. The finished Front Cover layout is shown in Figure 15.7.

Figure 15.7
Bart's Front Cover layout.

The next step in creating Bart's jewel case cover is customizing the Back Cover layout. Most of the work has already been done, because Label Creator will use the data that was entered earlier in the Disc Label and Front Cover layout. There are two remaining textboxes that Bart will need to enter: Date and Contents. The Date textbox can be any date that you want. In Bart's case, he is going to use the date of the Las Vegas trip. The Contents textbox is used to list what is on the DVD. Bart has decided to list the four Main Menu buttons in this textbox. With that said, let's see how the Back Cover layout is customized.

1. If Label Creator is not started, go ahead and start it from the Windows Start Menu, as shown in Figure 15.1.

2. Switch to the Back Cover layout button by clicking on the Back button that is located on the left-hand side of Label Creator's main interface.

3. You will notice that the DVD title has already been entered into the title portion of the left and right spine. Double-click on the Date textbox and type in a desired date.

UPDATING THE DATE TEXTBOX
As with all other textboxes in Label Creator, when the Date textbox is updated on either the left- or right-hand spine, the opposite one will be updated as well.

4. Double-click on the Contents textbox and type what is contained on the DVD. Bart's completed Back Cover layout is shown in Figure 15.8.

Figure 15.8
Bart's Back Cover layout.

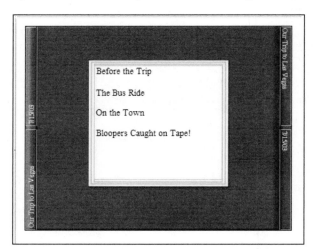

ADDING A NEW LINE IN A TEXTBOX
Remember, in order to start a new line within a textbox, you must press Ctrl+Enter.

TEXTBOX FORMATTING
Unfortunately, Label Creator's formatting abilities within a textbox are less than stellar. For example, any formatting done in the Contents textbox pertains to the entire textbox. You must bold everything or nothing. It is an all or nothing deal.

Printing the layout is the last step when creating a jewel case cover and a disc label. Unfortunately, this is also the most tedious step. You must manually set the paper type for each layout that is to be printed. Luckily for Bart, he is only using three layouts.

1. If Label Creator is not running, go ahead and start it from the Windows Start Menu, as shown in Figure 15.1.

2. Pull down the file menu and select Print. The Print window will appear, as shown in Figure 15.9.

Figure 15.9
Label Creator Print window.

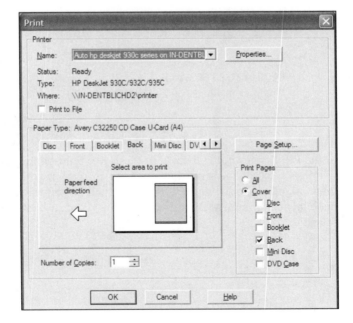

3. If you have more than one printer, select the appropriate printer from the Name drop-down menu.

4. Select the paper type by clicking the Page Setup button. This is done by selecting the type of paper to be used from the Current Paper Type drop-down menu. The Page Setup window is shown in Figure 15.10.

Figure 15.10
Page Setup window.

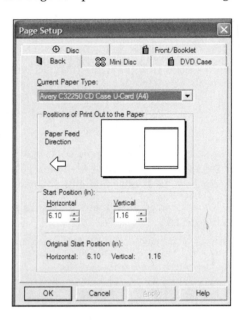

PAGE SETUP PER LAYOUT
You must manually set up the paper type for each layout to be printed.

5. In the Print Pages frame located in the lower right-hand corner of the Print window, select the layouts that you want printed. If you would like to print them all, click the All radio button. Bart will be printing the Disc, Front, and Back layouts. Figure 15.11 shows the Print window with the appropriate layouts selected.

Figure 15.11
Bart's Print layout.

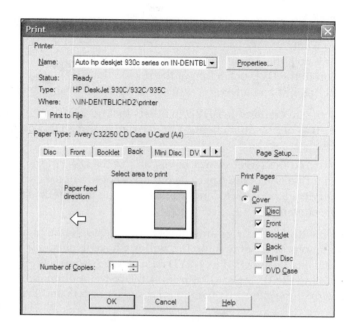

6.   If you would like more than one copy, use the up and down arrow buttons next to Number of Copies to select the number of copies to print.

7.   Click the OK button.

8.   Load the paper (see Figure 15.12) in the correct order as instructed by Label Creator.

Figure 15.12
Load paper in the correct order.

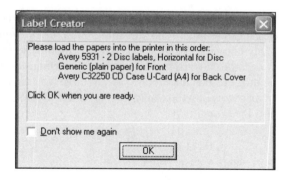

9.   Congratulations, your covers and labels are printed.

Bart needed to print a copy of the jewel case for each resident who requested it. Also, in order to access the layouts later and not have to re-create them, Bart saved them.

Lili: Creating Jewel Case Covers

Like Bart, Lili also wanted to package her new DVD. She wanted to do it in a way that would catch the eye of any potential clients. Unlike other promotional DVDs, Lili wanted hers to become an addition to the DVD collection of the person that she gives it to. Although this may be ambitious thinking, Lili had a few decisions to make in order to achieve her goals.

▶ Trying to conform her DVD to others that may be on the entertainment center shelves of potential clients, Lili decided to use a DVD case cover instead of the jewel case style.

▶ To avoid her target viewer having to put the DVD in the player just to see what is on it (the DVD Case Cover layout does not include a global contents textbox), Lili decided to create a new textbox on the back of the DVD case cover that lists the contents.

The work involved with Lili's covers and labels is much less than that of Bart's. This is due mostly to the limitations of Label Creator. Lili will not have to choose a theme, because there is only one theme that can be assigned to a DVD case cover. Also, the Front and Back Cover layouts are included in the DVD Case Cover layout. Due to the limitations discussed in this chapter, Lili has only three steps involved in creating her covers and labels.

▶ **Disc Label layout**—This step is similar to Bart's, but Lili will insert different text into the global textboxes.

▶ **DVD Case Cover layout**—As you can recall from Chapter 12, DVD case covers are special jewel cases that are longer than normal jewel cases. Because of their different sizes, a different layout is required.

▶ **Printing**—Printing from within Label Creator is the same for both Bart and Lili. The difference will be in selecting the paper type and layouts to be printed.

Lili should customize her Disc Label layout first before moving on to the DVD Case Cover layout. Although the DVD Case Cover layout has one assignable theme, you can still choose any theme desired for the Disc Label layout. For this DVD, she decided to go with the Kids data theme. As with any other Disc Label layout, she has to enter information into two textboxes— Title and VolumeID. To start out, Lili has decided to use Twue to You as the Title and Summer 2003 as the VolumeID, but this second textbox may change as her company matures. With that said, let's look at how she did it.

CHOOSING A DISC LABEL THEME

While it is possible to choose a theme for a disc label, keep in mind that the default DVD case cover and the disc label theme should coordinate.

1. If Label Creator is not started, go ahead and start it from the Windows Start Menu, as shown in Figure 15.1.

2. The default layout displayed when Label Creator is open is the Disc Label layout. If this layout is not selected, go ahead and select it now.

3. Click the Theme button and uncheck the Show Audio Themes check box (see Figure 15.4).

4. Choose the desired theme from the data theme list.

5. Click the OK button.

6. Double-click on the Title textbox, and type in the desired text.

7. Set the font type to Wendy Medium and the font size to 48. Press the Enter key.

8. Double-click on the VolumeID textbox and type in the desired text. Press the Enter key.

9. Set the font type to Wendy Medium and the font size to 48. Press the Enter key. The completed disc label is shown in Figure 15.13.

Figure 15.13
Lili's Disc Label layout.

Now that the Disc Label layout has been finished, it is time to move on to the DVD Case Cover layout. The text in the Title textbox (since it is a global textbox) will transfer from the Disc Label to the DVD Case Cover layout. Unfortunately, by default, a global contents textbox does not exist in the DVD Case Cover layout as it does in the other layouts. Lili still wanted one, so she created one of her own. Let's see how she customized the layout, including the new textbox.

1. If Label Creator is not started, go ahead and start it from the Windows Start Menu, as shown in Figure 15.1.

2. Click on the DVD Case Cover layout on the left-hand side of the Label Creator window.

3. Change the font size of the Title textbox on the right-hand side of the layout to 48 and the Title textbox in the spine to font size 24.

4. From the Objects toolbar, click the Text icon (see Figure 15.14).

5. The mouse pointer will change to a square. On the left-hand side of the layout, position the mouse in the upper left-hand corner of the location of the textbox to be created.

6. Click and drag the mouse from the upper left-hand corner to the lower right-hand corner of the textbox to be created; let go of the mouse button.

7. Double-click on the new textbox and type in the desired text.

8. In this example, the text color was changed to yellow in order for it to show up on the blue background. This is done by right-clicking on the textbox and selecting Properties from the menu that appears. In the Text Properties window (shown in Figure 15.15), in the upper right-hand corner of the window, change the text color to yellow.

8. The result of Lili's DVD case cover is shown in Figure 15.16.

Figure 15.14
Text icon.

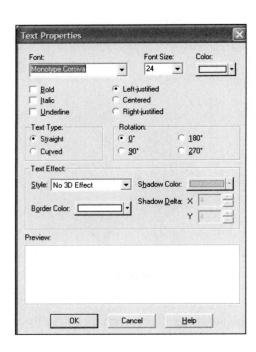

Figure 15.15
Text Properties window.

Figure 15.16
Lili's DVD case cover.

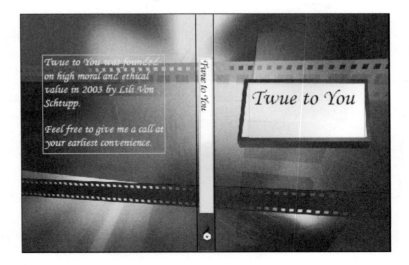

As stated earlier, printing Lili and Bart's projects is very similar. Since the two are so similar, I will quickly go over how Lili printed her covers and labels.

1. If Label Creator is not started, go ahead and start it through the Windows Start Menu, as shown in Figure 15.1.

2. Open the Print window by clicking the File menu and choosing Print from the menu that appears.

3. If you have more than one printer, select the appropriate printer from the Name drop-down menu.

4. Click the Page Setup button and configure the paper settings for the Disc Label and DVD Case Cover layouts.

5. Select the number of copies desired by incrementing the Number of Copies select box.

6. Click the OK button.

7. Load the paper in the order specified by Label Creator, and then click the OK button.

Finally, we have finished creating our labels and covers to package with our DVD media. Next, we will look at how to either burn the disc to a blank DVD or save the project to an image file.

Burning Your Disc

From this point forward, I am going to present the case studies together. At this point in the process, the two are quite similar. With that said, there are two things we will look at in this section.

▶ We will burn the work to DVD recordable media.

▶ To save for later use, we will also save each DVD to an image file. This is important for both case studies to do in case they want to make additional copies of their DVD.

PREVIEW YOUR DVDS

Make sure to do one last preview of your *entire* DVD before you burn it to disc—check all menus and buttons for problems. This will help in working out any last minute bugs that may exist.

First, let's look at the procedure to burn the project to DVD.

1. Make sure that DVD Builder is started. If not, click on the Windows Start Menu and navigate to Programs, then select Easy CD and DVD Creator 6 and choose DVD Builder from the menu that appears, as shown in Figure 15.18.

Figure 15.18
DVD Builder via
Windows Start Menu.

2. With the project loaded, click the Roxio burn button as shown in Figure 15.19.

Figure 15.19
Roxio burn button.

3. Select the desired number of copies by clicking the Number of Copies select box (see Figure 15.20).

4. Click the OK button (also see Figure 15.20).

Figure 15.20
Burn window.

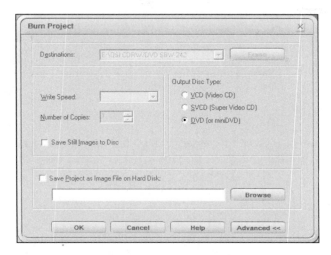

When the OK button is clicked, the burning process will start in high gear. During this process, the menus and movies are encoded into the MPEG format, and the project will be burned to the DVD.

Finally, we will look at the procedure to save the disc to image for distribution at a later time, without having to re-create the project.

1. Make sure that DVD Builder is started. If not, start it via the Windows Start Menu, as shown in Figure 15.18.

2. With the project loaded, click the Roxio burn button, shown in Figure 15.19.

3. Click the Save Project as Image File on Hard Disk check box—shown in Figure 15.20.

4. Click the Browse button that is located below the Save Project check box.

5. Using the Browse Image Files window (see Figure 15.21), navigate to the target location on the computer where the file should be saved.

Figure 15.21
Browse Image Files window.

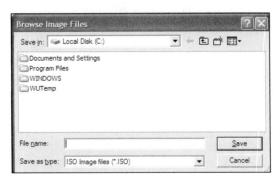

6. Once you've arrived at the target location of the image file, type a file name in the file name box.

7. Click the Save button.

CHECK HARD DISK SPACE

When saving your project to an image file instead of burning to a DVD, make sure that you have plenty of hard drive space on your computer. Microsoft Windows will most likely crash—or at the very least, slow to a crawl—if the hard drive runs out of space.

When the save button is clicked, the project will go through the exact same process as it did when burning the DVD to media. DVD Builder will inform you when this process has completed.

BURNING THE CASE STUDIES

If it seems like I skimmed over this last section, in a way I did! The reason for this is two-fold: First, the method to burn a DVD was covered in great detail in Chapter 5, and second, the method that was covered in Chapter 5—and briefly in this chapter—is the exact same for either case study (or anyone for that matter). If you have any questions about the burning process, please review Chapter 5.

Summary

This last chapter in our case study looked at the final touches of burning a DVD—creating jewel case covers and labels and also burning the DVD to the media itself. Label Creator is an application that is included in Roxio Easy CD and DVD Creator 6. This application uses global textboxes to update information such as Title, VolumeID, and Contents across the layouts.

The last section of this chapter dealt with either burning the DVD to disc or saving it to an image file for later use. Before burning the DVD to disc, make sure to preview it one last time to make sure everything links the way that it should. Both burning a DVD to disc and saving the project to an image file involve the same process. Simply put, when saving to an image file, the same encoding and menu rendering steps are used as if you were burning the DVD to the media itself. Make sure you have enough free space on your hard drive when saving your project to an image file, because it compresses all video, pictures, and menus into one file.

This concludes *DVD Burning Solutions*. You will find two appendices in the back of this book. Appendix A is a listing of 20 practical uses for a DVD. Appendix B is a glossary of terms that were used throughout this book.

As your DVD authoring career evolves, I hope that you are able to refer back to this book for any questions that may arise. Thank you for your time. I hope that you enjoyed reading this as much as I enjoyed writing it.

Appendices

Appendix A

20 Practical DVD Uses

Appendix B

Glossary of Terms

Appendix A
20 Practical DVD Uses

Now that you are armed with the fundamentals of authoring DVDs, the hardest thing left to do is figure out a use for it. This appendix will list 20 real-world examples (in no particular order) that will hopefully get your creative juices flowing so that you can think of some ways to use your new DVD burner. Keep in mind that this is not a complete list by any means, rather a brainstorming session to give you ideas to apply to your own life. With that said, let's get started.

1. You just purchased a digital camcorder and a digital camera. You have a child on the way, and you want to document every part of his life—including opening Christmas presents, potty-training, and his first birthday. When he is old enough, you want to give him something he'll be able to share with his children.

2. You work as a realtor for a new housing development, and you'd like to create a multimedia marketing tool that you can give to customers to take home with them. You want it to include a video tour of each house, specifications about the house, and approximate price for each upgrade to the house.

3. You are a corporate trainer for a large company. You like to reinforce your training with electronic visual aids. Also, you would like to be able to give new employees electronic copies of things such as policies and procedures, a safety video, and a welcome message from the CEO.

4. You are an aspiring film director, and you really like writing short films. You just graduated from college and would like to make a portfolio to hand out to potential clients. You want to leave them something that they can view on their own time.

5. Being a graduate student, you have to write a thesis and present it to your class. This thesis contains numerous videos and pictures. You could use presentation software—Microsoft PowerPoint for example—but the presentation would be too big to fit on a CD.

6. You are an IT professional who has been asked to conduct computer training for all personnel in the corporation. Unfortunately, you do not have a dedicated computer lab to house the training. Instead of scheduling time with each user in front of his or her computer, you can create a DVD for each training class.

7. You just bought an old Victorian-style house that you plan on restoring from the ground up. You decide that it would be neat to keep an electronic diary on the progress of the house. You could create a DVD that would show the condition of the house before the restoration started, track the progress as the house goes through various stages of transformation, and then a final walk-through of the completed house.

8. You are a freelance photographer who shoots weddings, bar mitzvahs, and so on. Being in the digital age, you want to offer something to your clients they will not be able to get anywhere else. Using a wedding DVD as an example, you would be able to offer slideshows of the ceremony and reception, video of the father-daughter dance, and even capture a video clip of the family member—there is always at least one—that had a little too much to drink at the reception.

9. You are interested in nature and would like to create a documentary of a safari that you are taking next year. Things on the DVD could include an audio commentary attached to a video of the tiger that tried to get into your car, a video of a zebra stampede across the plain, or a slideshow of a boat ride in the Amazon.

10. You are an avid music collector. Unfortunately, your CDs tend to take a beating because you are constantly swapping discs in and out of your CD player. A DVD could allow you to store a couple hundred CDs (in MP3 format) on one DVD, and you could store your original CDs in a safe place.

11. For insurance purposes, you would like to take pictures and digitally record everything that is contained in your house. To organize your content on a DVD, each room could have its own menu button.

12. Being an accountant, you must keep client data for a certain number of years in case the IRS performs an audit. Instead of having numerous CDs, you could consolidate all of these files on one DVD.

13. You are a high-school teacher who is in charge of both the yearbook and senior video each year—a senior video is produced by the graduating seniors thanking the administration and saying goodbye as they start another chapter in their life. Instead of publishing a yearbook in print form that will wear over time, you could produce a digital yearbook that would also include the senior video. You could organize the content by having a menu for each class—freshmen through seniors.

14. In the evenings, you tutor students in various subjects such as Math and English. Instead of using a standard workbook with exercises, you want to develop a DVD with exercises and review videos that the students can take home with them.

15. Each year you attend a large family reunion. At the last one, you were asked to research your "family roots" and present it at the next family reunion. You have found some great videos and pictures tracing your family back to the Civil War but are unsure how to present it; a DVD would be perfect to hand out as family members arrived.

16. You are a dairy farmer with a few hundred cows that are milked by means of an electronic milking machine, which is hooked up to a computer to track milk production. With a few hundred cows, the production data is quite large. A DVD could be used in order to archive old data in the event that you needed to access it at a later time.

17. You own a small Internet-based after-market car parts website that offers thousands of parts for a wide variety of cars. It would take hours for a customer to browse your online parts catalog. You would like to provide a link on your website to request a catalog be sent via mail. Instead of publishing a hard copy of your catalog, you could create a DVD that is organized similarly to your website so the customers could browse at their convenience.

18. You just retired after a 30-year career as a financial counselor. To achieve maximum enjoyment, you buy a beach house to spend each winter, but want to rent this house out when you are not there. You could create a virtual tour of the beach house to give to friends in your hometown in order to generate business.

19. Your son is on a little league team. Being the proud "baseball dad" that you are, you want to track the team's progress, shoot some video of the kids running around the bases, and maybe even interview the coach. You could create a DVD at the end of season highlighting everything that happened throughout the season to hand out to all of the parents and coaches.

20. You provide a service to the Motion Picture Industry that delivers new motion pictures to the theaters in your home state a couple of days before they are released. As you can imagine, there are a lot of movie theaters in one state. You want to provide directions, including maps, to each of your drivers that they can take with them on the road. You could provide each driver with a laptop and a DVD with directions from your headquarters to each serviced movie theater.

Appendix B
Glossary of Terms

Authoring DVDs can seem like an overwhelming task at first, but once you get the hang of the process, it will be self-gratifying. Appendix B is a reference to make learning the DVD authoring process easier. Let's get started, shall we?

Acquire Image. An application acquires an image from a TWAIN device.

Application format. The type of data that is written to the disc. There are many application formats to choose from: VCD, SVCD, DVD-ROM, DVD-VIDEO, DVD-AUDIO, or SACD.

Audio commentary. Audio narration that is recorded over a video or slideshow.

AVI. Stands for Audio Video Interlace. AVI is a movie format that is used with most Microsoft products.

Background. Picture or image that is used as the menu background.

BMP. Stands for Bitmap. BMP is a picture format that is good for printing and archiving high-resolution photos.

Bonding layer. The layer that holds the two substrates together. In a DVD-9 or DVD-18 disc, the bonding layer is transparent so that the laser can read both substrates from one side.

Broadcast format. The way that the DVD picture is displayed on the television screen. This can be either NTSC—used in North America—or PAL—primarily used in Europe.

Burning. Slang term for writing or recording data to a DVD, usually reserved for home use (as opposed to commercial manufacturing). The word "burning" is used because the disc will show a ring on the disc after the DVD is burned.

Captioning. Text that is added to video for the hearing impaired or if the viewer is not versed in the language on the video. Subtitling is an example of captioning.

CD-ROM disc. Removable disc media that has a maximum storage capacity of 700 Megabytes. The physical dimensions are the same as DVD media.

Chapter markers. Similar to an index in this book, chapter markers are used to index a video. This can be used in conjunction with scene selection menus to jump directly to a point in the video.

Chapter searching. A DVD feature that allows the viewer to jump straight to a chapter within a video.

Copy protection. Technology developed to aid in prevention of illegal copying of DVD content. Some examples include Macrovision and Content Scrambling System (CSS).

Copyright. A right of ownership to written pieces—either in digital or hard-copy format—that will protect it from being copied by someone else. This is an unregistered right, meaning that nothing has to be done on the author's part. Once the work is completed, it is automatically copyrighted.

Digital camcorder. An electronic device that captures video and stores it to a digital video tape. This type of camcorder (digital) can be hooked up to a computer and the video captured to a file(s) on the hard drive. Some common digital camcorder tape formats are DV (digital video) and Hi8.

Digital Camera. An electronic device that takes pictures and stores them digitally on the camera so they can be transferred from the camera to the computer, instead of print photographs.

Direct capture to burn. To save disk space, direct capture to burn can be used to transfer directly from a video capture device and burn to a DVD without using the hard drive.

Direct to Disc. *See Direct capture to burn.*

Disc format. Refers to the way that the DVD is physically constructed. The available disc formats are DVD-5, DVD-9, DVD-10, and DVD-18.

Disc image. Instead of burning a DVD project to disc, some DVD authoring applications can be saved to an image for later use. This image contains all menus, videos, pictures, and so on in a compressed ISO file.

Disc labels. Adhesive labels that stick to the DVD media. Normally used to describe the contents of the disc.

Disc media. Removable computer data storage. Some examples of this media are floppy, zip, CD-ROM, and DVD.

Double-sided. A DVD player uses both sides to read information on a double-sided DVD. The disc must be flipped when it is time to read the other side.

Drive bay. An expansion slot in a computer, designed to accommodate an IDE device (a DVD burner).

Drive jumper. Small piece of plastic that is used to set the IDE device as Master, Slave, or Cable Select.

Drive rails. Mounting brackets that are screwed into the IDE device so that the device can be installed into the drive bay.

Dual-Layer. Every DVD has two reflective layers that are used to hold information. A dual-layer DVD uses both of these layers to hold the information, whereas a single-layer uses only one of these layers.

DVD-5. Single sided, single-layer DVD. The maximum storage capacity of this disc format is 4.7 Gigabytes.

DVD-9. Single sided, dual-layer DVD. The maximum storage capacity of this disc format is 9.6 Gigabytes.

DVD-10. Double sided, single-layer DVD. The maximum storage capacity of this disc format is 9.6 Gigabytes, but the viewer is required to turn the DVD over after the first side has been shown.

DVD-18. Double sided, dual-layer DVD. The maximum storage capacity of this disc format is 17 Gigabytes. This format is not used often because of the manufacturing cost of the disc.

DVD. Stands for Digital Versatile Disc and is the topic of this book.

DVD-AUDIO application format. This format, also known as DVD-A, is intended to replace the Audio CD. Unlike an Audio CD, the DVD-AUDIO can produce surround-sound quality audio.

DVD decoder chip. Electronic chip that is used to decode the information as it is read from the DVD.

DVD Entertainment Group. Originally named the DVD Video Group. This group actively promotes the different DVD application formats.

DVD Forum. Originally named the DVD Consortium. This forum is composed of DVD hardware and software manufacturers that collect to exchange ideas related to DVD. In addition to exchanging ideas, they also endorse certain standards in DVD manufacturing.

DVD layout. Includes all design elements and how they are placed on the DVD. The position of the menu buttons is an example of a part of the layout.

DVD-R recordable format. This format follows the WORM (Write Once Read Many) theory. Once the disc is written, it is closed and cannot be written to again.

DVD+R recordable format. A competing format to DVD-R that follows the same standards as DVD-R. Keep in mind that not all drives can read both DVD+R and DVD-R formats.

DVD-ROM application format. This format is used for video games or read-only computer discs—a set of encyclopedias on a DVD would be an example.

DVD-RW recordable format. This format allows the disc to be written to more than once.

DVD+RW recordable format. A competing format to DVD-RW that follows the same standard as DVD-RW. Keep in mind that not all drives can read both DVD+RW and DVD-RW formats.

DVD-VIDEO application format. This format is used for either commercially produced or home-authored DVDs.

DVD Preview. Before burning the DVD project to disc, most DVD-authoring applications will let you preview it in real time. This allows any last minute bugs that may exist to be addressed.

DVD project. Includes the DVD layout, plus the videos, pictures, and audio that are added to the layout.

DVD substrate. Metal foil that is contained inside the DVD. Each DVD has two substrates that are used to reflect the laser so that it can be interpreted and then converted to audio or video by the DVD player.

DVD Workshop Area. The area in the main DVD Builder interface that handles the movie and menu organization.

ESD grounding strap. A wrist strap that grounds you to the floor and eliminates any static electricity that may be produced.

FireWire interface. An external interface developed by Apple computer that was designed for multimedia and has an extremely fast transfer speed.

First Play Video. *See Introduction Video.*

Floppy disc. Removable disc media with a maximum storage capacity of 2 Megabytes. The most common storage capacity is 1.44 Megabytes.

Frame rate. The amount of frames that are displayed on the television screen per second. A higher frame rate will reduce choppiness on the screen. *See Broadcast Format, NTSC Broadcast Format, and PAL Broadcast Format.*

Hybrid disc. A special type of audio disc that holds the current Audio CD on one standard and either DVD-AUDIO or SACD on the other layer. This type of disc allows DVD-AUDIO or SACD media to be played on a normal audio CD player.

IDE cable. Cable that is used to connect the IDE device to the IDE controller.

IDE controller. Connector built on to the computer's motherboard that IDE devices are plugged into.

IDE/ATAPI interface. An internal interface used in most personal computers today. An IDE device can be a hard drive, CD-ROM drive, Zip drive or DVD burner.

Import Multimedia. When the multimedia file—picture, video, or audio—already exists on the computer (it does not need to be captured), the file is imported into the DVD authoring application.

Introduction video. The video on a DVD that is shown before the Main Menu. This video cannot be bypassed. The FBI warning on all commercially produced DVDs would be an example.

Jewel case. Hard cover case in which most DVDs or CDs are stored.

Jewel case covers. Paper inserts that contain information about the DVD. These inserts are slipped into the front and back of the jewel case.

JPG. Stands for Joint Photographic Experts Group and is pronounced J-Peg. This is a standard picture format that is widely used on the Internet because of its tremendous compression.

Mark-in. Set this to the desired starting point of the video.

Mark-out. Set this to the desired ending point of the video.

Master/Slave/Cable Select. Three IDE settings that should be configured on each drive so that two IDE devices can be installed on the same IDE cable.

Menus. Primary means of navigation around a DVD and is similar to a website.

Menu buttons. To ease navigation confusion, these are used to organize the content on the DVD into submenus that are accessed via these buttons.

Menu button labels. The textual name that is given to a menu button.

Menu rendering. When the burn process starts, each menu is put into a format that can be displayed on a television.

Menu titles. A textual title that is given to a DVD menu.

Menu template. *See Theme.*

Movie. Within DVD Builder, a movie is a collection of videos or pictures. In other applications, a movie may simply refer to a video.

APPENDIX B

MP3. Stands for MPEG Audio Layer 3 and is an audio file format that is quickly becoming the digital audio compression scheme standard in the computing world.

MPEG-1 encoding. A video compression standard that produces VHS picture quality and is the standard compression for the VCD application format.

MPEG-2 encoding. A video compression standard that produces DVD picture quality and is the standard compression for (you guessed it) the DVD-VIDEO application format.

MPEG-4 encoding. The newest type of video compression, also known as DIVX, that can be put on a DVD. This compression is much more efficient than its predecessors—MPEG-1 and MPEG-2.

Multimedia CD. Developed by Philips and Sony as a competing format to Super Disc. The combination of these two formats became what we know as DVD.

NTSC broadcast format. Stands for National Television System Committee. NTSC is a broadcast format that has a resolution of 720 × 480 and a frame rate of 30 frames per second.

PAL broadcast format. Stands for Phase Alternating Line. PAL is a broadcast format that has a resolution of 720 × 576 and a frame rate of 25 frames per second.

QuickTime. Apple Computer's standard movie format.

Real-Time Recording. *See Direct capture to burn.*

Recordable format. The way that the application format is written to the disc. There are five different recordable formats: DVD-R, DVD-RW, DVD-RAM, DVD+R, and DVD+RW.

Resolution. The number of lines that are displayed on the television. The resolution is denoted in a A × B form, where A is the number of horizontal lines, and B is the number of vertical lines displayed on the screen. The higher the resolution, the better the picture will look.

SACD application format. A competing format to the DVD-AUDIO application format that stands for Super Audio Compact Disc. Unfortunately, SACDs cannot be played in a DVD player unless this functionality is specifically built-in.

Screening Room. The area in the main DVD Builder interface that handles video editing, previewing, and capturing.

SCSI interface. An internal or external interface that was originally used in all Macintosh computers and a select number of PCs. This interface is more expensive than IDE and is reserved mainly for computer servers today.

Scene Selection Menu. A special menu that shows each chapter marker within a video as its own menu button.

Single-Layer. Every DVD has two reflective layers that are used to hold information. A single-layer DVD uses only one of these layers to hold the information, leaving the other layer blank.

Single-Sided. In a single-sided DVD, one side is always used to read information, while the other side is used to attach a disc label.

Slideshow. A group of pictures that are shown for a specific amount of time before moving on to the next one. A slideshow can be created with or without background music.

Stand-alone DVD player. A DVD player that is connected directly to a television, not a computer.

Super Disc. Developed by Toshiba and Time Warner as a competing format to Multimedia CD. The combination of these two formats became DVD.

Super Video CD application format. This format was introduced as an upgrade to the Video CD format. It produces DVD quality video on a standard compact disc but at a cost of playing time. A SVCD can only hold between 35 and 72 minutes of video compared to a two hour DVD.

Themes. A collection of similar menu buttons, background, and fonts that are put together to give your DVD a common look and feel.

Toolbar. A set of buttons within an application that are grouped together by function.

Transcoding. Process of taking a digital file, usually in AVI or QuickTime format, and converting it to the DVD-compliant MPEG-2 format.

Transitions. Effects that are added between slides in a slideshow. These effects can be a fade in then fade out, dissolve in then dissolve out, fly in then fly out, and so on.

Trimming. A video can be trimmed to the right or left. For example, trimming right will remove any video that is to the right of the cursor position.

TV Safe Zone. To make sure that the menu buttons or titles are not cut off because of their position, the TV Safe Zone will display a box that all menu items should be kept in.

TWAIN. Platform independent interface standard that allows imaging devices (scanners, digital cameras, and so on) to communicate with image processing software.

USB 1.1 interface. The original USB standard that is included with all personal computers manufactured today.

USB 2.0 interface. The upgrade to USB 1.1 and is a competing technology to FireWire. This interface is faster than FireWire, but has not been as widely adopted.

VHS. Stands for Video Home System and is the format that a VCR uses.

Video Capture. Recording from either an analog (VHS) or digital (digital camcorder) source and saved into a computer file (usually AVI or QuickTime format).

Video capture card. An expansion card that is added to a computer in order to capture from an analog video device—a VCR or non-FireWire based camcorder would be an example.

Video CD application format. This format uses compact disc technology—this makes it considerably cheaper than DVD—and has a picture quality that is comparable to a VHS tape. VCD is popular in Asia, but has not caught on in North America.

Video clips. Within DVD Builder, video clips are videos that are captured or imported into a DVD Builder movie.

WAV. Stands for Wave file and is an older audio file format that is still widely used.

Working folder. A directory that is used to store captured videos and temp files that are used during the encoding process.

Zip disk. Removable disk media that is packaged in a hard plastic shell with a storage capacity of 100, 250, or 750 megabytes.

Index

INDEX

INDEX

V

VCD format, 19–20
  for burning software, 47
  decoders, 19
  Macintosh iDVD 3.0 and, 116
VHS, defined, 251
Video Capture button, DVD Builder, 57–58, 133–135
video clips, defined, 49, 252
video editing. *See* editing
VOB
  DVD Builder supporting, 135
  Roxio Easy CD and DVD Creator 6 with, 51

W

WAV
  defined, 252
  DVD Builder supporting, 52, 136
  MyDVD 3.5 support for, 98
  for slideshows, 156
  Ulead DVD MovieFactory 2.1 supporting, 74
websites
  iDVDthemepak.com, 120
  MyDVD 3.5, 97
  Ulead Web site, 73
  U.S. Copyright Office, 10
WG2 on DVD-ROM standard, 20
Windows 95 DVD burner interfaces, 29
Windows 98 DVD burner interfaces, 29
Windows 2000 DVD burner interfaces, 29
Windows NT, 29
  DVD burner interfaces, 29
Windows XP
  DVD Builder, getting to, 210
  DVD burner interfaces, 29
Wizard, MyDVD, 99–101
WMA
  DVD Builder supporting, 52, 136
  for slideshows, 156

WMV
  DVD Builder supporting, 135
  Roxio Easy CD and DVD Creator 6 with, 51
Workshop area. *See* DVD Builder
WORM (write once, read many) concept, 24

Z

zip disks, 6–7
  defined, 252

INDEX

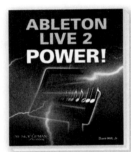